THE LANGUAGE AND EDUCATION LIBRARY 15
Series Editor: Professor David J. Corson
The Ontario Institute for Studies in Education

Race and Ethnicity in Multi-ethnic Schools
A Critical Case Study

James Ryan

MULTILINGUAL MATTERS LTD
Clevedon • Philadelphia • Toronto • Sydney

For my parents, Joseph and Shirley Ryan

Library of Congress Cataloging in Publication Data

Ryan, James
Race and Ethnicity in Multi-ethnic Schools: A Critical Case Study / James Ryan
The Language and Education Library: 15
Includes bibliographical references
1. Minorities–Education (Secondary)–Canada–Case Studies. 2. Discrimination in education–Canada–Case studies. 3. Multicultural education–Canada–Case studies. 4. Critical pedagogy–Canada–Case studies. 5. Ethnicity–Canada–Case studies.
I. Title. II. Series.
LC3734.R93   1999
373.1829–dc21   99-12740

British Library Cataloguing in Publication Data

A CIP catalogue record for this book is available from the British Library.

ISBN 1-85359-447-4 (hbk)
ISBN 1-85359-446-6 (pbk)

Multilingual Matters Ltd

UK: Frankfurt Lodge, Clevedon Hall, Victoria Road, Clevedon BS21 7HH.
USA: 325 Chestnut Street, Philadelphia, PA 19106, USA.
Canada: 5201 Dufferin Street, North York, Ontario M3H 5T8, Canada.
Australia: P.O. Box 586, Artamon, NSW, Australia.

Copyright © 1999 James Ryan.

Typeset by Bookcraft Ltd, Stroud.
Printed and bound in Great Britain by WBC Book Manufacturers Ltd.

Contents

Acknowledgements

This book became possible only through the efforts of many individuals. There are a number of these people to whom I am particularly indebted. Rouleen Wignall helped with the writing of the original proposals for the two studies that eventually supplied the data for the book. The funding which we received from an OISE Transfer Grant from the Ontario Ministry of Education and Training and from the Social Sciences and Humanities Research Council of Canada allowed us to bring a number of other people on board. Shawn Moore helped with classroom observations and teacher interviews. His meticulous and conscientious efforts produced much data of value. I am also grateful to Sandra Anthony and Mary Harris. Both women used their considerable interactional skills to get both students and parents to confide in them, and as a consequence, to provide valuable information about what was happening in the school. Also one of the educators in the school, a graduate student who can't be named, also helped us out by conducting a number of interviews with teachers. Others helped out along the way. John Tucker and Lorayne Robertson provided feedback to me on drafts of the manuscript. David Corson was also of considerable help. His overall encouragement and feedback on drafts of the material proved to be instrumental in the completion of the book. Finally, I am indebted to the students, their parents, teachers, and administrators of Suburbia Secondary School. Their willingness to give up their valuable time and provide us with their insights made this project possible. Finally, thanks to John.

Chapter 1

Representing Race/Ethnicity in a Multi-ethnic School

In a university department with which I am familiar, eight figures stand silent watch over the main corridor. They look out, bold and confident, their collective gaze effectively challenging anyone who approaches. It is difficult to escape this gaze. Anyone who wishes to get to the series of offices that lie beyond must risk being seen. For many, attempts to avoid the gaze will prove futile. Those who crouch or duck to escape notice as they pass will testify that the eyes follow their every move. This is not to say that no one has mastered the technique of slipping by these silent sentinels unnoticed. Many who work in the area pass regularly with impunity. They are able to do so by simply ignoring the sentries. This comes easily with time. Those who pass by their position day in and day out come to take them for granted, and as they do so, these impressive figures fade quietly into the woodwork of their surroundings. This is a luxury that only the residents of the area enjoy, however. Most visitors cannot help but notice the figures. Their prominent position in this key area makes it difficult, if not impossible, to miss them. For some of these visitors, these figures are striking. But for others, their presence is downright intimidating.

As you have probably guessed by now, these figures are not of the flesh and blood variety. They are merely images, photographs of eight people. These eight are, or were, living and breathing human beings. As I write, seven of them are no doubt going about their business. The eighth has passed on. The photographs adorn the left wall as one prepares to enter from the common area. Someone has arranged them in two rows of four. The upper four are directly above the bottom four, separated by a space of approximately four inches. A space of around the same dimensions separates photos that are in the same row. On the other hand, approximately three feet divides the bottom of the lower pictures from the floor, while the top row reaches around seven feet from the floor. Each photograph measures approximately eight by ten inches.

Most who see these photographs would probably say that they are tastefully done. Dark mahogany-grained wood frames of slightly different

1

shades border each of the pictures. A gold trim lines each of these frames, but it does not do so in a consistent manner. On some the trim is nearer the outside of the frame, while on others it crowds the inner edges. Three-inch borders separate the actual photographs from the frames. All are brown. Two, however, are distinctly lighter than the others. Balancing the assembly, these two pictures stand diagonally opposite one another. Inside these borders sit the actual photographs. They feature primarily the faces of the eight, although they also take in upper chests and shoulders. The photos are all in color except for one. All display similar, obviously professionally provided backgrounds, except for one. Unlike the others, this picture has obviously been snapped out of doors. In all of the pictures the subjects stare directly at the viewer, except this one. This individual is looking off to the side, and in contrast to others, is wearing a hat. The seven remaining subjects look boldly out. All have pleasant looks on their faces, although we can only see three sets of teeth. The names of each of the individuals are inscribed on a gold-trimmed plate, which sits on the brown border directly below the actual photo. Above the entire assemblage is a larger plate with the words *Professors Emeriti.*

The individuals depicted in the photographs display many differences. Because the images are restricted primarily to faces, viewers have to use their imaginations as to how the subjects differ from the neck and chest down, but many of the differences visible are those one would expect to find between and among the faces of most human beings. There is a wide variety in facial features. For example they differ in terms of size and shape of noses, ears, chins, foreheads and so on. Eyes, at least those that the viewer can pick out, are of different colors. Hairstyles also vary. But while the differences are many and evident to all who see these photographs, it is the similarities between and among these individuals that tend to attract people's attention.

These faces display four obvious similarities. The first is their age. The color of their hair, its absence in a couple of the cases, and the facial lines testify to the age of these individuals. They are all at least sixty years old. The second similarity is their affluence. Although faces take up much of the photo space, viewers can see at least part of their clothing. All are nattily attired and, with the exception of the outdoors subject, appear ready to attend a formal gathering. The third thing they have in common is their sex. A quick glance at all the faces and glistening foreheads is enough to alert the viewer to the fact that all of these people are men. Finally, all share the same skin color. All of these men are White. The latter two characteristics have made more of an impression on people than the first two. Apparently, as will become evident, age and affluence do not constitute as much of an issue as sex and race/ethnicity.

At one point controversy swirled around these photographs. They first became an issue as the department was gearing up to search for someone to fill a vacant faculty position. In an effort to break with a uniformly White male past, the unit had agreed to make an effort to hire someone who would diversify the current faculty complement. While the reasons for this decision no doubt varied among those concerned, most agreed that such a move seemed to make sense in a community where the immigrant population was pushing 50% of the total. It was at this time that one faculty member raised the issue of the photographs. He believed that they did little to encourage those who could not identify with the photographs to apply for the position. He went on to relate the case of a potential candidate who, after coming across the photographs, decided that perhaps this was not the place for her. The silent sentinels, it seems, conveyed to her an image of the unit with which she was not totally comfortable.

In the weeks that followed a struggle ensued over the photographs. In the process various faculty members voiced their respective opinions about the photographs and what they felt should happen to them. The means of communication for this was electronic, and all faculty in the unit were privy to what was going on. Individuals routinely copied their latest Email message to everyone. As one would expect, positions varied. Some strongly demanded that the photographs be removed immediately. Others were equally convinced that they should stay right where they were. Others again supported positions that were more moderate.

Not all chose to participate. No doubt the sensitive issues involved played a part in their decision to stay out of the fray. Being academics, however, those who did take part did not stop at merely declaring their wish for the photographs to come down, stay up, or be moved. Rather, these preferences were inevitably accompanied by multitudes of reasons and rationales. All who cared to voice their opinion supplied plenty of additional text to support their respective positions.

One way of understanding the clash over the photographs is to see it as a struggle over representation. In this situation these individuals were engaged in a clash over what images they felt were appropriate to stand in for, or represent, the department and/or particular individuals who were at one point associated with the department. Some believed that two rows of pictures of the White male founders in a prominent place was the way to go. Others felt that this sort of display was inappropriate. But this issue was not just about representation generally. It also concerned issues of race/ethnicity (and gender). In particular, it illustrated just one instance of a wider struggle over the representation of race/ethnicity. One group of faculty believed that the choice to display images of these particular (White) people in this unique way sent a message that was not particularly welcoming those who were not of European heritage. They felt that such a practice was typically exclusionary. The opposition, on the other hand, preferred to treat the issue as one of justice/reward rather than of race/ethnicity. They believed that these people deserved to be honored in this way because they had contributed so positively to the department and to their academic discipline.

What is not immediately obvious is that this struggle over representation took place on more than one level. The first and most visible area of conflict revolved around what to do with the photographs. One group wanted them taken down or moved, while the other felt that they should stay right where they were. The former believed that moving them would facilitate a shift toward a more inclusive department, while the latter felt that leaving them where they were would rightly acknowledge the history of the department and the contributions of worthy individuals.

The other level at which struggle occurred was not so obvious. Despite its sometimes surreptitious nature, this was nevertheless an arena where much wider and more pervasive conflict frequently occurs: the level of meaning. At this more fundamental level the conflict was not so much about what to do with the images on the walls as about what they meant. In other words, this struggle over representation was importantly a struggle over meaning. What was the significance of this set of photographs? How did people make sense of them? And perhaps most important, what sense eventually prevailed? And what effect did the prevailing meanings have on what was eventually done? The lesson to be learned here is that contests over representation generally revolve around struggles over what and whose meaning or sense will prevail.

At the surface level of description, the 'denotative' level (Barthes, 1972), where more specific or *literal* meanings become obvious, most would agree that the images on the wall represent human beings. Moreover, one only has to look at the caption over the photographs to realize just who these people are, or were. The differences in meaning emerge not on this denotative level, however, but on the more diffuse, ephemeral and wider level of 'connotation', where meaning is more loosely *associated* with a word or phrase. It is here that the senses the opposing parties made of the photographs parted ways, and as a consequence, clashed. While these photos meant many things to their supporters, one meaning in particular stood out. These images signified an honor. In this regard some faculty believed that the people on the wall had accomplished much for the department and their discipline during their tenure, and deserved to be acknowledged for this service by having their faces mounted in a prominent place. For these faculty, the photographs acquired their meaning within a sense-making scheme that recognized the practice of rewarding or honoring individuals in this way.

Their opponents, on the other hand, made sense of the photographs in a different way. For one thing, they tended not to see them on an individual basis. What was important for these people was the entire collection, and in particular, the place and manner in which it was displayed. They believed that these eight photographs stood not so much for the individuals they were meant to represent as for the department as a whole. For them, the fact that every one of these individuals had white skin gave the impression that the department was an exclusive rather than inclusive club. They made sense of the photographs in terms of race/ethnicity and privilege. To understand the photographs, these people tapped into a sense-making framework that acknowledged the pervasive nature of White privilege. In the logic of White privilege, these photographs represented just another way of ensuring the continuity of a privileged (White) club by marginalizing those different others who were seen as a threat.

As I hint above, the construction of meaning around these photographs is neither a simple nor straightforward process. This is because their meaning does not lie in the images themselves. Nor does it rest entirely with those individuals who interpret what they see on the wall. Rather it emerges in the dialogue between those who do the interpreting and the images that they perceive. This is not to say that interpretation is an individual thing. It is not. Constructing meaning – making sense – is fundamentally a social process. To accomplish this kind of task we require sense-making frameworks. These sense-making frameworks are in turn always anchored in discourse, that is, in *language in social use* (Fiske, 1996). We must appeal to a 'language' – sets of statements, images, practices, metaphors and so on that are organized in particular ways – in order to make sense of our experience. The elements associated with these discourses provide a medium that filters the different ways in which we can make meaning. While some may prefer to think of discourse as a multi-institutional and transindividual archive of images, words and practices for constructing knowledge about an area of experience (see, for example, Foucault, 1972), it is also very much an active process. In other words, discourse is both a noun and a verb (Fiske, 1996). We might just as well speak of 'discourse' as of 'discoursing'. The fact of the matter remains that in order to make sense of any aspect of our experience, we must first place it into discourse. This is just what the faculty members did. One group made sense of the pictures by locating them in a kind of justice/reward discourse, while the other placed them in a discourse of White privilege. Without placing them in some discourse they would have not made any sense.

Discourse is not just a 'discursive' or 'linguistic' concept, however. It is an attempt to combine language and practice: what people say and what they do (Hall, 1997a). A basic assumption of this perspective is that meaning depends not just on language but on the social practices with which it is associated. Making sense of something always occurs in the context of some other forms of social organization which provide a space where linguistic practice can take place. The sense that people made of the photographs, for example, depended in important ways on the fact that they were associated with a very particular form of institutional organiza-tion. Because discourse is closely associated with forms of social organization, it also conveys, and is subject to, power. Power works on and through individuals as they take up the positions offered to them in discourse and as they become objects of discourse (Foucault, 1980). But discourse is not merely a technique of power. It is also the terrain on which struggles over wider issues occur (Fiske, 1996). Men, women and children regularly contest meaning as they look to see to their interests.[1]

What happened in the university department was first and foremost a struggle over representation. The faculty members of this department clashed over the images that they felt were the appropriate ones to stand in for their unit. At an obvious and immediate level the struggle was over what to do with the photographs. At another more ephemeral and diffuse level, it concerned the meanings that were attributed to these photographs. The respective groups sought to promote their respective sense of the images by placing their experience of the images into discourses that promoted their interests and confirmed their experiences, and by subse-quently circulating this sense. One of the areas that this struggle over representation touched was race/ethnicity. While the supporters' discourses generally side-stepped this issue, their opponents' highlighted its central role. Employing a discourse of White privilege, for example, they contended that, among other things, displaying photographs of all-White males in this way discourages different others from wanting to become part of this university community.

As I write, the photographs still stand in their original place, a testimony to the outcome of the skirmish. As it turned out, the supporters' discourse, reinforced as it was by the immanent authority of the status quo, prevailed over their opponents'. In the end the sense that the former made of the photographs counted for more than the latter's when the time came to make, or rather, not make a decision. The discourse of White privilege had obviously not made sense to enough people, or the right people, for a change to be made.

This does not mean that the battle is over, however. Indeed this brief exchange represents a minor skirmish in a much wider clash over not only how race/ethnicity is to be represented, but also how people are to live their lives. While the battle over the photographs had, and still has, a local and fairly specific element to it, it also extends far beyond the walls of the department. The terrain on which it is being waged is in many important ways a global as well as a local field of representation. How members of this educational community make sense of theirs and other's lives is tied closely to what kinds of opportunities they and others will have and what kinds of lives they and others will eventually lead. In the case at hand the sense that people made of the photographs influenced in crucial ways what they eventually did about them. These decisions tie into decisions and practices being made or accomplished elsewhere that have a profound effect on the day-to-day lives of all men, women and children.

This book describes how this process works itself out in another educational setting, a multi-ethnic secondary school, Suburbia Secondary School (a pseudonym). In situations like this one where there is an abundance of racial/ethnic diversity the process of representation is perhaps more intense, and thus more obvious, than it is in other more monocultural settings. While this school setting provides an ideal laboratory for exploring the representation of racial/ethnic diversity, I did not go out looking for places that would provide this sort of opportunity. In fact quite the opposite occurred. In a sense it was this multi-ethnic setting that offered up the phenomenon of representation as a way of understanding many of the things that were happening around diversity. It became apparent at a point during the study that the various processes associated with representation were responsible for much of what happened around issues of racial/ethnic diversity. As a consequence, what began as an empirical study designed to explore how teachers responded to racial/ethnic diversity in their classrooms, became an examination of how the processes associated with representation shaped the ways in which students and educators understood and reacted to diversity in and around the school. As the various themes associated with representation emerged, it became evident that these processes were also responsible for extending opportunities to some students while at the same time penalizing others.

The empirical data associated with two related studies supplied the foundation for this book, which explores particular aspects of the struggle over racial/ethnic representation. However, the book does not focus exclusively on the school itself. Rather, in what follows I account for the context, including a history, in which this clash over representation occurs. In a number of the chapters the data provide a starting-point for exploring the various issues that these data introduce. A central premise of the book is that the struggle over how race/ethnicity is represented is generally conducted under conditions that are not equal. I document these conditions by illustrating the ways in which race/ethnicity has been represented in the past and in the present, starting with selected cases and situations at Suburbia Secondary School.

The lens I employ to explore this process of representation is discourse. In this sense the struggle over representation is a struggle over discourse. The book explores how these struggles arise in the school over (1) difference, race and racism, (2) stereotyping practices, (3) curricular images, (4) student identity and community and (5) language. My purpose in writing this book is to make plain the ways in which the representation of race/ethnicity works in a multi-ethnic school. My hope is that those who read it will be motivated enough to attempt in their situations to provide conditions that allow for the construction and circulation of discourses that work *for* rather than *against* groups that have traditionally not been well served by prevailing racial/ethnic discourses. Before moving on, however, I present a brief overview of the book.

Representing Race/Ethnicity

In the contemporary world, representation generally, and the representation of race/ethnicity in particular, will increasingly continue to play a vital role in how people live their lives. This is so for a number of reasons. The first is that world population and immigration patterns are changing. Among the countries to notice these changes are the Anglo-dominated ones of the 'West'. Canada, the United States, Great Britain and Australia, for example, have all in the past two decades experienced a noticeable shift in the people who are traveling from other parts of the world to settle in their lands. At one time most immigrants emigrated to these countries from Europe. Now they come from all parts of the world. In fact fewer now travel from Europe than from Asia, Africa and South America (Statistics

Canada, 1993, 1997; US Bureau of the Census, 1995; Australian Bureau of Statistics, 1995; Owen, 1994). Many of these immigrants settle in the larger cities. In Toronto, Canada, for example, immigrants constitute around 42% of the city's population (Statistics Canada, 1997). Moreover by the year 2000 visible minorities are expected to make up 54% of the city's population (Carey, 1998). As expected, these changes are generating many changes in school populations. In the same city, as far back as 1988, one school district reported that one-third of the total day-school population and two-thirds of the mothers of this same student population were born outside Canada (Handscombe, 1989).

The representation of race/ethnicity will play an important part in people's lives for other reasons as well. It will continue to be an ongoing concern because of ways in which processes associated with representation have changed over the years. Over time humanity has moved from a heavy reliance on oral media, to print, and most recently, to electronic media. This evolution has been, at least in part, responsible for the current proliferation of images. It is difficult for anyone living in the Western world not to encounter persistently the images associated with these media. The images that emanate from books, newspapers, magazines, advertisement posters and billboards, televisions, movie screens, computers, among many other sources, have become an integral part of our lives. Not only may we discover that these images are increasingly accessible; many of us may find that we cannot do without them. These images, or at least most of them, are however 'racialized', that is, they are necessarily filtered through a 'racial' lens. Some are more obviously associated with race than others. Images of O.J. Simpson, Clarence Thomas (Fiske, 1996), or of police rousting mostly Black offenders in 'real life' cop dramas (Andersen, 1995) on television speak perhaps more forcefully than the eight photographs in the university department. The bottom line here though is that all these images, and in particular the ways in which they are perceived or interpreted, will have a profound effect on how people think about issues of race and ethnicity and what they eventually do about these issues.

One other comparatively recent change in the contemporary world also renders issues of racial/ethnic representation increasingly important. Associated closely with changing immigration patterns and the proliferation of contemporary images is the increasing uncertainty that many people experience today. For example, many men and women now find cause to dispute what once were time-honored truths (Anderson, 1990). While some may recognize the limitations of physical and social sciences, others take advantage of contemporary opportunities to question a wide variety of knowledge claims. The seemingly infinite array of perspectives and views, which may come packaged in forms that range from scientific journals to talk shows, continues to undermine the idea that there is one true and ultimately knowable world out there. What this has done is to destabilize, to a point, a structure that has in the past provided more or less uniform, and often debilitating, ways of understanding race. This destabilization has in recent years provided more opportunities for traditionally marginalized groups to have their voices heard by allowing them some space in which to shape the ways they are represented. Given the importance of contemporary representations, then, it will be crucial to find ways of constructing and circulating images, and understandings of them, that work in the interests of the marginalized.

While representation processes work away steadily in and through most contemporary institutions, they are particularly apparent in schools. Indeed representation constitutes a crucial part of learning. Students learn as they are presented with images of many aspects of life through a variety of media. This is not to say that representation operates exclusively in the formal learning process itself. It also surfaces in many other forms and situations, as is evident in the case of the photographs above. What will become apparent in this book is that the ways in which race/ethnicity has been, and currently is, represented in schools, as in other areas of life, provide advantages for some and disadvantages for others. This has come about over the years as schools and the people who teach and learn in them have routinely provided, and been provided with, what are regularly interpreted as negative images of certain groups and positive images of others. Students do not encounter these representations just in the formal curriculum, however. They also circulate in and through the interactions they have with their fellow students and with teachers and administrators.

Over the past three or four decades teachers and scholars have increasingly acknowledged the disadvantages that certain racial/ethnic groups face in schools. Some of these people have gone so far as to attribute causes to this phenomenon and to prescribe solutions. Some belong to an approach that has come to be known as 'multicultural' education. Proponents of many different varieties of multicultural education promote a wide range of preferred practices. One fairly common theme revolves in important ways around representation. In this regard many multiculturalists believe that students should be presented with positive images of the 'cultures' of various racial/ethnic groups. They contend that exposing students to the life ways of previously unknown groups will lead to, among other things, a greater understanding of, and tolerance for, different others; improve communication between and among groups; and enhance the self-perceptions of members of the groups featured (Sleeter & Grant, 1987; Gibson, 1976; May, 1994). Another more recent approach, 'antiracist' education, although taking issue with the more superficial aspects of this process of representation, nevertheless also features positive representations in the classroom. Citing approaches by Jeffcoate (1979) and Hatcher and Shallice (1983), Rattansi (1992) notes that positive images are inherent in antiracist efforts to present Black histories primarily as narratives of resistance and struggle against racism.

Both multicultural and antiracist approaches have made significant contributions to education. Their analyses of advantage and disadvantage and their suggestions for practice have, among other effects, drawn attention to the injustices faced by groups of racial/ethnic students, motivated practitioners to adopt more inclusive teaching practices, and increased the life opportunities of some students. But despite these positive achievements, most multicultural and antiracist approaches are not (as yet) equipped to analyze the process of representation in schools. While representation remains an important part of their respective approaches, it does not figure directly in to the ways in which representation works outside of curricular images through, for example, the so-called 'hidden curriculum' and all interactions that take place in schools. Rattansi (1992) also maintains that multicultural and antiracist representations which are uniform and positive and sometimes essentialist, often gloss over the divisions and differences within groups. Finally, most multiculturalists and antiracists do not account for how the images presented in the classroom come to mean things to students. They do not take into consideration the ways in which students make sense of curricular materials or the interactions they have with fellow students and teachers.

Understanding the process and effects of racial/ethnic representation in schools requires that we attend to the process of meaning. This is because the images that students and educators encounter in schools do not themselves possess inherent or enduring meanings. Nor does the meaning of these images become immediately apparent or automatic to those who apprehend them. Rather, the pictures, words and figures that take precedence in classrooms and around schools are merely signs or symbols that those who see or hear them must interpret in order to make sense of them. Meaning is constructed in the dialogue between individuals and the images and symbols that they perceive. The meaning that students take from, for example, texts, classroom talk or school rules emerges out of their respective relationships with these particular symbols. This does not mean that constructing meaning, or making sense, is an individual thing. It is instead a fundamentally social process. Men, women and children make sense of life by placing their experience into socially generated sense-making frameworks, or discourse. They can make sense of racial/ethnic issues only by taking up positions in these historically generated, institutionally grounded discourses.

Because making sense of race/ethnicity (or 'discoursing') is a social process, it is always enmeshed in relationships of power. Discourse revolves around power in at least two ways. The first is that it operates as a technique of power (Foucault, 1972, 1980). Racialized discourses structure or filter in important ways the possible alternatives for interpreting race/ethnicity. Individuals must take up a position in a discourse before they can make sense of the images they encounter. In this context they are subjected to discourse. As a technique of power, discourses also 'construct' the objects about which they concern themselves. Thus, certain groups of people are assigned certain characteristics by virtue of the prevailing discourses about them. Males of African heritage, for example, may take on various characteristics in racist discourses.

Discourse does not operate exclusively as a technique of power. Discourses do not simply roll over everything in their paths. Rather they are always contested and contestable (Fiske, 1996). This is not to say that all struggles over meaning and discourse are equal, however. As I illustrate in the subsequent chapters, certain groups have had, and continue to have, distinct advantages over others in the construction and circulation of certain racial/ethnic discourses. The result of this inequality is that certain discourses that favour Whites/Europeans/Anglos over other groups prevail in schools and elsewhere. But because they are contestable, they can also be challenged, resisted and replaced. Thus it remains for all those interested in social justice to challenge these debilitating discourses and to find ways of constructing and circulating discourses that work in the interests of the marginalized.

Suburbia Secondary School

The struggle over representation finds its way into many areas of school practice at Suburbia Secondary School. Suburbia is located in a rapidly growing and highly diverse suburb of a large Canadian city. According to school officials, the community for which the school caters has residents who are both struggling and well off financially. Even so, many students who attend this school are from so-called middle-class backgrounds. The larger metropolitan area in which this community is located, like many others across North America, has become more visibly diverse with the change in immigration patterns over the last 10 to 20 years. Most immigrants no longer emigrate from Europe as they once did. In 1991, for example, most people who traveled to this country came from Hong Kong, Poland, China, India, the Philippines, Lebanon, El Salvador, Sri Lanka, Vietnam and Guyana, to name just a few of the places of origin (Statistics Canada, 1993). Many settle in the larger cities. In 1991 immigrants constituted fully 38% of this city's population (Statistics Canada, 1993). By 1996, this number had grown to 42% (Statistics Canada, 1997).

Suburbia Secondary School reflects this diversity. Visitors to the school are immediately struck by it. One such visitor observed that the school was a 'replica of the United Nations'. This diversity was recently confirmed by a school-administered survey which indicated that students identified with over 60 different heritages. Students of Italian (18%), Filipino (14.7%), Portuguese (9.5%), Chinese (8%) and Polish (6.3%) heritage constitute the largest groups. The school itself is only four years old, and has a student population of approximately 1700. Like many other schools in the area it has already experienced the need to employ portable classrooms to accommodate the burgeoning student population. The school staff are comparatively young, many of them hand-picked by the principal and school administration, and almost all are of European heritage.

Suburbia looks like many of the newer schools in the rapidly expanding area in which it is located. From the outside the building appears to be long and low. Its two storeys take up a considerable amount of area. The grounds that surround it, however, take up even more space. Indeed one can easily imagine a small subdivision of houses fitting nicely into the entire school property, which includes three parking lots, 12 portable classrooms and a football field. The building itself is inconspicuous. Its light-colored brick exterior blends easily into the suburban terrain that surrounds it. This terrain continues to change, however, as houses perpetually consume the once prominent pastures. The interior of Suburbia is as pleasing as its exterior. The front doors give way to a large foyer where students regularly congregate before class in the morning, at lunch, and after school. A large cafeteria borders one side of this space. Locker-lined corridors extend in a square formation around this central foyer. These corridors lead to classrooms, a large gymnasium, an auto shop, a woodwork shop, science labs and computer labs, among other types of specialized rooms. Observant visitors will notice that cameras on the grounds, in the corridors and in some of the rooms follow their every move.

In many ways the school is typical of many others in the area. Before, between and after classes there are hundreds of young people going in all directions. The following passage is from field notes that I wrote during one of my first visits. It is an image that has stuck with me since that time. Over the next weeks I witnessed many similar scenes. Many, but not all, were as benign as this event.

> I arrive just before classes begin, get directions from the office to Jennifer's class, and start toward the class. The halls are filled with kids it seems from an infinite number of backgrounds. Caucasians are definitely in the minority. The halls are filled with students going every which way, but there is little disruptive behavior. I look over and see a teacher open the door from the inside for a group of waiting kids. When he sees them he gently smiles, and without a word, lets them in. They smile back as they enter.

I refer to the heuristic approach that I employ to understand issues of racial/ethnic representation at Suburbia as a *critical case study*. In some respects it shares elements common to traditional case-study research (Bogdan & Biklen, 1998; Stake, 1994; Yin, 1994; Merriam, 1988). It involves a detailed examination of one setting and, if only in a limited sense, constitutes an exploration of a bounded system. The empirical data that provide the basis for my account come from within the boundaries of what can fairly easily be identified as a particular school community. This is also, as Adelman, Jenkins and Kemmis (in Merriam, 1988:10) contend, 'an instance drawn from a particular class'. This study is a particular example of the manner in which race/ethnicity is represented in (multi-ethnic) schools, a process which quite obviously occurs in many similar and not so similar situations. A detailed exploration of this one particular setting has much to offer that can help us understand the much broader phenomenon. A case-study design can accommodate a range of methods, but the approach adopted here is primarily qualitative in nature. Qualitative methods are employed because, as Merriam (1988) notes, they are best suited to exploring the human complexities associated with the construction of meaning in social processes. As we will see below, the processes of representing race/ethnicity in a multi-ethnic school revolve in important ways around the social construction of meaning.

The critical version of case-study research that I employ here departs in a number of respects from the more traditional approaches. In particular, it is not based on induction, goes well beyond the limited notion of context employed in many case studies, and eschews the presumption of so-called neutrality. Case-study research has traditionally revolved around the principle of induction, that is, it proceeds on the assumption that the data provide the grounding for the generation of generalizations, concepts or hypotheses (Merriam, 1988). Advocates of this approach fail to acknowledge, however, that no researcher can go into a situation *tabula rasa*, that is, with no preconceptions. In order to make sense of any situation, a researcher, just like any other human being, must fit what he or she perceives into a particular, already existing discourse. Social scientists will therefore inevitably characterize a research setting through the filter of the theoretical baggage they bring with them (Angus, 1986). In this study, I readily acknowledge that the way I characterize what happens at Suburbia Secondary School is shaped, at least in part, by a critical tradition of social science and its associated discourses. In fact I credit these discourses with helping me characterize what happens here in ways that I hope will be helpful to readers.

To their credit, a number of case-study advocates emphasize the holistic, contextual nature of human interaction (Yin, 1994; Stake, 1994). They acknowledge that the 'variables' associated with the phenomenon under study cannot be separated from their context and trust that case-study research will be able to capture the ways in which experience is rooted in context. Unfortunately their concept of context is a limited one. It rarely extends much beyond the immediate setting of interest in the case study. In doing so, it fails to account for wider social patterns, structures, and discourses that in fundamental ways shape the thoughts, words and deeds of those in the particular situations that are of interest to case-study researchers. In this sense, this notion of context also fails to account for the history of these social patterns. The critical approach that I employ here attempts in the same manner as critical ethnographers (May, 1994; Angus, 1987) to locate what happens in a particular situation within a context which includes wider social patterns and the history of those patterns. To this end I provide a history of racial/ethnic representation, and account for various contemporary manifestations of it that extend beyond Suburbia Secondary School.

Finally, case-study researchers attempt, sometimes implicitly, to maintain neutrality in their approaches, although many would acknowledge the impossibility of maintaining 'objectivity' in their inquiries. By this, I mean that they look to describe settings 'as they really are' (May, 1994), rather than adopting explicitly ideological positions. The likelihood of anyone being able to adopt a stance that in some ways does not support some position, implicitly or otherwise, is not possible, however. Everyone must place themselves somewhere, whether they are unwittingly buttressing the status quo, or knowingly working toward changing it. The position I adopt here is one that I hope works in the interests of those marginalized groups traditionally not favored by processes associated with racial/ethnic representation. I acknowledge that the various discourses associated with historically rooted social patterns and unequal power relationships have generated conditions that penalize certain groups and individuals. My intent in this book is to reveal the sometimes taken-for-granted ways in which this process works and provide suggestions to change these patterns, so that those marginalized by them can enjoy the same life chances and experiences as those who ha· e traditionally benefited from these arrangements.

Two separately funded studies provided the basis for what follows. The first, a study funded by the Ontario Ministry of Education and Training, was initially conceived as an inquiry into the ways in which teachers, students and parents were responding to student diversity in Suburbia Secondary School. During the course of the study I, as principal investigator, worked with three other people – a research officer and two graduate students. We divided up the tasks associated with the data collection and met regularly to discuss such things as emerging themes and future strategies.

The first task involved talking to teachers and observing a select few in the classroom. We chose four teachers for intensive two-day classroom observations, on the basis of their differences in teaching experience, subject expertise, and gender. Although we were not able to arrange to sit in on their classes, we did manage to talk to the only two teachers on the staff who were not of Caucasian background. These observations were accompanied by in-depth interviews that centered on teaching practice and around incidents that occurred during the course of the observations. We also interviewed many other teachers, guidance counselors and administrators. In all we talked to 25 staff members.

We also talked to and observed students. First we shadowed six students for two entire school days each. Like the teachers, they were selected to represent as much variation as possible. We initially looked for potential candidates to shadow in the classes where we were observing teachers, and made our final decisions after comparing notes on them. We gathered data both from these observations and from in-depth interviews. Student focus groups were another means of gathering information. We also talked individually to students who we thought might provide us with unique insights on diversity. For example, we sought out and interviewed one student who reacted in a constructive way to one particularly ugly racist act. In all approximately 40 students voiced their opinions on matters of diversity.

Finally we interviewed six parents or sets of parents. Initially we attempted to talk to the parents of those students we shadowed. Where this was not possible we interviewed parents who were of similar background.

In the initial stages of the study we met regularly in order to compare notes and pick out promising themes to pursue. These themes included difference, race and racism, stereotyping, curriculum, student identities and communities, and language. They emerged early in the study, while we were having our initial conversations with students. These students drew our attention to the tendency of both teachers and fellow students to hold and act on beliefs that revolved around these areas. Eventually we came to tie all these together under the larger rubric of 'representation'. We decided at this early stage to pursue this phenomenon and we subsequently looked for it in our observations in classrooms, hallways and the cafeteria, and we asked pointed questions about it when we talked to teachers, students and parents. After all the data were collected, I isolated all descriptions and/or opinions regarding these themes, and organized them for presentation in a systematic way.

The second study was part of a larger one funded by the Social Science and Humanities Council of Canada (SSHRC), designed to explore how administrators respond to racial/ethnic diversity in their school communities. This study comprised three parts, each of which called on different methods. The first two were qualitative in nature, while the third entailed a quantitative approach. The relevant portion here was the second part of the qualitative phase. In this phase I shadowed a school administrator for two weeks in efforts to try to understand how he approached racial/ethnic diversity on a day-to-day basis. The administrator worked at Suburbia Secondary School. Besides concentrating on some of the themes that had emerged in the other qualitative portion, I also took the time to pay attention to some of the representation themes that had emerged in the previous study at the school, which included, among others, difference, race and racism, stereotyping, curriculum matters, student identity and community, and language.

On the days that I followed the administrator I would arrive at the beginning of school and shadow this individual until he went home after the day had ended.[2] In his company, I toured the halls, inspected the grounds, visited classrooms, attended meetings with administrators, teachers, students, sales people, central office personnel, social workers and many others, listened to him conduct business on the phone, and watched him engage in a host of activities too numerous to mention here. Of course, there were times when he needed to meet with others in private when confidential matters were being discussed. At those times I would find something else to do. When it was possible I would ask him questions about his job, particularly on diversity issues. Many of these conversations were spontaneous in nature, but I did manage to record some of what was said between us. During the day I would keep a rough record of what I saw and heard that I felt was relevant to the study. In the evening I would sit down and reconstruct these events from the rough notes. The recorded interviews were also transcribed. Both the field notes and the interviews were eventually analyzed along with the interviews of the other administrators, using the NUD*IST software package.

Exploring Representations of Race/Ethnicity at Suburbia

The struggle over representation finds its way into many areas of school practice at Suburbia Secondary School. One of these areas is the way in which teachers and students understand and react to what they see as differences. One of the most significant of these differences is race/ethnicity. For most who spend time within Suburbia's walls, race/ethnicity is a category which everyone acknowledges and responds to. Some understandings and responses are positive, at least on the surface. Others are negative, that is, racist in nature. Some are blatantly so, while others are more subtle.

Racist discourse of this sort has a long history. Reaching back to at least 16th-century Europe, it took shape when privileged groups struggled with others to protect their interests while rigid social hierarchies of the time dissolved and new forms of social organization and means of production emerged. Racist discourses functioned to help these people secure their positions in life by providing rationales for the ways in which they subjugated and exploited others, both at home and in their colonial efforts abroad. These discourses accomplished this task by drawing distinctions and establishing hierarchies between (privileged) Europeans and others. Scientific discourse also helped in the cause by attributing racial worth to biological causes.

Racist discourses have survived pretty well over the years, although the ways in which they now operate may not be as straightforward as they once were. In the increased complexity of life, contemporary racism takes on many guises, meshing with a multitude of other forms of advantage, disadvantage and difference, including class, gender and (dis)ability.

These discourses do not go unchallenged, at least to the extent they once were; for example, various individuals and groups at Suburbia are actively engaged in challenging racist practice and discourse. But while the more obvious forms of racism are generally easy to identify and often provide the grounds for resistance, educators and students may not always recognize the more subtle forms.

One of these more subtle ways in which racism works through representational practices, at Suburbia and elsewhere, is through stereotypes. People routinely accept and employ stereotypical portrayals of groups that often work to the latter's disadvantage. While traditional approaches to analyzing stereotypes have produced some positive outcomes, such as drawing attention to oppressive patterns of racism and associated forms of social control, they do have their shortcomings. For one thing, they tend erroneously to see stereotypes as self-contained negative and mistaken images. As a follow-up exercise, proponents of this view routinely recommend the replacement of these depictions with good and accurate portrayals. In doing this, however, they fail to see the ways in which discourses work through these images. A more useful approach sees stereotypes as forms of discourse that individuals employ to make sense of what they see about them. A number of these stereotypical discourses prevail at Suburbia! Both teachers and students commonly make sense of groups of students in ways that unjustly penalize them. For example, many believe that African students possess unique physical capabilities but are less able intellectually than other students, particularly the Asian students, whom they see as the most gifted academically. These beliefs lead both teachers and students to interact with these groups in ways that do not always promote the latter's opportunities in school. The fact that it is these sense-making practices and not others that are more generally accepted is the result of a one-sided struggle. In the case that I highlight in Chapter 5, the sense of the more powerful teachers and more numerous students prevailed over the ways in which African students saw themselves. Of course the struggle over these discourses goes beyond the school; in the media, for example, discourses that depict African males in these ways circulate freely.

Perhaps one of the more obvious ways in which race/ethnicity is represented at Suburbia is in the curriculum materials. As in other schools, teachers rely heavily on texts, novels, films and other resources to assist them in their instructional practices. The ways in which these materials touch on issues of race/ethnicity, and in turn often marginalize various groups, can be traced to colonial times. Throughout that period European colonizers used curriculum resources to circulate demeaning discourses of those they colonized in order to justify their questionable treatment of these indigenous people. Although discursive treatments of non-European groups in curriculum resources have improved over the years, a residue of this negativity nevertheless persists (Pahl, 1995; Wilson, 1995; Walker, 1993; Sleeter & Grant, 1991; Whately, 1988; Lewis, 1987; McDiarmard & Pratt, 1971). The struggle in schools over what resources students should be exposed to and the meaning of these materials continues. At Suburbia, for example, teachers and a group of students battled over whether or not to include a particular novel in the curriculum. The sense that these students attributed to the book differed from that of teachers and other students. The teachers believed that the book was a classic, while the students felt that it was offensive. Because students felt so strongly about it, they demanded that the book be removed from the syllabus. The teachers disagreed. In the end, however, the teachers' sense of the book prevailed and their positions of power made it possible for them to ensure that it was retained as part of the curriculum.

Struggles over representation present themselves at Suburbia in yet another way. They surface regularly as students represent themselves to others in the process of constructing their identities. These identities are reflected in the choices students make about what kind of music they listen to, the clothing they wear, the discourses they employ, the activities in which engage, and with whom they associate. In the process they shape their own little communities, communities that sometimes form along racial/ethnic lines. At Suburbia, divisions among and between groups are obvious, although the boundaries between the respective groups are not as rigid as some would believe. Indeed many students count as their friends other students who are associated with different heritages. Whatever boundaries do exist between and among groups originate not with the individual groups themselves, but with debilitating forms of global culture that engender efforts on the part of marginalized groups and individuals to construct identities in ways that sometimes exclude different others. Students feel perpetually pressured to 'become somebody' in an anonymous, uncaring and debilitating world. Yet constructing an identity is rarely accomplished without a struggle. At Suburbia students constantly battle with school authorities over their personal choice of friends and associates, clothing, music and language.

The final area of struggle over representation concerns, not the content of the representation, but the medium: language. Language becomes a concern in a school where many different tongues are spoken. At Suburbia students speak over 60 varieties, but the language of instruction is – with the exception of a few classes where French, Canada's other official language, is spoken – English. In class most teachers expect students to speak English, regardless of what their parent tongue may be, whereas in fact they display a wide range of competencies in English, from those who speak it very well to those who barely understand it.

Language is much more than just an instrument of communication, however, or a tool that facilitates through its communicative capacities the intellectual development of students. Language is also a symbol that communicates value to those who are associated with its various networks. Those who participate in language conventions assign worth to language users on the basis of the ways in which they employ these conventions, both in the classroom and out. This attribution of worth does not occur through natural or preordained processes. Rather it is the result of struggles between and among groups who vie to have their various conventions, styles and meanings accepted as legitimate and accorded corresponding value. The results of these struggles are evident in Suburbia where certain English language styles are favored over others. This favoritism is evident in those conventions which are generally employed in the classroom and beyond, and in the attitudes of students and educators towards them.

At Suburbia everyone is engaged in the practice of representing race/ethnicity. Indeed the seemingly basic act of making sense of texts, other human beings, or oneself, and/or communicating this sense to others, implicates everybody in this process. Unfortunately here, as elsewhere, the sense that prevails does not always work in the interests of all groups. Instead it often favors those of White/Anglo/ European backgrounds in the way it attributes meaning to racial/ethnic differences, constructs various stereotypes, produces selected readings of curriculum materials, and prompts young men and women to construct identities that set them apart from others. Even the medium that students use to communicate their sense of the world confers advantages and disadvantages on them. Those students who speak English well have more advantages than those who speak it poorly or with an 'accent', or choose in certain situations to speak another language altogether. But as I have emphasized above, these sense-making frames are not simply imposed and accepted. They are the result of struggles. In a number of instances students and others actively contest prevailing meanings. Although the reality here is that many of these contests are one-sided affairs and that student efforts to resist these meanings more often than not fall short of their intended target, the fact that these meanings are human constructions and that they are contestable suggests there is hope for those looking to challenge, resist and replace oppressive discourses.

In order to help students who have been placed at a disadvantage by virtue of their perceived racial/ethnic associations, schools need to challenge debilitating discourses and find ways to construct and circulate other methods of making sense that work in the interests of all. In doing so they need to target not just local, but also more global manifestations of these discourses. One place to start is to help both teachers and students understand, critique and challenge media discourse. Another obvious target is curriculum resources. In both of these areas it is important not only to develop decoding skills, but also to join together with others to pressure media outlets, publishers and the corporate interests that run them in ways that will encourage these to sponsor alternate voices in their communications. Educators interested in providing opportunities for traditionally disadvantaged students also need to attend to language and identity issues. In doing so, they must reinforce as far as possible the value associated with students' ways of expressing themselves. These and other such efforts are needed if in the future students are to be rewarded rather than penalized for their group affiliations. Challenging and replacing oppressive racialized discourses with ones that work in the interests of those not always served well by schools will be a key to improving the life chances of these students and ensuring that their life situations improve.

The chapters that follow elaborate on the themes that I have touched on here. The next chapter describes the relationships between and among education, diversity and representation.

Notes

1. The concept of discourse that I employ here is not consistent with most notions of ideology, particularly those that see it as 'false consciousness' or as a medium that distorts reality (Giddens, 1979). Like Foucault (1980) the view of discourse that I support here does not rest on the presumption of a reality or truth 'out there' in the world. As will become evident it the following chapters, perceptions of reality and truth are always shaped within particular discourse regimes. Reality becomes whatever these discourses allow it to be. Unfortunately the discourses that have dominated social life have often not served up realties or truths that have worked in the interests of all groups equally.

2. Shadowing, like most observational techniques, is fraught with difficulties. Perhaps the most obvious is the possibility that those being observed will alter their behavior in the presence of a researcher who is doing the observing. The nature of the situation is likely to have an impact on the extent to which this may occur. If, for example, those who are being observed are acutely aware of the

researcher, the presence of this person may alter the pattern of their behavior. This is perhaps even more probable where one person is the object of observation, as in the case of shadowing. The possibility that this may happen is unavoidable. What we tried to do in these situations was to establish a relationship with those being shadowed to make them feel as comfortable as possible, so that they would be more likely to continue with their normal routines even in our presence. While it is difficult to say how successful we were, we were reasonably sure that all of the students and the administrator eventually became more or less comfortable with our presence. Classroom observations presented us with some of the same issues. However, the fact that there were 30 to 40 other individuals in the same room, and that students were used to people coming in to observe for other reasons, tended to minimize our presence. We also did what we could so as not to stand out. For example, I stopped taking my laptop computer into the classrooms to take notes, because it tended to attract the attention of some students.

Chapter 2
Education, Diversity and Representation

Formal educational institutions have responded to ethnic/racial diversity in a number of ways over the years. Early initiatives to homogenize diversity have given way, at least in some realms of policy and practice, to approaches that value (particular) differences. These latter responses, however, continue to be complicated by the changing nature of contemporary diversity in the Western world, of which there are two main aspects. The first is the change in character of the Western populations. Changing immigration patterns now mean that many teachers, themselves of European heritage, are instructing students who have emigrated from all parts of the world. The second change is associated with comparatively new patterns of representation. The disintegration of knowledge certainties, the proliferation of media images, and the race to cultivate new market niches and consumer identities will ensure that contemporary forms of diversity will continue to expand and evolve.

Educational Responses to Diversity

Providing a general overview of Western responses to diversity in the area of formal education is not always a straightforward matter. This is so for a number of reasons. First of all such responses, like the responses to diversity in general, vary over time and space. Not all regions have reacted or continue to react in consistent or similar ways. Nor do responses by dominant groups to what are perceived as differences occur in parallel time frames. A region may adopt a certain policy or practice years after it has been certified by another area, abide by it for a time, then revert back to previous ways of doing things. There can also be considerable overlap or differences in the various discourses and actual practices. Academics and policy-makers may recommend one set of policies and practices, but teachers may follow their own set. At the same time certain teaching practices may display elements of very different, sometimes inconsistent and contradictory, ways of doing things. For example, teachers may preach respect for a wide variety of beliefs, but in actual teaching practice negate those very same beliefs. Regardless of any such contradictions, however, responses ultimately reflect the times in which they occur. Reactions are ultimately associated with current discourses on the meaning of various kinds of difference.

Government and educational institutions have until recently responded to perceived diversity in one general way. Many of these agencies have seen education as the means by which groups and practices viewed as 'different' could be assimilated into the mainstream or dominant state of affairs. Although there were exceptions, most individuals who controlled such organizations instituted policies and carried out teaching practices that were designed to do away with many of the differences they saw in the students who attended their schools. They adopted these strategies because they believed that the qualities which they perceived in these different others were less worthy than their own and, as a result, represented a threat to a status quo which they valued. European colonizers, for example, looked upon the differences they saw in the people around the world whom they encountered, and eventually subordinated, with a measure of fear and a sense of superiority. But colonizers were uncomfortable not only with the differences they perceived abroad. They also looked with suspicion and a haughty disdain upon those different others who lived in their own backyards. Those who held such views believed that education had an important role to play in ensuring that these threatening differences be eliminated. This approach to education was thought to be in the interests of both the educators and those destined to be educated. Supporters of the position felt that everyone would be better off if these different others could be made to recognize the error of their ways and to embrace the values and practices of those who dominated the institutions of the day.

This approach was reflected in the ways in which European colonizers and their descendants treated indigenous people. Europeans believed the latter to be 'savages' and 'heathens' who lacked the proper manners and skills needed to get along in life. They saw their task as principally educative in nature. In 16th-century North America, for example, individuals like Sir George Peckham believed that taking control of the education of young indigenous people would provide the means through which they could be shaped into the sort of human beings of whom most Europeans would approve. Education, in his view, would bring these savages

> from falsehood to truth ... from the highway of death to the path of life ... from superstitious idolatry to sincere Christianity ... from hell to heaven ... Besides the knowledge of how to till and dress the ground, they should be reduced from unseemly customs to honest manners,

from the disordered riotous routs and companies to a well-governed commonwealth, and with all that should be taught mechanical operations, arts and sciences. (Gue, 1975:8)

These sorts of belief and their related practices have persisted until well into the 20th century. In Canada, for example, aboriginal education continues to be characterized to varying degrees by a lack of respect for, and trust in, Native people (Ryan, 1996b); processes which highlight and devalue what are perceived as differences (Ryan, 1989); and pedagogical practices that systematically erode Native beliefs and practices (Ryan, 1992a, b).

This treatment of difference is not and has not been directed exclusively at indigenous people. Those who controlled education saw schooling as an important tool for dealing with the differences they perceived not only in the immigrants who found their way inside their borders, but also in those men, women and children of the 'lower' classes who represented 'otherness' of which they did not approve. School promoters of British descent in 19th-century Upper Canada (Ontario), for example, were wary of the large numbers of Irish immigrants whom they saw as 'harbingers of a worse pestilence of social insubordination and disorder' (Prentice, 1977:56). They also felt threatened by the poor who they believed were increasingly composed of 'brutes and criminals, of men, women and children who were essentially in a "state of nature" and in desperate need of civilization and education' (Prentice, 1977:180). Education, so they thought, would provide the means through which these immigrants and the poor of the lower classes could be taught such things as Christian love, order, the sanctity of property and correct social behavior. Ideally education of this sort would encourage them to abandon their supposedly faulty habits and attitudes and to take up those more consistent with the interests of the upper classes. The school promoters were confident that education would discipline these groups, diffuse threats to the prevailing social order and foster good relations between immigrants and the poor, on the one hand, and the rich on the other.

While some regions and individual educators still hold these views, other approaches to diversity have emerged in the latter part of the 20th century. Perhaps the best known of these is 'multicultural education'. This educational response to diversity arose as an alternative to the assimilationist models that preceded it. Nurtured in the reactionary movements of the 1960s, it looked to celebrate, rather than eliminate diversity. Beyond this, it is difficult to make general statements about multicultural approaches, simply because there are so many variations of them. Many sorts of program fit into the multicultural education rubric, since the term itself often means different things to different people (see, for example, Gibson, 1976; Sleeter & Grant, 1987). These meanings may shift from country to country and from region to region. What is more, they often reflect very different historical contexts. Great Britain, the United States, Canada and Australia, for example, have very different histories of race relations, and as a consequence the ways in which multicultural education has been initiated may also differ. In the United States multicultural education emerged from the demands of mobilized ethnic/racial groups seeking to do something about their subordination, whereas in England and Australia it was principally Whites who debated such issues (Olneck, 1990; Sleeter, 1989).[1] Finally, there is no guarantee that practitioners and academics will agree on the nature and substance of multicultural education practices. Scholars may be writing and debating about issues that rarely show up in the classroom.

For simplicity's sake, I will choose one variant of multicultural education to illustrate its characteristics. I have selected this one for two reasons. First, it is a fairly common type, and second, it is often this particular version that antiracists identify when they critique multicultural education. Labeled 'benevolent multiculturalism' by May (1994), it encompasses such types as 'multicultural education for cross-cultural understanding' (Gibson, 1976), 'culturally responsive education' (Gibson, 1976), 'a human relations approach to improve interpersonal relations' and 'promotion of cultural pluralism by raising consciousness' (Sleeter & Grant, 1987). Unlike assimilationist approaches, which assume that different others come to school culturally deprived, benevolent multiculturalism is based on the notion that these young people (and their parents) are simply culturally different (Ogbu, 1992). Unlike the former approach, differences are not assigned a differential status, at least in principle. Instead proponents of these strategies look to celebrate differences in culturally plural schools and societies. At the same time they look with disfavor on policies and practices that are designed to 'melt down' differences and produce monocultural (that is, dominant cultural) communities.

While there are differences even within this strand of multicultural education, the concept of culture nevertheless assumes a pivotal role. Proponents feel that bringing certain aspects of what they see as culture into the classroom will generate a number of desired outcomes. First, exposing unknowing others to elements of various 'cultures' of which they will have had little previous knowledge will lead to greater understanding and tolerance of different others and improve communication between and among groups (Sleeter & Grant, 1987; Gibson, 1976). Second, learning about their own culture in the classroom will provide ethnic minority students with the opportunity to improve their self-esteem and develop 'cultural pride' (May, 1994:37). Proponents of this view maintain that when combined with the incorporation of cultural processes in classroom interaction, these improved self-perceptions will allow those who possess them to fend off the effects of potentially inhibiting cultural discontinuities and will in the end enhance student achievement (Erickson, 1987b; Ogbu, 1992). Many of these practices and related discourses persist today, often alongside other similar approaches. Multicultural education thus conceived has however had its critics, on both the right and the left of the political spectrum. In fact the most recent response to diversity, antiracism, often takes as its starting-point a critique of this particular form of multiculturalism.

Antiracist education emerged as an alternative to multicultural education in the 1980s. It represented, in part, the reaction of radical educators and scholars to the conservative challenge to the liberal gains of the 1960s and to the apparent inability of multicultural strategies to improve the position of ethnic and racial groups. Antiracists were particularly critical of the way in which multiculturalists employed the concept of culture. They felt that highlighting the surface manifestations of what was essentially an apolitical version of culture, as they believed proponents of multicultural education did, could do little to change the position of ethnic and racial minority students. They took issue with the notion that cultural discontinuities were responsible for the inability of certain groups to master the school curriculum. For antiracists school failure (and the subsequent position of racial minorities generally) was intimately tied to the enduring patterns of subordination and domination that characterized relationships between generally White, middle-class groups and various racial minority groups. In other words, the real problem was not that the various groups were different, but that certain groups were subject to systemic racist practices, both in school and out. The antiracist argument was that by attending to such surface cultural or lifestyle phenomena as 'saris, samosas and steel bands' (Troyna, 1993) educators deflected attention away from the structural inequalities that drove racist practice, inhibited school achievement, and inevitably limited the life chances of many ethnic/racial minority students. Antiracists also took care to emphasize the place not just of 'racial' patterns of domination, but of the complex relationships between and among all forms of domination, including those that revolve around race, class, gender and health/disability.

Not surprisingly, multicultural advocates take issue with the claims of some of the antiracists, and in particular the latter's criticisms of multicultural approaches. The most repeated view is that antiracists set up a straw figure which they then proceed to dismantle. Sleeter (1989), for example, maintains that antiracists oversimplify multicultural education, mistakenly assuming that all multiculturalists advocate the single 'human relations' approach at which their criticisms are directed. Multiculturalists respond that the field is more complex than the antiracists claim, and that few if any contemporary approaches conform to the narrow picture they paint of multicultural education. Sleeter goes on to say that multicultural education, like antiracist education, can be seen as a form of resistance to oppressive social relationships. Indeed more recent advocates of multicultural education (Nieto, 1992; May, 1994), like Sleeter herself, acknowledge the role of subordination and domination in the educational process and the place of strategies to counteract these debilitating patterns. Others (Gillborn, 1995; Carrington & Short, 1989) maintain that actual classroom and school practices which antiracists and multiculturalists advocate display more similarities than differences.[2]

Despite some overlap between the two approaches, one sticking-point remains – the nature and place of culture in analysis and recommended practice. Antiracists are correct in pointing out that emphasizing superficial and apolitical aspects of culture obscures the structural nature of disadvantage. But excluding culture from analyses and recommended practice altogether – throwing the baby out with the bathwater – is not helpful either. One recent study that attempts to resolve this culture/structure divide is May's (1994) enlightening description of Richmond Road School in Auckland, New Zealand. In it he shows how the gap between emancipatory theory and practice can be bridged. At Richmond Road, culture retained a pivotal role in this process. Advocacy for cultural pluralism, however, was complemented by the practice of structural or institutional pluralism. The principal, Jim Laughton, and all those who were associated with the school, worked to ensure that elements of non-Anglo culture which they introduced were lodged in the very structure or organization of the school. They accomplished this by producing curriculum materials that represented non-Anglo perspectives; changing the traditional authority relationships between teachers, students and community members; featuring child-centered pedagogy; abandoning grades and embracing vertical *ropu* (family groupings) with their emphasis on inclusiveness, mutual support and extended relationships; entrenching home languages (and culture) in the curriculum; and eliminating traditional school assessment patterns. Those associated with Richmond Road

School believed that increasing the life chances of minority students demanded that the school not only recognize, but promote, honor and celebrate differences, and that it help students acquire the skills necessary to function in a society that does not always favour the efforts of marginalized groups. As May (1994) illustrates, these methods turned out to be reasonably effective in accomplishing these goals. Moreover the school was able to survive the death of the architect of these programs, Jim Laughton, at least for a time.

Many of those who read May's account will be inspired by the accomplishments of Jim Laughton, the teachers, students and community members associated with Richmond Road School. Their efforts and the efforts of many multicultural and antiracist teachers and scholars rightly deserve to be applauded. They have introduced many ways of thinking about and practicing education that have increased the visibility and legitimacy of racial/ethnic diversity, and in some instances provided greater opportunities for marginalized groups. Nevertheless the various multicultural and antiracist approaches to education are not without their shortcomings. As is evident above, antiracists are quick to point out what they see as the failings of some versions of multiculturalism. More recently, however, especially in Britain, antiracism has come under fire not just from conservative groups, but also from those on the left of the political spectrum (Gillborn, 1995; Rattansi, 1992). Critics have pointed out how multiculturalists and antiracists may either ignore or misread the ways in which culture is represented in their respective positions. Rattansi, for example, takes issue with the way in which a number of multiculturalists and antiracists see fit to represent culture, faulting them for, among other things, the essentialism he discerns both in their respective positions (see below) and in the exclusively positive images they promote for what they themselves perceive as reasonably well-defined groups.

The practice of representation, as Rattansi points out, is a key element in both multicultural and antiracist approaches. In this regard both promote the use of positive images in the classroom. Multiculturalists attempt to combat racial prejudice by providing students with 'positive' images of 'other cultures'. By using these images to teach students about various groups, proponents hope that they will come to a better understanding of these different others and consequently treat them with respect. Antiracists rely on a similar strategy. Citing approaches by Jeffcoate (1979) and Hatcher and Shallice (1983), Rattansi notes that positive images are inherent in antiracist efforts to present Black histories primarily as narratives of resistance and struggle against racism.

Rattansi takes issue with this practice of exclusively presenting positive images. He finds a number of faults with the approach. The first is that it leaves both multiculturalists and antiracists open to the same charges of propaganda and indoctrination as they themselves sometimes direct towards textbooks, authors and teachers. Advocating 'correct' representations while at the same time purging 'incorrect' ones provides fodder for complaints about a top-down authoritarian or totalitarian conspiracy. In this regard conservative opponents, multiculturalists and antiracists all share the same epistemological terrain. According to Rattansi (1992:34)

> all share the misleading assumption that it is possible to produce a singular, incontestable, objective and accurate representation of the reality external to the literary or photographic of any other text. They thus ignore or obscure a different democratic objective: that is, the search for mechanisms for giving voice to a range of representations, and for encouraging a critical dialogue and interrogation of all intellectual and political frameworks.

Rattansi also contends, citing the views of Black artists, that the reduction of diverse Black histories, experiences and cultures to no more than a response to racism inhibits the productive exploration of the economic, cultural and sexual differences within Black communities. Indeed 'positive' images tend to privilege middle-class, heterosexual and family respectability. Such a reduction also tends to block the creativity of, in this case, Black artistic imagination and practices of representation. By favoring the presentation of only certain images, multicultural and antiracist positions fail to account for the complex ways in which representation works. They do not always acknowledge the role of readers in constructing meaning, the interpretive frameworks which all readers must call on to make sense of texts, the manner in which they take up positions in this process, and the effect that this has on them. Rattansi (1992:35) argues that

> both multicultural and antiracist critiques ignore the actual literary and pedagogic devices involved in the construction of subject positions for the child/reader in school texts. They neglect *how* texts construct meanings as opposed to *what* they supposedly mean. As a consequence, the complexity of the processes by which texts which form part of particular school disciplines – history or geography, etc. – have effects on the 'subjects' of schools, the students, is also neglected. Too often, all the protagonists make simplistic assumptions about the ease with which subjectivities are produced by racist or antiracist texts.

The possibility of any straightforward correspondence between a particular group and an image of it is further undermined by the realities that characterize group dynamics. Rattansi believes that in their attempts to teach about 'other' cultures in the classroom, multiculturalists consistently oversimplify the highly complex, contextually variable and perpetually changing group dynamics that typically characterize encounters both within minority communities and in their relationships to dominant groups. He contends that group boundaries are continually being drawn and redrawn as divisions and alliances emerge and fall away. This implies, he suggests, that the foundations of teaching about 'other cultures' need to be reconsidered; that the shape and character of ethnic formations is too complex to be reduced to formulas around festivals, religions, world-views and lifestyles, which fail to take into consideration 'the shifting and kaleidoscopic nature of ethnic differentiations and identities and their relation to internal divisions of class and gender' (Rattansi, 1992:39).

Rattansi also contends that antiracists are not immune from charges of essentialism. He maintains that by focusing (for understandable reasons) on unitary conceptions of the 'Black Struggle', antiracists have tended to reify the notion of community. As Rattansi points out, 'Black' here denotes not simply an often successful political alliance against racism. It also 'operates as a profoundly cultural category, an attempted representation of particular experiences and a particular construction of unity around those experiences' (Rattansi, 1992:40). Recently, however, some groups have reacted against these characterizations. Rattansi notes that British Asian and Afro-Caribbean groups have protested the homogenization of different histories, cultures and needs implied in the use of a single category. Others have pointed to the marginalization of minority groups not included in this category. And still others have begun to explore and express identities not exhausted by the experience of and struggle against racism.

The point Rattansi emphasizes here is that efforts to work for social justice in increasingly diverse schools require that educators attend to issues of representation. There are a number of reasons for acknowledging the place of representation in this process. The first is that it is becoming increasingly apparent that educators and social scientists are unable to construct mirror images of naturally existing groups in society, much less exclusively positive images, as some multiculturalists and antiracists attempt to do. Recent perspectives in the philosophy of science, outlined below, describe the futility of attempts to accurately represent a supposed real world in this way. Jameson (1984) refers to this condition as a 'crisis of representation'. Another reason for acknowledging issues of representation is the recent explosion of modes and means of representation. The proliferation of communication vehicles, including electronic media images and the rapidly expanding nature of the content which they transmit, continues to multiply the ways in which people can know and understand the world, experience life and live out their dreams. Finally the changing nature of groups themselves complicates attempts to represent what are thought of as static communities. Changing immigration patterns over the past couple of decades have contributed in a substantial way to the perpetually evolving nature of diversity in Western countries.

Changing Populations

Changing immigration patterns over the last two decades have brought on changes in the traditional population base of a number of Western countries. This is particularly true in the case of Great Britain and its former English-speaking colonies. More men, women and children from non-European countries than ever before are traveling to take up permanent residence in Great Britain, the United States, Canada and Australia. Technology is partly responsible for these changes. Advances in commuter travel have made it easier for people to journey long distances. More important though for these changing population flows are changes in immigration policies. Canada and Australia, for example, initiated changes to their policies over two decades ago. Before this they were discriminatory in character, explicitly favoring European immigrants, while at the same time excluding people who were not from European countries. The result, naturally, was that European settlers outnumbered others by a considerable margin. But even though such discriminatory policies have been abandoned, non-Western populations continue to be placed at a disadvantage. The United States policy reflects this implicit discrimination. By favoring immigrants, other than refugees, who either have family who are already citizens or else have valued or needed skills, these policies exclude many in the Third World who would have difficulty acquiring such skills. Despite this advantage, however, European immigration has declined significantly over the past two decades, while non-European has increased substantially.

In Canada, as in Britain, Australia and the United States, immigration patterns have changed over the last century. Give the discriminatory policies in place before 1960, it may not be surprising to hear that from 1913 to 1957 the United Kingdom accounted for 37% of all immigrants (Statistics

Canada, 1993). By 1974, however, these numbers had changed. At this time immigrants from the United Kingdom comprised 17.6%, while places such as India, Hong Kong, Jamaica and the Philippines now accounted for 5.8, 5.8, 5.1 and 4.3% respectively of the total immigrant population (Statistics Canada, 1993). The next two decades brought yet more changes. By 1989 Asian immigrants outnumbered Europeans by almost two to one, with 94,645 immigrating from Asia, 50,725 from Europe and only 7045 from Great Britain (Statistics Canada, 1990). In 1991 Hong Kong was the largest supplier of immigrants, at 9.7%, followed by Poland at 6.8%, China at 6.0% and India at 5.6%. Many other immigrants reported countries of origin such as the Philippines, Lebanon, Vietnam, El Salvador, Sri Lanka, Guyana, Iran, Greece and Italy (Statistics Canada, 1993). Canada's growing diversity is perhaps best highlighted by the fact that it employed 126 categories to account for its various ethnic groups in 1991 (United Nations Yearbook, 1994).

The population of the United States has also become more diverse over the last two decades. Its reported foreign-born population of 9,740,000 in 1970 increased to 19,767,000 in 1990 (US Bureau of the Census, 1995). Of these 4,017,000 were born in Europe. Only 17.9% of this number have immigrated to the United States between 1980 and 1990, however. This contrasts sharply with the percentage of those people who emigrated from Asia, Mexico, the Caribbean, Central America, South America and Africa in the last 10 years. The US Bureau of the Census (1995) notes that of the total number of American citizens born in the aforementioned countries, 56.1%, 49.9%, 40.4%, 67.4%, 52.1% and 59.3% respectively immigrated during this time. In another indicator of diversity, this same agency reported that resident non-European ancestries include 1,113,000 Hispanic, 11,587,000 Mexican, 1,955,000 Puerto Rican, 1,505,000 Chinese, 1,005,000 Japanese, 23,777,000 African and 8,708,000 American Indian. Finally, there are 31,845,000 people in the United States who speak a language other than English (US Bureau of the Census, 1995).

Australia's changing attitudes towards immigration have reflected many of these same trends. These changes have meant that officials do not keep track of the origins of settlers, at least in published records, as they once did. The Australian Bureau of Statistics *1995 Year Book Australia* does note however that there is considerably more diversity than their categories might indicate. It shows, for example, that those first-generation citizens who were born in Lebanon include Catholics, Orthodox, Shi'a Muslims, Sunni Muslims, Druze and Armenians. As in Canada and the United States, Australia's settler population has seen an increase in non-

Europeans. Between 1971 and 1991 numbers indicate an increase in citizens born in Latin America from 12,879 to 71,955, in Africa from 33,709 to 99,058, in Southern Asia from 39,960 to 110,494, in East Asia from 28,113 to 199,515, in South-East Asia from 38,440 to 377,844 and in the Middle East from 44,352 to 167,587 (Australian Bureau of Statistics, 1995). Percentages of settler arrivals reflect a similar shift. While immigrants from the United Kingdom and Ireland decreased from 44.6% to 9.2% of the total immigrant population during this time, those coming from Hong Kong, Vietnam, India, the Philippines and China increased from 0.3% to 10.4%, 0% to 7.8%, 0% to 5.4%, 0% to 5.2%, and 0.3% to 3.6%, respectively (Australian Bureau of Statistics, 1995).

Generally speaking, immigrants tend to gravitate toward particular areas. Many prefer to settle in urban surroundings. In Britain 44.6% of 'ethnic minority' groups live in Greater London, while only 10.3% of persons from 'white' groups reside in these same areas (Owen, 1994). Furthermore, many of these settler groups tend to congregate in particular districts. Those of Pakistani heritage who live in the south-east region, for example, cluster around north-east London, Slough and Luton. Australia displays many of these same trends, although groups tend not to segregate themselves the way they do in Great Britain. Sydney and Melbourne have the largest concentrations of non-English settlers (Australian Bureau of Statistics, 1995). The same holds true for Canada. In 1991, immigrants respectively accounted for 38, 30, 24 and 22% of Toronto's, Vancouver's, Hamilton's, and Kitchener's total populations (Statistics Canada, 1993).

The immigrant population by itself is producing major demographic changes in school populations, particularly in these larger urban areas. Data gathered from one Toronto school district in 1988 indicate that one-third of the total day school population and two-thirds of the mothers of this same student population were born outside Canada (Handscombe, 1989). The Ontario Ministry of Education and Training (1993) indicates that nearly 70% of all foreign-born youth live in Greater Toronto, over half are of single non-European ethnicity, two-thirds are visible minorities, 50% have a mother tongue that is neither French nor English, and one-third have immigrated to Canada since 1981. The age of immigrants is also significant – many of them are either of school or of child-bearing age. In 1987, 28% (42,970) of the total immigrant population were 19 years old or younger, while 50% (76,834) were between the ages of 20 and 39 (Statistics Canada, 1990). Suburbia Secondary School perhaps reflects the diversity of many schools in this area. A recent school-administered student survey indicated that students associated their ethnic identity with 63 different countries. Italy (18%), the Philippines (14.7%), Portugal (9.5%), China (8%) and Poland (6.3%) constituted the largest groups. Of the total of 1700 students, only 76 reported either that they had no ethnic heritage or that it was Canadian.

Changing immigration flows that bring more non-Western people to the English-speaking world constitute only one part of the increase in perceived diversity in the First World. Growing skepticism about science and certainty, the increasing public availability of information, and the impact of electronic patterns of communication and representation are also increasing the ways in which people understand and experience their lives.

A Crisis of Representation

Increasingly scholars are indicating that efforts to represent groups in ways some believe to be accurate are pointless. Like Rattansi (1992), above, they maintain that it is impossible to present a picture of, for example, a certain group of immigrants to the West that corresponds to the way such a group really is. Many of the critics of this one-to-one correspondence view of knowledge are philosophers. Some maintain that these challenges to traditional views of knowledge and science have engendered a crisis of sorts. In the foreword to Jean-François Lyotard's now classic work *The Postmodern Condition* Jameson (1984) employs the term 'crisis of representation' to refer to the problems of legitimacy that science and knowledge production are facing in the contemporary world. Lyotard sought to expose the fallacy of the traditional foundations of science, but the crisis to which Jameson refers clearly has wider applications. Indeed, it is not just philosophers who are experiencing doubt these days. Many ordinary men and women find cause to dispute what at one time may have been time-honored truths, scientific or otherwise. While some may simply recognize the limitations of physical and social sciences, many others are caught up in contemporary trends that lead people to question all kinds of knowledge claims. The questioning associated with these social conditions may include the growing legitimacy of diverse (non-scientific) sources of knowledge and information, the rapid expansion of publicly available perspectives, views and scenarios, and the proliferation of electronic information sources. This questioning will not only continue to create a more diverse world, but will also reshape the ways in which we experience our realities.

How then can we understand what social scientists and philosophers mean by 'representation'? And how is it associated with doubt and diversity in our contemporary world? One way to look at representation is to view it as a form of reproduction. An artist, for example, may attempt to reproduce a particular setting on stretched canvas. Applying a range of colored paints to such a surface in a discriminating way allows the artist to capture what can be a very large, complex, multidimensional scene in a relatively small two-dimensional space. The fact that the different characters, figures or etchings on the canvas stand for elements of the original setting permits those who look upon the painting at another location to identify this original scene or another similar one (at least if this indeed is the artist's intent). In a similar way the technology associated with photography allows a person to reproduce a particular setting, freezing it in time.

The capacity for reproduction and representation has changed over the centuries. The earliest human beings developed systems of signs which they meant to stand for or signify something other than the sign itself. Although they did reproduce some of these signs on cave walls and other surfaces, the earliest preferred mode of employment was oral, and was used most often in the context of interaction with fellow human beings. The sounds associated with what would eventually come to be called 'words' stood for something; that is, they possessed meaning. The words could represent to others a number of things, including identifications of particular states of affairs. Language allowed men and women to reproduce, for others, versions of what was happening or had already happened in different times and places. In some communities such narratives played an important role in their governance and continuity. In these instances, certain figures were empowered, often by virtue of their memorizing capacities, with the authority to recite epic poems or myths (Lorrimore, 1994). These narratives were generally invested with the capacity to adapt to changing circumstances. Narrators simply absorbed any new knowledge and potentially contradictory information into new versions of these perpetually evolving myths. In some circumstances story-tellers would recite the myth in such a way as to allow listeners to personalize what they were hearing so that they could adapt it to their own particular circumstances (Scollon & Scollon, 1981).

As oral societies gave way to literate ones a different kind of representation emerged . Writing made it possible to freeze time. In contrast to oral communities, where representations were perpetually evolving, the more or less permanent nature of words on parchment or paper allowed men and women to construct static representations of ideas and states of affairs. In a sense these words and the ideas to which they referred were thought to stand on their own. Readers could attribute meaning to these words without necessarily knowing the context in which they were written or the intentions of the author (Goody & Watt, 1968; Goody, 1977; Havelock, 1978). This decontextualized form of representation also complemented a scientific view of the world. It allowed for the habitual separating-out of various cultural elements from what, in many oral societies, was an indivisible wholeness.

> Writing facilitates the segmentation of nature, its dissection into categories, and the systematic ordering of all elements of experience into separate areas of intellectual activities. This taxonomic division of life goes hand in hand with syllogistic reasoning. A more general relationship between words and their referents and the looser connections with the particularities of person, place and time frees statements up for their dissection and manipulation. It allows men and women to marshal an argument by defining the relevant ideas, breaking down problems into constituent elements, analyzing and specifying relevant relationships, and finally, employing rational syntheses. (Ryan, 1994a:256)

Science emerged with literacy and pushed to the limits the kind of representation that the latter made possible. Scientists presumed that scientific techniques allowed it to generate accounts that corresponded to a presumed static, solid and obdurate world 'out there'. Jameson (1984:viii) points to science as having 'an essentially realist epistemology, which conceives of representation as the reproduction, for subjectivity, of an objectivity that lies outside it – projects a mirror theory of knowledge and art, whose fundamental evaluative categories are those of adequacy, accuracy and Truth itself.' In other words science, in this view, presumes to have the unique ability to represent or reproduce the one and true nature of the world as it really exists. It is this capacity that Lyotard maintains is losing credibility in the postmodern world, prompting those like Jameson to speak of a crisis of representation.

There are a number of critiques of this traditional view of knowledge and science. Two are particularly useful. Both Lyotard (1984) and Foucault (1979, 1980) offer insightful criticism of the traditional realist scientific paradigm. Lyotard directs his efforts at what he believes to be science's faltering legitimizing mechanisms. To begin with, he believes that science is simply a narrative – a form of language game – since scientific claims must always be made within a language. What makes it different from so-called ordinary narratives is its acceptance as a privileged discourse, one that takes precedence over others. Maintaining this status, however, has required that it appeal to sources outside of itself. This represents a change from the self-legitimizing character of premodern story-telling. Here the narration acquired its authority by virtue of its conformance to social custom. Science, on the other hand, is incapable of legitimizing itself. It cannot employ its own rules or techniques to verify these same rules. As a consequence, science finds itself in the position of appealing to other narratives to guarantee its authority. Lyotard (1984) refers to these as 'meta-' or 'grand' narratives. They are different from the usual kind of narrative in that they are overarching and synthesizing stories that provide coherence and meaning at the local level. Lyotard mentions two such metanarratives – emancipatory and speculative. He contends that legitimacy is conferred on science because of its role in freeing humanity from the bonds of oppression and its ability to contribute to the unity of all knowledge.

The substance of Lyotard's challenge is his contention that these legitimizing metanarratives have declined in their influence and, in doing so, have undermined the authority of scientific knowledge. In fact he goes so far as to 'define postmodern as an incredulity towards metanarratives' (1984:xxiv). It's not that he believes that people reject these narratives out of hand, but that they are finding it increasingly difficult to accept them (Burbules, 1995). Lyotard attributes this skepticism to the changes in technology and capitalism that have occurred since the Second World War, the seeds of which can be found in the 19th century. These changes have rendered science incapable of ensuring its emancipatory or knowledge-unification goals. He contends that although emancipation is an admirable goal, it has nevertheless become evident that it is misguided. This is because oppression has shown itself to be a more complex phenomenon than many proponents of emancipation would admit. He believes that the sites at which conflict occur reflect multiple forms of oppression that interact and play off one another. As a consequence these context-dependent struggles cannot be reduced to single and unified forms of domination and subordination. To illustrate his point he provides examples which show that actions taken in the name of emancipation may produce outcomes that run counter to the ideal. A unified totality of knowledge also seems hopelessly out of reach. Universities no longer police knowledge, traditional disciplines dissolve with regularity, and new areas of knowledge proliferate.

Have these grand narratives indeed lost their credibility? And if so, what does this mean for scientific knowledge? Ironically, Lyotard (1984) is somewhat ambiguous about the emancipatory metanarrative. He insists (p. 37) that 'the grand narrative has lost its credibility, regardless of what mode of unification it uses', having just stated (p. 35) that emancipation is 'gaining new vigor'. While Lyotard demonstrates *logically* that emancipation in a postmodern world is a misguided ideal, he seems also to concede, at least up to a point, that men and women may still subscribe to emancipatory narratives. West (1991) takes Lyotard up on this very question, charging in fact that Lyotard presents an exclusively Western view. West (1991:5) maintains that Lyotard 'and his friends hanging out on the left bank' overlook 'the religious and ideological and national revivals in Eastern Europe and the Soviet Union'. He asks 'Who is he talking about … whom does he have in mind?' But the fact that emancipatory meta-narratives may not be a thing of the past may have little to do with scientific knowledge. Lyotard argues that prescriptive statements associated with emancipatory discourse and the denotative statements of speculative discourse are logically distinct, that is, they have their own sets of rules. He maintains that 'there is nothing to prove that if a statement is true, it follows that a prescriptive statement based on it … will be just' (p. 40). In other words one cannot get 'an ought from an is', a value from a fact, or vice versa.

The bottom line here is that while emancipatory grand narratives may be alive and well, their existence cannot enhance the legitimacy of science. Science then becomes just another discourse that has to compete on an equal footing with other discourses, a state of affairs that erodes even further the speculative unity of knowledge. Metanarratives associated with emancipation or other legitimizing narratives such as efficiency persist,[3] but as increasing numbers of diverse scientific and non-scientific claims compete for legitimacy, the idea of the possibility of the unity of all knowledge continues to recede.

Foucault's work (1979, 1980) complements Lyotard's. Though Foucault also takes issue with the authority of science, he directs his attention to the relationship between power and knowledge. In doing so, he turns the traditional view of this association on its head. Many scientists and social scientists have looked on the practice of science as a means of representing existence the way it really is. Scientific methods are able to accomplish this task because they are thought to be able to be objective or neutral. Indeed science's authority is derived at least in part from its supposed ability to transcend the social (and personal) relationships under which scientists and social scientists labor, including relationships of power. Foucault, however, maintains that just the opposite is in fact the case – power is intimately intertwined with knowledge. He contends that

> truth isn't outside power, or lacking in power … Truth is a thing of this world: it is produced only by virtue of multiple forms of constraint. And it induces regular effects of power. Each society has its regime of

truth, its 'general politics' of truth: that is, the types of discourse which it accepts and makes function as true; the mechanisms and instances which enable one to distinguish true and false statements, the means by which each is sanctioned; the techniques and procedures accorded value in the acquisition of truth; the status of those who are charged with saying what counts as true. (Foucault, 1980:131)

Like Lyotard, Foucault believes that authoritative knowledge – truth – is produced by men and women in and through privileged discourses. But he takes this idea one step further. He emphasizes the fundamental role that power plays in the establishment of knowledge. For Foucault, these discourses derive their value from power, and not from their (supposed) capacity to represent the world as it really is.[4] The fact that the products of scientific investigations are often thought to be true can be traced not to their specialized techniques, but to their position in relationships of power.

Foucault and Lyotard highlight one side of the current crisis of representation. From a philosophical point of view, they both take issue with the idea that science is uniquely capable of reproducing portraits of a real world 'out there'. Both contend instead that what are believed to be true representations of life always emerge in and through constructed discourses. Lyotard explains science's fading legitimacy; Foucault reveals the role of power in the production of knowledge. Lyotard alerts us to the fading hopes for the unity of all knowledge and the subsequent proliferation of different representations of reality; Foucault notes that those representations that will count or dominate will be those that are backed by favorable relationships of power.

Employing logical arguments, philosophers have long since disposed of the notion of accurate representation (see also Cherryholmes, 1994). It is only recently, however, that skeptical attitudes towards scientific claims have surfaced among the public. Faced with ever increasing numbers of competing and contradictory claims, people are beginning to acknowledge the limitations of science. Hargreaves (1994:57) argues that men and women no longer depend as they once did on expert knowledge, received wisdom or established beliefs to guide them along the path of life.

The knowledge explosion ... has led to a proliferation of expertise; much of it contradictory and competitive, all of it changing. This has begun to reduce people's dependence on particular kinds of expert knowledge, but also created a collapse of certainty in received wisdom and established beliefs. Sunshine is good for you, then it is not. Alcohol is assumed to be detrimental to one's health until it is announced that modest levels of red wine actually reduce cholesterol levels. The reported release by the Colombian drug cartel that cocaine is high in fiber, is a joke that points to the disconcerting pervasiveness of perversity of such scientific certainties. Science no longer seems to be able to show us how to live, at least with any certainty or stability.

Hargreaves goes on to illustrate how what were once thought to be 'incontrovertible findings of educational research' have subsequently been shown not to be the case. As an example, he illustrates how later research into the topic of direct instruction has produced different findings from early explorations. The consequence of this state of affairs is that those responsible for choosing school curricula can no longer rely on (social) science to guide them. The case of Lola, Montana typifies the dilemmas that often arise in such situations (Anderson, 1990). In this situation two groups of concerned individuals squared off in a battle over school curricula: on the one side, educators and parents who promoted 'global perspectives', 'moral reasoning', and 'values' clarification'; on the other, their opponents, offended by the fact that their children were not being instructed in the rudiments of patriotism and in traditional Christian and American values. These sorts of scene are being played out all over the Western world. Inevitably, however, what will count as knowledge and be included in the curriculum will be the version favored by those in power. Whether an indigenous view of North American history, a creationist view of the world, or an antiracist program will become part of the curriculum will depend on what kind of pressure and power groups of teachers, administrators, parents, school board trustees or legislators can bring to bear on the decision-making processes.[5]

The availability of these diverse ways of knowing has increased dramatically over the past few decades. The expansion of electronic media is at least partly responsible. These now provide an infinite range of information sources to anyone who cares to tune in to the appropriate channels or visit the right websites. Indeed the mass media are almost wholly responsible for the growing heterogeneity that many in the so-called First World are now experiencing. The number of options with which they provide consumers and the form of communication which they adopt are both responsible for the growing diversity in the contemporary world.

Electronic Representations and Consumption

The ways in which people communicate and the manner in which they make representations has changed over the course of the 20th century. Although they still communicate with each other orally and on paper, the time they devote to electronic media has increased dramatically over the past 30 years. People who live in the First World spend considerable time watching television, viewing movies at the theatre or in their home, interacting with electronic games such as Nintendo, surfing the Internet, and sending and receiving facsimiles and Email. In 1987, for example, almost 100% of Canadian households had a television, 50% had two sets, 45% had video players, while 68% enjoyed the choice that they received from their cable subscriptions (Young, 1989). In 1994 Canadians averaged 22.7 hours in front of the television over the course of a week. Teens watched less, at 17.1 hours per week (Statistics Canada, 1994).

The shift to electronics has brought on a change in the structure and character of communication. Among other things, contemporary communications technology has contributed to an annihilation of space and time. Transmissions criss-cross the globe in seconds, rendering what were once borders and boundaries irrelevant. In a sense these technologies are supplanting the 'horizontal' organization of people with 'vertical' organizational forms (Morley & Robins, 1995). Men and women are now increasingly connected electronically rather than geographically. The character of electronic communication is also unique. At no other time in history has the technology for reproducing the real been so effective (Denzin, 1991). We now have the ability to capture life in vivid color and almost unlimited detail. The medium generally responsible for these reproductions, however, is not only a system of representation that produces meaning. It is also a means of production that turns out standard products (Gardner & Shephard, 1984 in Andersen, 1995:19). As a consequence, advertising assumes a key role in this process. Indeed Andersen (1995) goes so far as to claim that advertising is the essence of postmodern culture.

The global nature of these communicative networks invites predictions that the world will become more homogenized. The idea here is that since improved communications techniques now situate us all in a type of global village, we are destined to become very much like one another. In a sense the mass media do offer opportunities for men, women and children to share experiences. Electronic media can create new communities, as it were, across their spaces of transmission, bringing together disparate and different groups around the common experience of television. National broadcasting services like the BBC have played a key role in promoting national unity at the symbolic level. They have done so, in part, by linking individuals and families to a national centre and offering audiences an image of themselves and of their nation as a knowable community (Morely

& Robins, 1995). To insist, however, that we will all share a common world culture is to miss the paradoxical nature of these communicative processes. Ang (1995:163) maintains that 'the global village, as the site of the culture of capitalist postmodernity, is a thoroughly paradoxical place, unified yet multiple, totalized yet deeply unstable, closed and open-ended at the same time.' Rather than inhibiting diversity, integration fosters it. Even though more people will be connected to one another, the sheer number of these interdependencies increases exponentially the potential for a diversity of relationships between and among what were once distant and disparate worlds. Perhaps the greatest potential for diversity, however, rests not with the quantity of relationships, but with their character. The potential play of differences that accompanies these electronic representations allows for multiple interpretations of them.

The work of Baudrillard (1981, 1983) is helpful in sorting out the nature and effect of electronic representations. Unfortunately he is often derided and misunderstood, particularly by American critics (Denzin, 1991). His cynical and biting characterization of American culture (see, for example, Baudrillard, 1988) is no doubt at least partly responsible for this reaction. Another reason for his negative reception may be his tendency to totalize his descriptions. Reading his work, one might easily come to the conclusion that he believes contemporary life to consist exclusively of tours through theme parks and time in front of the television watching rock videos and commercials. As Poster (1995), Ang (1995) and others point out, however, there is much outside these images. People still spend much time conversing and interacting with each other on a face-to-face basis. Nevertheless, despite some of his excesses Baudrillard's work provides a good starting-point for interrogating the representations that accompany contemporary media culture.

Baudrillard is preoccupied with the concept of 'mediation', that is, he directs his efforts towards understanding the nature and effect of the signs that men and women employ to communicate with one another. He believes that the processes associated with the signs' capacity to represent reality have changed over the years. In premodern times, he contends, there was a straightforward three-way relationship between 'sign' (e.g. word), 'signified' (concept) and 'referent' (object). A word, for example, was thought to stand unambiguously for something in the real world. When someone spoke of a tree, listeners generally understood what the speaker was referring to. The sign (the word 'tree'), its meaning (the concept of tree) and the designated object (the actual tree) coincided nicely with one another. This relationship began to change, however, as the world (that is, Europe and the West) moved from the Renaissance through the industrial age to postmodernity. According to Baudrillard, signs went from reflecting, perverting, and masking the real world to finally having no relationship with it whatsoever. The mass media now disrupt what supposedly was once the direct unmediated relationship of men and women to a material world. The media's floating signs and images produce endless series of simulations, which play off one another in what Baudrillard refers to as a 'hyperreality'. This simulated reality is taken to be more real than the reality for which these signs presume to stand. It achieves this, in part, by changing the thing that it treats, altering forever the 'original' (Poster, 1995).[6]

Baudrillard also highlights the change in the type of sign generally employed in electronic media. Postmodern culture is now characterized by figural (non-discursive) rather than discursive signs. This shift has consequences for the way in which men and women experience what they see. Lash (1988), for example, contends that unlike discursive signification, where interpretation is bound by sets of rules, figural signification is subject only to the unhindered mobility of the eye in a continuous visual field. To signify via figures is to signify merely through a resemblance to referents. Signifiers or symbols which resemble referents, however, are less likely to be clearly distinguished from them in the way discursive signifiers normally would be. In media culture, in fact, referents often act as signifiers in their own right. The result is that what we have now are proliferating chains of signifiers that are able to float free from objects and are available for use in an infinite variety of associations. The possibilities for diverse interpretations escalate significantly in a world where meaning depends not on the relationship of sign and referent, but on relationships between and among infinite arrays of changing signs. For Baudrillard the explosion of these free-floating signifiers signals a loss of meaning, since there is no possibility of fixing meaning of any sort in a world where signification has tumbled out of control.

With his characteristic flair for overstatement, Baudrillard misreads the contemporary status of meaning. While signification may well have become more complex or arbitrary, this does not mean that the images that are part of media culture have no significance (Anderson, 1995). Rather, their meanings may not be quite as obvious as say, those that accompany discursive signs. Even in this visual realm, men and women tend to categorize or classify figural signs in an effort to make sense of them (Featherstone, 1991). Although people will in many cases have to work harder to sort through the glut of images and the expanded range of potential interpretations which goes with them, there is every reason to believe most will experience a degree of success in the process, rock videos notwithstanding, even though they may not take the time to reflect on many of the more subtle media meanings. To understand why a certain degree of agreed-upon meaning will always be part of this culture, one need only look to the productive forces which drive the world of images. Indeed those producers that sponsor ads literally cannot afford to generate meaningless images. To do so would defeat the very purpose of their advertisements and threaten their all-important profit margins. But while Baudrillard may overstate the elusive character of meanin⸴, he nevertheless provides an important service by alerting us to the rapidly expanding diversity that is driven, in part, by media culture.

Television advertisements like the Shady Brooks Farm one for turkey provide a good way to understand how significations proliferate (see Andersen, 1995). This particular advertisement consists of a series of idyllic pastoral scenes, punctuated by images of turkey parts, a family meal setting, and a boy eagerly devouring turkey. The trusted voice of Burgess Meredith provides an accompanying monologue that emphasizes the connection between the freshness of such country settings and the taste of turkey. The advertising strategy employed here is not one that informs the viewer about the product's value. Instead, it ties value and meaning to the product by associating one image with the next at a connotative level. Andersen maintains that associative techniques of this sort derive meaning not through reasoning channels, but through the association of fast-moving images. In this case, as in many others, the distinction between referents and signifiers collapses. The character of the associations makes it possible for viewers to assign a variety of meanings to sunshine, golden hay and turkey that might be very different from their meanings in normal contexts. Andersen (1995:82) proposes that

> powerful visual juxtapositions, the *lingua franca* of advertising, encourage the viewer to engage in associative drift, producing a range of meanings derived from that engagement. The beautiful images of fields of grain, blue skies, sunshine, and babbling brooks at Shady Brooks Farm evoke any number of possible associations. The viewer might drift from love of country to the serenity of nature, all the while experiencing nostalgia for a past never actually experienced – sensations that mingle with feelings of warmth, tranquillity, leisure, and freedom.

Desire and pleasure play an important part in the cultivation of consumers. They are also a key to understanding the steady advance of diversity. Television programming attempts to attract consumers by actively engaging in strategies that provide positions of pleasure for viewers through the representations they construct. Andersen (1995) argues that a certain amount of ambiguity in meaning is necessary to excite and engage the viewer. Without gaps of significance, desire has no place to invest itself. Neutral or definite representations do not always hold our interest. Inevitably, however, possible meanings in a television commercial converge around a desired meaning. The associative drift is in the end employed to direct the viewer's attention, as far as it can, toward the featured product in such a way as to entice them to take up a favorable attitude toward it.[7] But meanings cannot be imposed on viewers, and there is always the possibility that different groups with different ideological positions will attribute different meanings to what they see in a television advertisement, a soap opera or a news program (Ang, 1995).

Heterogeneity is not just the consequence of a surplus of meaning. The reason for the contemporary explosion of differences can also be traced to the fact that producers actively exploit the instabilities associated with diversity (Ang, 1995). Indeed the current culture of consumerism is founded on the idea that the constant transformation of identities through consumption is pleasurable. This state of affairs has emerged with the change in the nature of social hierarchies over the past century. The fact that identity is no longer tied, as it once was, to stable patterns of status such as class means that men and women are now compelled to perpetually reconstruct themselves (Ang, 1995; Taylor, 1991). For many, lifestyle provides the opportunity to shape an identity and, in the process, acquire status and emotional fulfillment (Featherstone, 1991). Now that lifestyle is no longer tied to traditional patterns of class, for example, consumption of the *symbolic* quality of the material goods and services that constitute the adoption of a particular lifestyle provides men and women with the means to fulfill their deepest desires. More than ever before, people are acquiring pleasure from the act of carefully choosing, arranging, adapting and displaying goods, services and other pastimes. They acquire a degree of fulfillment as they become part of what their houses, clothes, professions and leisure pastimes, including the television programs they watch, signify. Meanwhile producers scramble not only to search out new markets, but to create, often through advertising techniques, desires in consumers which they then satisfy, or claim to be able to satisfy, through the products and services which they sell (Andersen, 1995).

Producers are increasingly organizing their production processes so as to both engender and take advantage of consumers' perpetually evolving desires. Flexible specialization practices, which may include small batch runs, 'just in time' delivery methods, contracting-out of various services, and aggressive marketing strategies, allow producers to target specialized markets and tap into (or develop) a range of particular tastes. In television, audiences are increasingly being thought of in terms of 'niches', made up of flexible tastes and preferences. Producers tailor their shows not for universal anonymous audiences, as had been the case in the past, but for specific audiences (Ang, 1995). The result has been an enormous increase in the choice of programs and in viewing practices. Local and regional cable outlets and 24-hour satellite stations provide a seemingly in.finite range of programming choices, including news, sports, comedy, drama, mystery, history, music, nature, weather, documentary, 'talk', 'infomercials', reality-based police action, to name just a few of the options. Viewers also have at their disposal many more ways by which they can watch small-screen entertainment. Remote control devices facilitate quick perusals of current programming options. Video recorders allow viewers to watch preferred programs at the time (and place) of their choosing. People can also now watch television at sites other than their living-rooms, including campsites, laundromats, bars and so on. This dogged pursuit of new and perpetually evolving market spaces, which involves at least in part the cultivation of new desires and wants,[8] creates an escalating and ultimately uncontrollable proliferation of difference and identity or 'identities-in-difference' (Ang, 1995). Because these desires are for the most part not material but social, and therefore limitless, the heterogeneity that accompanies consumer capitalism will continue to advance virtually unchecked.

While this expanding diversity may know few bounds, it nevertheless will necessarily conform to identifiable patterns, which will themselves be subject to constant change and diversification. As mentioned previously, those who produce media images often have a stake in seeing that these kinds of pattern find their way from their productions to those who consume or apprehend them. To increase the chances of a successful transfer these people generally include incentives for consumers to interpret images in some ways rather than in others. This is the case with issues that touch on race/ethnicity. Consumers of media fare are often provided with rewards for interpreting race/ethnicity in preferred ways. Many of these patterns, although complex, are certainly identifiable. And though they have evolved over the years, sometimes for the better, they continue to favor White/European groups (Fiske, 1996; Merelman, 1995; Shohat & Stam, 1994; Wilson & Gutierez, 1995). The gains that have characterized non-White groups in television comedies and soap operas, for example, stand in stark contrast to the negative ways in which they continue to be portrayed in broadcast journalism. I will say more about this in Chapter 5.

The consequences of the proliferation of media images for representing race/ethnicity in schools are many. One that stands out is the intensity of interaction that this form of technology engenders. In contrast to times gone by, there are few boundaries to the communication of discourses that both print and electronic media favor. Contemporary technology now makes it possible for media discourse to find its way into most nooks and crannies, not only in the Western world, but in many other parts of the globe as well. Indeed Morgan (1995:54) contends that 'no place on earth is immune from modern media.' The technology has also enabled these messages to travel much faster today than they could in past decades and centuries. What this has done is to collapse boundaries between what at one time were considered separate and distinct categories of experience. It has, in other words, engendered a kind of 'de-differentiation' in contemporary life, where these once separate units of existence collapse into one another (Ryan, 1996c). As discourses and practices circulate freely, resisting efforts to confine them, boundaries between institutions (including schools) and other realms of existence become increasingly blurred . The result is that media discourses find their way easily into schools, influencing the ways in which students and teachers see one another (Morgan, 1995). This applies to discourses of race/ethnicity just as it does to most other media discourses. Indeed the ways in which students and educators perceive race/ethnicity, in schools as elsewhere, will in some measure be associated with those discourses that dominate print and electronic media.

Diversity and Contemporary Schooling

Students, teachers, administrators, parents, trustees and others associated with schools can look forward to a future where schools display considerably more diversity than they have in the past. Many of the conditions cited above will, in one form or another, find their way into the classroom. As a consequence, we can expect schools in the First World to come to display many of the following characteristics.

- Teachers, many of whom are of European and Anglo heritage, will find in their classrooms students from all over the world. This trend is already apparent, particularly in many of the bigger cities, and is likely to continue for some time.

- Many more students entering schools in English-speaking countries such as Canada, the United States, Great Britain and Australia will be arriving at school unable to speak English. In some of the larger schools between 50 and100 locations around the world will be represented in the classrooms.

- Schools will cater to more transient student populations. But it will not solely be immigrant families (who may be having difficulty settling in) who will be moving. The changing nature of production will increasingly require a more mobile work-force (Eitzen, 1992).

- Educators will encounter ever greater ranges of different and sometimes opposing views of schooling from the diverse communities which they serve. But it will not be just recent immigrant families who bring a range of attitudes to the table, so to speak. Men and women of European and non-European heritage whose ancestors immigrated some time ago will also express considerable variations in views.

- Schools will increasingly serve as the battleground over which opposing views will be fought. Inevitably those who are able to muster the most resources will see their version of knowledge inserted into the school curriculum.

- The influence of science and social science will continue to dwindle. Educators will increasingly realize the impotence of (social) science to provide them with guidance in teaching or in helping them sort out what version of knowledge they should include in their subject matter.

- Student consumption patterns will enhance diversity in schools. Students will increasingly take advantage of the wide range of consumer options available to them to express themselves in the ways they see fit.

- The ever more fluid and rapidly shifting patterns of student identity will not always be traceable exclusively to heritage, ethnicity or race. Students will be continually combining elements of ethnicity, for example, with consumer offerings to forge 'hybrid' spaces for themselves.

- Patterns of domination and subordination will become more complex. Even though privileged groups will continue to benefit from the effects of power, they will not be able to control it. Rather, power will increasingly work its way through the production, circulation and consumption of meanings associated with continually evolving forms of representation.

Representing Race/Ethnicity in School

Improving opportunities for traditionally marginalized groups requires that those concerned understand and use contemporary forms of representation. Unfortunately, teachers and scholars have not to date paid enough attention to the crucial role that the process of representation plays in providing and denying life chances. While some multicultural and antiracist approaches have taken impressive strides in advancing the study and practice of educating a diverse student population, they have not generally acknowledged, in any substantial ways, the manner in which the process of representation has operated to generate meanings that work in the interests only of certain groups. Nor have they always taken advantage of available opportunities to subvert oppressive sense-making practices and replace them with ones that work in the interests of the marginalized. Instead, as I have illustrated above, they tend to rely on the practice of representing exclusively positive images of what are thought to be fairly distinct groups in schools.

Attending to the process of representation becomes increasingly urgent in the contemporary world. This is because the means and modes of representation are increasing at a rapid rate. Traditional scientific processes of representing life are being seriously questioned and the current electronic media are now providing more and more ways for individuals to understand their world and themselves. These processes are in turn complicated, at least in the Western world, by changing immigration patterns. These changes accentuate the need for us to understand how both traditional and newer forms of representation are working on today's students and how they operate in favour of or against the interests of certain groups and individuals.

Notes

1. Olneck (1990: 168) neverthless maintains that 'irrespective of who enunciates it, the predominant voice in American multicultural education is not the autonomous voice of racial and ethnic minorities'.
2. These include such things as the appointment of ethnic minority teachers, whole-school approaches to school reform, collaborative teaching and learning arrangements, peer tutoring, child-centered and process approaches to learning, involving minority parents and fostering bilingualism and multilingualism (May, 1994).

3. Usher and Edwards (1994) maintain that 'performaty' cannot be considered a grand narrative because it lacks a teleological quality. There can never be an end to efficiency.
4. Cherryholmes (1994) provides a good overview of the argument against the notion that language can represent reality.
5. Such decisions may not always come about after intense reflections. Power operates perhaps more efficiently through unconscious choices that are based on taken-for-granted assumptions about life.
6. The following may illustrate this point. When a rock singer who was in the process of filming a video at the site of a monument in North Africa was asked how she felt about her surroundings, she replied, with reference to the monument's replica in Disney's Epcott Centre, that she kept thinking that she was at Disney World rather than at the monument that the replica was designed to copy.
7. Advertisers may also insist that the programs that run the commercials or the magazines which display the ads project the appropriate images, that is, that their tone is not negative or in any way disrupts the product's promise to meet the consumers' unmet needs (Andersen, 1995).
8. Obviously producers cannot control consumer desire. While they can market-test their products and provide a range of possible attractions, it is in the end up to the consumer to choose or bypass the product.

Chapter 3
Representation, Meaning and Discourse

Representations of life, perhaps now more than ever, play a crucial role in the lives of men, women and children. This is not to deny that they have always been instrumental in determining how people live their lives. Representations of past and present events, and of the individuals and groups of people who make them possible, have always been an integral part of social life. Until recently, however, they were largely taken for granted. With the exception of a few social scientists, people generally did not single them out for attention. All this has changed over the past couple of decades. Today the process of representation is receiving more attention than ever before. Contemporary social scientists, social commentators and the lay public increasingly acknowledge the role that images of social life play in what they feel, believe, do and say. This recognition has been motivated, at least in part, by the proliferation of images in contemporary life and by the accompanying awareness of the complexity of the process of representation itself. Media outlets produce images of every imaginable aspect of life and, through a variety of rapidly evolving technologies, circulate them in large numbers to consumers, who may perceive them in any number of ways or treat them with a certain degree of skepticism. But regardless of how these contemporary representations are treated or perceived, there is growing consensus that such images play a key role in the conduct of social life, and by extension, in the education of young men and women.

Representations of life also play a key role in perceptions and treatment of differences. This is particularly true in the case of race/ethnicity. The ways in which racial/ethnic images are presented to television-watchers, moviegoers, web-surfers, art lovers, to readers of tabloid journals, academic treatises and crime novels, and of course to students, will make a difference to the manner in which these individuals perceive and react to issues, events and people with which and with whom they associate race/ethnicity. As illustrated in the previous chapter, a number of multiculturalists and antiracists support such a view. They believe that the presentation of positive images to those who apprehend these images will engender perceptions and actions that will work in the interests of various racial/ethnic minority groups. But while the efforts of many of these scholars and practitioners have been positive, they tend to pay more attention to one aspect of representation at the expense of another. Many of these individuals emphasize the content of the images and often ignore the process. As a consequence, what these representations contain or mean generally takes precedence over how they became established in the first place. In order to understand the impact of representations of race/ethnicity on the life chances of students, we must understand both the products and processes associated with these representations.

Understanding the processes involved in representation requires that we carefully consider the concept of culture that these processes employ in their analyses and practices. Unfortunately the concept of culture currently employed by some multiculturalists, and in critiques of their position by antiracists, is not always helpful in this respect. Indeed a concept that portrays culture generally as the way of life or a set of traits unique to a particular group does little to enable an understanding of the processes, as well as of the products, of representation. A more helpful view sees culture as a symbolic domain, where meanings are perpetually produced, circulated and consumed between and among people who share them in varying degrees. Representations are a cornerstone of this perspective. In the position that I outline below, they become symbols that people must necessarily interpret as they make sense of the situations they encounter. The products are then the meanings and associated practices that emerge from this process. These meanings do not lie within, or inhere in, the images or representations, but are constructed in this sense-making process.

This is not to say that individual men and women generate their own meanings. Rather they must necessarily take up positions within historically produced discourses or sense-making frameworks in order to make sense of the signs which they encounter. These discourses do not however stand alone. They are in turn an intimate part of the social structures, institutions, and daily social practices in which they are embedded. Even though they may act as powerful guides, discourses do not exclusively determine the sense that men and women make of the world, but are also sites where struggles over meaning occur. Meanings are perpetually contested, confirmed and/or negated by the manner in which people do and say things.

Culture and Representation

Deciding on a concept of culture that will enable a helpful under-standing of the process of representation in a multi-ethnic school can present challenges. This is because, as Williams (1958) contends, 'culture' is one of the three most complicated words in the English language. Certainly there is an infinite array of concepts from which to choose. 'Almost 50 years ago, Kroeber and Klockholm (1952) identified hundreds of meanings for the term. The more traditional concepts of culture, however, have been framed within a 'high' versus 'mass' opposition. According to Hall (1997a) the 'high' notion was said to embody the best that has been thought and said in a society. The sum of these great ideas often found their way into what would eventually be considered classic works of literature, paintings and so on. 'Mass' culture, on the other hand, generally referred to widely distributed forms of popular culture, reflected in publishing, art and enter-tainment, which became part of the lives of so-called ordinary people. At one time people attached greater social value to the 'high' version than they did to the 'mass' one, but today these distinctions do not stand up as they once did; the multiple forms of contemporary media have blurred the once distinct boundaries. Even so, this modern version of culture does little to help us understand how the various forms come to stand for or represent their respective 'cultures'.

More recently 'social scientific' concepts of culture have assumed a more prominent role in assisting people to understand social life. One of the most popular is the anthropological version. Its designers first used it to try to understand what they believed to be the distinctive life ways of people who were very different from themselves. Anthropologists believed that this concept enabled them to study the hunting and gathering bands or resi-dents of small villages in whom they were interested. Generally speaking, they saw culture as the distinctive way of life of a particular people, community or group. Although many did acknowledge the process side of life, the emphasis was clearly on the visible manifestations (products) of it. Key elements of this perspective therefore included (distinctive) artifacts and behaviors around which boundaries could be drawn. In time this view would prove attractive to a number of groups, including multiculturalists. Both multicultural scholars and practitioners have, over the years, adopted a view of culture that more or less resembles this anthropological concept.

Following the anthropological view, a number of multiculturalists emphasize the traits associated with respective ways of life. In this perspec-tive, culture is something that individuals and groups possess. Nieto

(1992:110), for example, maintains that 'everybody has a culture'. Cultures include both visible and less tangible items. They are reflected in, among other things, 'foods, holidays, dress, and artistic expression' as well as 'communication style, attitudes, values and family relationships' (Nieto, 1992:111). As illustrated above, representation of these aspects of culture in the classroom and around the school in general are important to multicultural approaches. Proponents of many of these approaches believe that exposure to various groups' ways of life, reflected in foods, holidays, dress and so on, will help them understand these different others, and in doing so, extend to them the respect that is rightfully theirs.

Nieto and many other academics emphasize both the visible and intangible aspects of groups' life ways; many practitioners seeking to promote respect for various minority groups may however find few alternatives but to emphasize the more superficial and visible traits they associate with 'culture'(Hoffman, 1997; Wax, 1993; Turner, 1993). As a consequence schools may regularly feature heritage days where various groups display such things as foods, costumes and dances (Wong & Cowan, 1998; Ryan, 1997). This is the 'saris, samosas and steel bands' syndrome that Troyna (1993) and other antiracists criticize for deflecting attention away from more serious systemic problems that limit these students' life chances. Yet in criticizing such practices, antiracists implicitly endorse the view of culture they embody.

This perspective on culture carries with it at least one more belief. Implied rather than explicitly stated, this assumes that groups and their accompanying 'cultures' are naturally bounded entities. Some multiculturalists believe that various minority groups are in themselves distinct, and the 'cultural traits' that they share with other members of the group are unique (Hoffman, 1997). It is easy to see why this concept made sense to anthropologists. They were interested primarily in premodern societies and groups who lived in comparatively small communities, and as a consequence they generally had little difficulty in drawing distinctions between these groups and others. Some social scientists, however, seriously question the suitability of this anthropological concept for contemporary societies (Erickson, 1987a). It is a view that does not always reflect the blurred boundaries, shifting contours, and continuous creation, recreation and negotiation of cultural identities (Hoffman, 1997). It also has difficulty accounting for crucial systemic inequalities that characteristically penalize certain groups and individuals in the contemporary world. To get around this latter limitation a number of scholars prefer to see 'culture' and 'structure' as distinct, albeit related, phenomena (Nieto, 1992; Solomon, 1992; May, 1994).

Unfortunately this view of culture does little to help us understand how the process of representing race/ethnicity works. This is not to say that scholars such as Nieto and May have not generated useful perspectives. Indeed, they have both produced insightful work. In doing so they have not relied exclusively on the anthropological view of culture, but have employed other concepts, including 'structure' which they use both to analyze the current situation and to prescribe desired action. On the other hand, those who rely exclusively on the concept of structure do not always take into consideration the complex process in which the representation of traits comes to assume various forms. In other words, they do not always help us understand how these representations come to *mean* something to those who apprehend them. Thus, those interested in providing the basis for an understanding of representations of race/ethnicity would do well to employ a concept of culture that acknowledges the centrality of the *construction of meaning* in the process.

There are many concepts of culture that feature meaning, including anthropological ones. Despite the fact that some multiculturalists tend to emphasize other aspects of it, many versions of the anthropological concept generally include meaning as an important part. For example, some anthropologists see culture as a 'system of ordinary, taken-for-granted meanings and symbols with both explicit and implicit content that is, deliberately and non-deliberately, learned and shared among members of a naturally bounded group' (Erickson, 1987a:12). More recently social scientists have attempted to adapt meaning-oriented concepts in ways that are more appropriate for understanding the contemporary world. Geertz (1973), an anthropologist himself, maintains that the concept he espouses is essentially a 'semiotic' one. For him culture consists of the webs of significance that humanity has spun for itself. Exploring it, he believes, requires not an experimental science in search of laws, but an interpretive one in search of meaning. Williams (1981:13) also provides a view of culture that acknowledges the place of meaning in a complex contemporary society. He sees culture as 'a signifying system through which necessarily a social order is communicated, reproduced, experienced and explored'. He believes that a view of culture that acknowledges meaning and the role of a wide range of activities and institutions is more appropriate for understanding the contemporary world.

The social organization of culture, as a realized signifying system, is embedded in a whole range of activities, relations and institutions, of which some are not manifestly 'cultural'. For modern societies, at least, this is a more effective theoretical usage than the sense of culture as a whole way of life. (Williams, 1981:209)

The notion of culture as first and foremost a signifying system covers considerably more ground than does the trait-oriented anthropological one. And while it acknowledges traits, it does not privilege them. Hall (1997a) contends that in this view culture is not so much a set of things as a process, a set of social practices. These practices revolve around the production and exchange of meaning, the 'giving and taking' of meaning between members of a group or society. Proponents of this position feature meaning because they believe that the symbolic domain is at the very heart of social life. According to Hall, cultural meanings organize and regulate social practices, influence our conduct, and consequently have real practical effects. In this sense culture permeates all social life. It is involved in all those practices which are not simply genetically programmed into us, as for example are reflexes. Culture is implicated in those practices which carry meaning and value for us, which need to be meaningfully interpreted by others, and which depend on meaning for their operation. In short culture is that domain which encompasses all that is human.

This concept of culture is well suited to assisting those interested in understanding the process and effects associated with the representation of race/ethnicity, in school and out. This is because in this perspective, representation assumes a pivotal role. It is a view of culture that recognizes that social life takes shape as people construct, exchange, and interpret representations of that life. They are able to engage in this kind of interaction because they share similar concepts, ideas and images that enable them to think and feel the world and thus to interpret it in broadly similar ways (Hall, 1997a). To belong to the same culture, then, is to belong to roughly the same conceptual and representational universe and, as a result, to know how concepts and ideas correspond to the signs that represent them and refer to the world. This is not to overstate the shared nature of these sense-making practices. Meanings vary within every group. In any culture, there is always more than one way to interpret and represent.

Representation, Language and Meaning

Representation is also linked in intimate ways with language. In fact representation is the process responsible for producing meaning through language. 'Language' is used here in the broadest sense to refer to a particular organization of signs, and consequently need not be restricted to, for example, the French or the English language. Signs may include words, sounds, notes, clothing, facial expressions, electronically produced dots, lights and so on. They stand for or represent what we want to say, to enable us to express or communicate a thought, a feeling or an idea. Thus a pattern of music notes is part of a particular 'language of music', designed to convey meaning (and feeling) to those who care to listen.

The view that I endorse here revolves around the idea that meaning is *constructed*. This means that we are responsible for producing meaning. We do this by using languages in systems of representation. Such a view differs from so-called traditional views of representation, which assume that meaning lies naturally in the objects and events out there in the real world. We come to recognize this meaning with the help of language, which functions transparently, like a mirror, to represent or reflect the true meaning as it already exists. Foucault (1970) maintains that in the Classical Age humanity believed that it was not the maker of the (social) world, but the clarifier of it. Humanity's role was to design a system of signs whose elements would correspond to the primitive, already ordered, nature of the world. By aligning the order of signs to mirror the natural order, humanity was thought to be able to produce knowledge. The classical view, according to Foucault, broke down, at least in part, because it could not account for, or represent, the process of representation itself. The constructivist view, by contrast, does account for the representational process.

Hall (1997) maintains that men, women and children all construct meaning by using two systems of representation. The first system consists of the manner in which objects or events are correlated with concepts that can stand for objects, events or people in the world. The concept or idea of 'a sheep', for example, must be aligned with the sheep standing in the field over there. Hall refers to this aspect of representation as a 'system' because he believes that we are not simply dealing with random collections of individual concepts. Instead he acknowledges that people are perpetually engaged in classifying, organizing and clustering concepts and establishing complex relationships among them. The principle of similarity and difference is key in establishing relationships that distinguish concepts one from another. For example, although we know that birds and planes both fly, we are able to differentiate between the two concepts by appealing to other dimensions of these concepts. We know that one is part of nature, and the other is a human construction.

The giving and taking of meaning depends on more than just the fact that people may share similar concepts. Hall (1997) maintains that we must also be able to represent and exchange concepts. This is made possible through Hall's second system of representation – language. This system enables us to translate our shared conceptual world into a common language. It does so by providing sets of publicly available signs that stand in for, or represent, these concepts or ideas. Any of these signs is capable of representing something. A sign does not have to be a word or a particular kind of visual image in order to function as a symbol, however. An article of clothing can stand for an idea or concept just as easily as a word or sentence in a novel. Thus when we hear certain sounds, read particular words, or see visual images we are able to correlate them with various associated concepts. These signs are in turn organized into patterns we refer to very broadly as 'languages'. These common languages enable us to translate our thoughts into words, sounds, or images and then to use them to express meaning and communicate with other people.

The question remains as to how people know what signs represent what concepts and objects. This is a key question, for meaning depends in important ways on this relationship. Hall's (1997) answer is that the relationship is governed by 'codes' or sets of rules. He maintains that these codes allow us to fix meaning, at least to a point, by specifying what signs stand for what concepts, and vice versa. Codes act to stabilize what is always an arbitrary relationship between these two realms in a way that allows people who share broadly similar conceptual terrain to give and take meaning from one another. Thus those who are aware of these rules can communicate in a reasonably effective manner with others who share the same cultural and symbolic universe. These codes, however, like meaning, are not fixed by nature or by gods. They are in fact social conventions, cultural covenants that are learned by language users who pass them on to others. Because these rules are tied to perpetually changing social conventions, they govern, but do not represent, a closed system. Indeed Hall (1997) contends that meaning continues to be produced through language forms that can never entirely be predicted. We can never be sure that the person on the other end of a communicative act, interpreting or decoding an encoded message, will attribute the same meaning to it as the sender. As a consequence, meaning will always continue to shift and slide. And as it does, the codes of a culture will also imperceptibly change.

Over the years social scientists have approached the problem of culture, representation and meaning in a number of ways. One influential perspective is semiotics. Developed first by French linguist Ferdinand de Saussure, this provides a 'linguistic' model of how culture and representation work. The approach is based on the assumption that all cultural objects that convey meaning work like languages. In this sense, semiotics revolves around the study of signs. In fact de Saussure (1974) referred to it as the 'science of signs'. By studying the configuration of signs, he hoped that the semiotician would come to understand how meaning was produced. He believed, however, that the sign was not simply a self-contained symbol. Rather, he broke it down into two elements. The first of these he called the 'signifier'. The signifier was a form which might take the shape of, for example, a word, or a photograph, or a piece of clothing. He called the other part of the sign the 'signified'. The signified was the concept or idea which the signifier triggered or to which it referred. De Saussure believed that both elements were required to produce meaning. The key for him though was the (systematic) manner in which these two were related to one another.

De Saussure's contributions to our understanding of the process of representation and meaning production are many, but his version of semiotics does carry a number of shortcomings (see, for example, Hall, 1997). Perhaps the most obvious of these revolves around his exclusive focus on language itself. He devotes considerable attention to signs and the role that they play as part of language in the production of meaning. In doing this, however, he diverts attention away from the manner in which language functions in actual social situations. Indeed it is difficult to ignore the fact that meaning depends in important ways on larger units of social organization. People interpret signs in situations that are in some manner already organized for them. As a consequence, the meanings that they eventually attribute to these signs will be associated in some way with this form of social organization. A word may take on a very different meaning in an institutional context such as a university classroom from that which it receives in a courtroom or over a family dinner. Because semiotics focuses almost exclusively on how signs function within language, it is not equipped to account for the ways in which meaning is associated with these other forms of organization. It does not adequately attend to the way in which language may be organized into more systematic forms like narratives, statements, or groups of images that work across texts or institutional settings; nor does it study issues of power, and the role that inequitable power arrangements play in the process of representation and the production of meaning. In the end, semioticians' preoccupation with how language works leads them to pay less attention to the effects and the consequences of representation.

An approach to representation that does account for the more social aspects of meaning production is discourse. Because a discursive approach accommodates the wider social environment to a greater extent than semiotics does, it is a more appropriate lens through which to explore the representation of race/ethnicity in schools.

Discourse

The version of discourse that I outline here owes much to the work of Foucault. It does not, however, endorse completely all aspects of his ideas. Indeed this would be difficult, since Foucault's view of discourse changed over the course of his life. He moved from a type of 'pseudo' structuralist position in *The Archeology of Knowledge* to a 'poststructuralist' stance in much of the work that followed in *Discipline and Punish, The History of Sexuality* and so on. Over the course of this transformation he abandoned, among other things, his quest to uncover impersonal and abstract codes that governed discursive practice and acknowledged a limited role for the subject or individual in this process. While borrowing some of Foucault's earlier ideas on discourse, I endorse, for the most part, his later poststructuralist view. In doing this I also rely on interpretations (Dreyfus & Rabinow, 1982; Cousins & Houssain, 1985; Hall, 1997a) and adaptations (Shohat & Stam, 1994; Fiske, 1996; Hall, 1997a) of his later work. Not all of the latter follow Foucault to the letter. Fiske (1996), for example, emphasizes the contested nature of discourse.

One of the advantages of employing a discursive perspective to understand the representation of race/ethnicity in schools is that it emphasizes the social nature of this process. This is not to say that semiotics does not see representation as a social process. It does. In this sense both semiotic and discursive analysts believe that language plays a vital role in the production of meaning in the process of representation. But this is where their similarities end. Semioticians highlight the importance of abstract systems of signs, whereas discourse proponents emphasize the socially situated nature of language. For the former, meaning emerges from the relationship of these abstract signs. The latter contend that meaning is produced as and when language is used in particular social situations, even though 'differences' may play a role. Discourse proponents maintain that language cannot be separated from the social situations in which it is employed. Fiske (1996) contends that discourse is a language in social use. He and others believe that it is not a purely 'linguistic' concept, but one that encompasses both language and practice. In doing so it attempts to overcome the traditional distinction between what people say and what they do (Hall, 1997a).

A discursive perspective assumes that the production of meaning in the process of representation depends on much more than merely the signs of a language. Indeed the social situations in which language is used provide both barriers and possibilities for language users. People cannot simply say anything they please at the time and place of their choosing. Rather they will find themselves in a 'space' that is already organized for them. For example, they step into situations that invite them to talk or reason in certain ways about certain topics. If they wish to make themselves understood or if they are to understand others they are required not only to employ the appropriate linguistic models and logic, but also to acknowledge the social conventions that accompany these situations. As Hall (1997a:44) explains:

> Just as discourse rules in certain ways of talking about a topic, defining an acceptable and intelligible way to talk, write or conduct oneself, so also, by definition, it rules out, limits, and restricts other ways of talking, of conducting ourselves in relation to the topic or constructing knowledge about it.

Another important aspect of discourse to keep in mind is that it is very much an active process. In other words, discourse is both a noun and a verb. Perhaps it may be more appropriate to use the term 'discoursing', rather than simply 'discourse' which is more suggestive of the noun form. In this regard discourse is not so much concerned with meaning *per se* as with the process of *making sense*. As men and women engage in symbolic activities, the sense-making that is necessarily associated with these actions brings together the various elements of discourse. Fiske (1996) suggests that there are at least three levels or dimensions of discourse. The first is a topic or area of social experience to which its sense-making is applied. The second dimension includes a social position from which this sense is made and whose interests it promotes. Fiske's last dimension is a repertoire of words, images and practices by which meanings are circulated and power applied. The latter two dimensions suggest that the process of sense-making always involves more than simply a linguistic operation. Fiske indicates that it is intimately part of 'non-linguistic' forms of social organization. He goes on to say that because power is a necessary element of these forms, these sense-making processes will always be contested enterprises. Whatever sense prevails in given situations will necessarily be the outcome of a struggle. I will now elaborate on these various aspects of discourse.

The first of Fiske's (1996) dimensions of discourse revolves around areas of social experience. Sense-making is always applied to a part of our experience. The conditions that are associated with this experience, however, do not display their own sense. That is, the meaning of any experience does not emerge from the nature of that experience itself. Rather it comes to make sense only in the manner in which it is placed into discourse. It is through discourse or 'discoursing' that we make sense of the raw material of our experience. Sometimes this process may be audible or visible, as for example in a text, in speeches or in conversations with others. At other times it may work silently, while we are attempting to work out for ourselves the sense of a certain situation. Though the areas of experience to which sense is applied are in principle infinite in number, the ways of making sense of these respective areas are not. For example, as Foucault (1972, 1988) points out, it was only within a particular discursive formation that 'madness' could appear as a meaningful part of people's experience. But people could only make sense of the associated behaviors in this way after certain definitions of madness were put into practice by the medical profession. The same applies to how we see those acts which we now make sense of as homosexual in nature. While these behaviors have always existed, 'homosexuals' only appeared on the social landscape after the medical profession shaped their theories of sexual perversity in the 19th century, and subsequently circulated and entrenched their ideas in moral, legal, medical and psychiatric discourses, practices and institutional arrangements (Hall, 1997a).

Another condition of discourse is that its sense is always made from a particular social position. This is in fact a process that works in both directions. On the one hand, discourse 'constructs' subjects and subject 'positions', yet on the other, the manner in which subjects or individuals enter into discourse, to make sense of such items as texts or photographs, for example, will often depend on their prior social position. The position that I endorse here acknowledges the partial role of the individual subject in this sense-making process. While not going so far as to eliminate the subject altogether, as structuralists do, this perspective does not see a central role for it. In this respect I endorse Foucault's (1970, 1972, 1980) critique of the traditional conception of the subject. He takes issue with a view of it as a stable and autonomous entity fully endowed with consciousness. He also opposes the idea that individuals are the source of all action and meaning, and consequently have a privileged position when it comes to understanding what they say. Foucault's initial reaction to the subject, in line with his earlier structuralist leanings, was to eliminate it from the process of meaning production. Later he did find a place for it, but he never restored it to its position as the centre and author of representation. Although his subject did acquire a certain reflexive awareness of its own conduct, it would have only a partial role in the practice of representation.

Foucault contends that the subject is produced within discourse. Hall (1997) observes that this production takes place in two different senses. Firstly, discourses produce subjects that are objects of discursive practices. For example, discursive practice produces 'madmen' and 'homosexuals', in ways described above. Those who display characteristics associated with these constructs are readily identified by others and themselves as these kinds of people. But secondly, merely entering into discourse to make sense of our experience will have an impact on who we are or who we become. In this sense we become ourselves as we engage in this process. Discourses provide places for individuals to occupy in order to make sense of their experience. If we want to understand something we can only do so from the positions that these discourses provide. Hall (1997a:56) supplies a particularly lucid account of this complex process. He says that discourse

> produces a place for the subject (i.e. the reader or viewer, who is also 'subjected to' discourse) from which its particular knowledge and meaning most makes sense. Not all will become subjects of a particular discourse. But those who do must locate themselves in the position from which the discourse makes the most sense, and thus become its 'subjects' by 'subjecting' themselves to its meanings, power and regulation. All discourses then construct subject-positions from which they alone make sense.

But while discourse may well construct subjects, it does not do so in a way that leaves these individuals with no choice. This is because a text, a photograph or a painting requires the reader or viewer to complete its meaning. Indeed meaning is constructed and sense made in the dialogue between readers/viewers and texts or photographs. In order for men and women to take meaning, however, they will have to identify with the position set up by a particular discourse. If they do not, then they will not be able to make sense of their experience, at least within this discourse. It is in this regard that the prior social position of a subject becomes important. This prior positioning will inevitably have an impact on how meaning gets completed. Everyone brings with them their racialized, classed, gendered etc. positions, and with these their often very different experiences of the world. The consequence is that not all individuals will be able or willing to identify with the positions set up for them by certain discourses and to take the meaning associated with these discourses. In other words, some discourses will simply not make sense to everyone. This is because they may not work in people's interests and/or may simply not conform to their experiences. In the case of the photos on the wall described at the outset, the respective parties in the disagreement made sense of them in different ways, resisting or refusing to occupy the space set up for them by their opponents' discourse. In a later chapter we will see how students of African heritage simply could not identify with the same discursive positions that teachers and non-African students used to make sense of the race-related activities of an early 20th-century southern American town. In both of these cases it was evident that the respective discourses and discourse positions did not work in everybody's interests, nor did they necessarily conform to everyone's experience.

Another element of discourse is that it requires a repertoire of words, images and practices to circulate meanings and to apply power. Each discourse has it own style and employs various words, images and practices in its own fashion. In this regard, discourses display a measure of regularity in the way their respective statements, concepts, metaphors, objects of reference and thematic choices are deployed. In other words, these elements of discourse are related to one another in a systematic manner. For example, a particular discourse can only give rise to a limited number of statements. These statements are in turn related and constrained by their respective fellow statements. Only certain statements can stand next to one another if they are to make sense as part of a particular discourse. Moreover, some metaphors or concepts will simply not fit with some discourses, and some discourses are not suited to making sense of some areas of our experience. A neo-conservative discourse brings with it a repertoire of words, images and practices that allow certain people to make sense of, say, education in certain ways. It tends to emphasize certain themes or concepts, like 'choice', and is better suited to generating sense about certain areas of school experience such as management, than about others such as equity. A neo-conservative discourse also works in the interests of those who easily identify with the discourse positions set up by its words and images, and would tend to confirm the experiences of those who employ its repertoire.

As I have emphasized here, discourse includes much more than simply language or languages. It is intimately associated with socially organized practices or institutions. Foucault's work revolves around the production of meaning in institutional settings. He is not so much concerned with meaning *per se*. Instead his focus is knowledge. Much of his work turns on the manner in which knowledge operates through discursive practices in institutional settings to regulate the conduct of men, women and children. In this respect non-discursive practices are just as important in producing knowledge as language practices. Foucault's contention is that knowledge statements inevitably lie in some institutional register. Spoken claims to knowledge, for example, are always made in the context of an institution. Understanding both the meaning and the authority that such claims carry with them requires that listeners understand who has the right to make statements, the site from which these statements emanate and the position that the speaker occupies. The sense that we make of what our respective doctors say to us about our health (but not necessarily about our golf game) requires also that we take account of the institution of medical practice, including its history, its prestige, the science associated with it, the training which doctors go through, the techniques that they employ, and so on. The bottom line here is that knowledge depends not simply on words, but also on the associated institutional practices.

One of Foucault's most profound contributions to our understanding of the process of representation is the idea that knowledge and power are inseparably linked. He contends that knowledge is always enmeshed in relations of power because it is always being applied to the regulation of social conduct. It accomplishes this through discourse in two ways. The first is in the manner in which people are constituted as objects of the discourse or knowledge. Social sciences play an important role in this process. Social scientists employ techniques to generate knowledge about humanity which is then turned around to govern what humanity does. They are able to do this, at least in part, by virtue of the status of their claims, that is, through their appeals to truth. Thus psychologists are supposedly able to determine through the techniques that they employ whether or not people are 'normal'. They will be able to tell us, among other things, who among us are 'mad', by identifying the deviant activities that are associated with this state. To prevent such behavior in the future they may suggest methods for ridding individuals of these proclivities, or simply leave this task to other authorities. Hence the ways in which social science produces images or representations of what turn out to be certain categories of people play an important part in the regulation of social conduct.

Power also works through discourse in another way. It operates as people take up roles not just as objects of discourse, but also as subjects. As alluded to previously, in order to make sense of a given area of experience we must enter into discourse, that is, we must take up the positions made available in the discourse. In doing this we must necessarily submit to the rules and conventions of the discourse, accepting its logic and the sense it allows us to make of the object of concern. In other words, discourse structures the ways in which we look at things. In this regard we become its subjects by subjecting ourselves to its meanings, power and regulation. In all of this process we become the bearers of knowledge; but this knowledge is necessarily always limited. This is because it presents us with a finite set of ways in which we can make sense of particular images or representations. For example there are 'racialized' and racist discourses that extend positions which make sense of black masculinity in particularly unflattering ways (Hall, 1997b). Those who are able to identify with these positions have little choice but to make sense of various images of African males in these specified ways. Yet as they do so they breathe life into these discourses, ensuring their continuity and the debilitating effects that they have on people of African heritage.

The presence of power in the process of representation makes it a *political* process. Fiske (1996) maintains that the way in which our experience is put into discourse and made sense of is never determined by the nature of the experience itself. The process of representation does not allow us simply to mirror the objects, events and people in our experience. As emphasized above, this process is socially constructed, and because it is, it is always subject to the forces that shape our social reality, including, in this case, power. Social power, then, gives our experience one set of meanings as opposed to others. But discourses do not simply immobilize everything in their paths. Discourse events are not just sites where power is uniformly applied. Rather, as Fiske (1996) contends, they are also important sites of struggle. This is where Fiske claims he departs from Foucault. He maintains that Foucault describes discourse primarily as a technique of power in a monodiscursive society. He himself argues, on the other hand, that we live not in a monodiscursive but in a multidiscursive society, where discourse is not just a technique of power but also evidently a terrain of struggle. In the contemporary world discourse does not simply repress, marginalize, and invalidate other discourses, but it is also the medium in which both discourse and other forms of life are contested. It is here that meanings are challenged, resisted, negotiated and transformed, as various groups and individuals vie to have their sense of the world supersede that of others.

There are many ways in which the politics of representation plays itself out in the struggle over meaning. Fiske (1996) provides us with a few ways in which men and women struggle over and through discourse. Such contests can revolve around struggles: (1) to 'accent' a word, to turn the way that it is spoken or used to advance certain interests; (2) to choose certain words or images; (3) to recover repressed words or images; (4) to link or 'disarticulate' certain images with other events; and (5) to gain access to public discourse or media so as to have one's voice heard.

These contests rarely occur on equal terrain. Inevitably certain discourses and those who identify with them will have an advantage over others. Understanding these inequalities requires an understanding of the history of relationships between the respective groups and the social power each has been able to mobilize through discourse to promote its interests. Thus we are better able to comprehend the often debilitating representations of African males when we become familiar with the history of the relationship between Europeans and Americans and the African people they enslaved. The overwhelming power that the former had over the latter allowed them to circulate a sense of African males that worked in their interests, legitimizing an inhumane but lucrative practice and easing their consciences in the process (Gilman, 1985). Many of these meanings endure to the present, although as marginalized groups continue to find ways to make their voices heard they are increasingly being contested (Fiske, 1996; Merelman, 1995; Hall, 1997b).

One of the more obvious characteristics of this view of discourse is its pervasive nature. Hall (1997a), Fiske (1996), Laclau and Mouffe (1990) and Foucault (1972) all assert that nothing meaningful exists outside of discourse. This of course does not mean that there is nothing outside of discourse. Indeed many things may well exist outside of discourse. The point here though is that despite their existence we will know nothing of them. This is because we can only know or make sense of things when they are put into discourse. There is a non-discursive reality, but it has no terms of its own through which we can access it. Because it does not have its own meaning, whatever meaning it does acquire will always be through discourse. Even though we may be able to draw a distinction between the physical or natural world and the social and discursive world, the two worlds will always be intimately related.

Despite discourse's pervasive nature, people do nevertheless make sense of images on different 'levels'. Barthes (1972) makes a distinction between two levels or orders of meaning. He contends that representation occurs on both descriptive and implied levels. The former he refers to as the 'denotative' level and the latter as the 'connotative'. The first level is primarily descriptive. It revolves around a relationship between the signifier and signified at the most obvious and consensual level at which objects mean something. At this level many people will often agree on the meaning of a photograph or a text. Those who see the photographs in the hallway, described in Chapter 1, will probably make the connection between the image of the person and the 'real' person, although of course the meaning of each photograph will vary with the ways in which the respective viewers know the individual depicted. On the other hand, most of those who read *To Kill a Mockingbird* will understand the author's general descriptions of the southern American town in similar ways. Most readers will agree on what the characters do and say. But the descriptions of these events, and the photographs, carry a significance that goes beyond this descriptive level.

Barthes (1972) maintains that people also make sense of things in their experience on a more connotative level. At this level the more descriptive meanings link up with broader themes, what Hall (1997:38) refers to as the 'wider semantic fields of our culture'. Viewers or readers make sense of photographs and texts in terms of wider realms that may include general conceptual frameworks and the value systems of a society. Meanings at this level, however, are more ephemeral and unstable, and as a consequence, are inevitably subject to greater change than the more descriptive meanings (Lidchi, 1997). They also tend to be the subject of struggles. Thus, as we will see in Chapter 6, the respective meanings that students and teachers attach to the descriptions of African Americans in *To Kill a Mockingbird* differ. They also give rise to a struggle over these meanings. For a good illustration of denotative and connotative meaning see Lidchi's (1997) account of the representation of *Custer's Last Stand*.

Conclusion

Discourse provides a useful lens through which to explore the representation of race/ethnicity in a multi-ethnic school. It can prove helpful for a number of reasons. First, a discursive framework acknowledges that human beings are responsible for shaping representations of race/ethnicity, in schools and elsewhere. People do this as they make sense of the things they see, hear and feel. This sense emerges as both students and educators interpret the signs that they apprehend. These signs may take the form of words, pictures or musical notes, among others. Thus what students and teachers take away from a textbook picture of a Native North American, for example, will depend on the meaning that they attribute to it. This does not mean that students or teachers can interpret the picture in any way they please, rather that how they interpret this image will be limited by the currently available patterns of words, images and practices that filter the possible ways in which they can make sense of it. In this view, students and teachers alike can only make sense of the picture by placing it into one discourse or another.

A discourse framework also acknowledges the role of 'non-discursive' forms of social organization in the sense-making process. Indeed these so-called non-discursive practices provide a 'space' for certain kinds of linguistic practices to take place and for certain meanings to emerge. It is in this sense that discourses are intimately associated with forms of power. Prevailing power arrangements make available limited ranges of pattern of words, images and practices, from which teachers and students choose in order to make sense of the words, deeds and pictures of Native North Americans. Because Native North American and other non-European groups have traditionally been less favored than Europeans, the prevailing discourses teachers and students use to make sense of their associated images do not always work in these groups' interests. But while discourse is a technique of power, it is also a terrain on which meaning is contested. It is here that various groups struggle over which discourses are to prevail. Of course, since the power differential has consistently favored certain groups over others, these contests are often one-sided. Thus the prevailing sense that teachers, students and others make of Native North American and other non-European groups does not always work in such groups' interests, either. Even so, the fact that meanings are contestable does suggest that there is hope for those who wish to replace dominant and debilitating discourses with ones that work in the interests of the traditionally marginalized.

The next chapter explores a number of these issues. In particular it examines what racial/ethnic differences mean to people and how such differences come to influence what people do. In an attempt to understand the nature of these racial/ethnic meanings I trace their origins and describe how these discourses show up at Suburbia Secondary School.

Notes

1. Fiske (1996) and others have perhaps exaggerated what they claim is Foucault's monolithic view of power. Foucault did acknowledge that the exercise of power was accompanied by struggle. For example, in making a case against semiotics, he says 'I believe one's point of reference should not be to the great model of language and signs, but to that of war and battle. The history which bears and determines us has the form of a war rather than a language; relations of power not relations of meaning.' (Foucault, 1980: 114)

Chapter 4
Difference, Race and Racism

Today difference plays an important part in the formal education of most students. This of course is not just a recent occurrence. Differences between and among communities, students, teachers and institutional structures have been a part of formal education for some time now. What has changed today is that selected differences that show up in schools are now highlighted more than they once were. There are a number of reasons for this. One is that teachers in many Western countries may notice that they do not share as many things with the students who attend their classes as they once did. Changing immigration patterns over the last couple of decades now mean that schools, particularly those in larger cities, may no longer be populated exclusively with students of European heritage, but with young people from all over the world. This is just as true for Great Britain (Owen, 1994), Australia (Australian Bureau of Statistics, 1995) and the United States (US Bureau of the Census, 1995) as it is for Canada (Statistics Canada, 1993).

These changes in immigration patterns have led many educators and students to acknowledge certain kinds of difference, to attribute certain meanings to them, and to react on the basis of these meanings. In particular, many notice first and foremost any racial/ethnic differences and adjust their subsequent actions in ways that take these meanings into consideration. At Suburbia Secondary School the meanings are not all positive. In fact the sense that students and educators (often unwittingly) attribute to these differences frequently acts to place some groups of students at a disadvantage.

These meanings of course are not unique to Suburbia, nor are they unique to the age in which we now live. They have a history. Indeed understanding how contemporary racial/ethnic or 'racialized' meanings come to play such an important place in interactions in today's multi-ethnic schools requires some knowledge of the origins of racial/ethnic discourses and the conditions that accompanied their emergence. We will be able to get a better idea of why students and educators may sometimes make sense in negative ways of the thoughts, words and deeds of the members of certain racial/ethnic groups if we learn something about how certain

72

Europeans who lived around the 16th century set about safeguarding the privileges they enjoyed by rationalizing, through the representations they employed, the ways in which they exploited other people.

This chapter provides a way to understand various racial/ethnic meanings that circulate at Suburbia Secondary School. It first describes how various students and teachers make sense of the differences they perceive at school. In an attempt to provide a context for the differential value that they place on racial/ethnic differences, I outline a brief history of racist discourse. Next I show how contemporary forms of racism reveal themselves at Suburbia, describing instances where racist discourses surface and racist acts are committed. The chapter ends by illustrating the manner in which racist discourse and practice is contested at Suburbia.

Difference at Suburbia Secondary School

Everyone who walks through the front doors of Suburbia Secondary School will immediately become aware of a multitude of differences. Many, however, take a number of these differences for granted. For example, few people in the Western world would pay much attention to differences between the vertical structures – the windows, doors and walls of this school – even though they do play an important part in the division of space. Visitors to the building would be more likely to attend more closely to the ways in which this space is allocated. Those looking for the principal, therefore, would pay particular attention to the differential space allocation in the building in order to deduce where they might find him. Other differences might be important for others who use the building. For instance, it would probably be in the interests of most students to be able to recognize the difference between fellow students and teachers. One difference that most visitors who were born in this country notice when they first come to the school is the physical appearance of the students – skin color, hair type, facial features and so on. Many who are not used to this sort of diversity comment to the staff that they are amazed to see so much variation in the 'cultures' of the students. For some, the school is a virtual 'United Nations'.

'Culture' also plays an important part in the way students, teachers and administrators perceive their school environment. At Suburbia 'culture' is simply a code word for race/ethnicity. Many teachers believe that students' 'heritage', 'ethnicity' or 'race' has a perceptible impact, both on how they interact in school and on the extent to which they are able to master the curriculum. Some see this diversity as an asset – something which enriches the school and the individuals who are part of it. Jeremy, a veteran teacher, believes that the school is 'richer': 'It's richer because you realize that you're seeing [the community] the way it's going to be in 15 or 20 years. I think it makes the school richer in a lot of different ways.'

Others see these differences more as problems. James, another teacher, cites various communication difficulties. He says that students from abroad often 'misinterpret the signal ... they have their interpretation and that's it. And that's one of the biggest problems that we have in this school.' Students notice these kinds of difference, too. Julia, for example, who is from South America, perceives 'Canadians' as 'cold', and as a consequence interacts with them differently from the ways in which she interacts with people from her own part of the world.

Students and teachers make sense of what they see as 'cultural' (racial/ethnic) differences in both positive and negative ways. I have already cited one instance of a positive kind of evaluation. Negative reactions to differences also surface regularly. Jane, for example, does not approve of the way a certain group of her students speak. She says:

> I don't really like it when they go, when they say, 'Oh yeah man', because I think that's sort of an inappropriate way to talk informally to somebody. So I kind of, I guess sometimes I might say 'Well I'm not "man".' You know, like, come on, let's talk in a polite way.

Negative reactions to perceived 'racial' or 'ethnic' differences do on occasion take on much more serious proportions. Racist in character, these kinds of reaction find their way into the speech and actions of both teachers and students. Racist discourse and practice are not unique to Suburbia, however. Nor are they recent phenomena. Rather they find their way into most Western institutions and organizations, and have been part of these social forms for quite some time. Understanding contemporary forms of racist discourse and practice as they surface in Suburbia requires therefore that we know something about their history.

Differences, Race and Racism

While the establishment, recognition, evaluation and use of differences (and similarities), including race, may be part of what we do every day of our lives, these processes are not simple ones. First of all, marking off a slice of existence, drawing a boundary around it and naming it involves establishing relationships between it and other phenomena. A thing is what its neighbors are not. A door is not a window, nor a teacher a student. Despite this, the respective relationships which they have with one another will provide important clues to their identities. Another important consideration is the variable nature of the meaning(s) of a particular set of differences/similarities. Meanings change and so do the actions to which they give rise. The position and role of a teacher may mean different things to Grade 1 students and to graduate students, and these differences will be likely to prompt different actions on the part of these respective groups. Finally, those who seek to understand this process need to come to terms with conditions under which certain discursive categories are established, understood, evaluated, and used. Of particular concern here is how some groups and individuals come to designate in discourse certain distinctions as important, and the affects these distinctions have on themselves and other groups of men, women and children. How and why, for example, do certain physical characteristics come to be important markers of distinction? How are they evaluated? Who is at the forefront in establishing and evaluating these differences? And what effects do they have on various individuals and groups? Understanding how 'cultural differences', race/ethnicity and racism play a part in the lives of young men and women in contemporary schools rests with the answers to these and similar questions.

At one time physical differences and other assumed, associated differences between groups of people did not play a significant role in social relationships. Despite the fact that Ruchames (1969) claims that 'racial thought is as old as civilized man', the idea of race did not appear in discourse until the early 17th century, and it was not until the 18th century that it surfaced in scientific discourse (Miles, 1993). Before this time most people paid little attention to such differences because, among other reasons, most stayed in relatively close proximity to their birthplace, at least by today's standards, where differences between groups of people were not always obvious. Even those who traveled great distances did not always notice these kinds of difference. Shreeve (1994) maintains that neither Marco Polo nor the 14th-century Arabian explorer Ibn Battutah ever thought in racial terms, because traveling by foot and camelback rarely allowed them to cover more than 25 miles in one day. It simply never occurred to them to categorize people in racial terms when the differences they noticed from day to day were quite minimal.

This all changed with ocean-going transport. But it was not ocean travel in itself that brought so-called racial differences to a point where they would eventually play such a pivotal role in organizing social relationships. A number of fundamental changes to the social fabric of 16th- and 17th-century Europe prompted men and women to notice and to place certain evaluations on what would in time be referred to as 'racial' differences, and consequently to make sense of these differences in very particular ways. These transformations did not occur in isolation from one another. Rather each was closely tied to the other. In fact they could not have emerged without the presence of one or more of the other conditions. One such change involved the dissolution of what for years had been fixed hierarchical relationships between and among groups of people (Taylor, 1991). Up until the 16th and 17th centuries in Europe a person's station in life and the privileges that accompanied this position were determined at birth. The son of a 'nobleman' inherited advantages that the son or daughter of a 'serf' could never realistically expect to come his or her way.

The transformation at this time and in the following centuries from an agrarian-based production process to one that favored the mass production of goods generated a threat to many of the privileges enjoyed by the nobility, while at the same time presenting new possibilities for others not born of so-called noble blood. In the scramble to establish and legitimize the manner in which privileges that accompanied this new order were distributed, individuals looked to certain strategies. One of these strategies coincided with the establishment of 'nation states'. These entities provided an ideal legitimizing mechanism for establishing and enforcing laws that made it possible for a relatively small group of people to maintain their privileges, often at the expense of a much larger group. For example, regulations regarding the ownership of land and other resources favored those who had the means to acquire them and penalized those who did not, a situation which lent itself to the exploitation of the latter.

The idea of the nation state provided a further rationale for the differential distribution of privileges by giving rise to the concept of a group or groups of people who shared certain valued characteristics with one another, while at the same time setting themselves apart from others who did not display these same positive traits. This discourse became particularly useful as industrialists began to employ ocean transport in order to secure resources and labor that would ensure greater profits for their enterprises. Indeed the establishment of so-called racial differences and their inevitable endowment with value, often associated with colonial ventures, provided those who currently enjoyed advantages with a justification for dominating and exploiting other human beings, and in the process, maintaining their own privileged positions. The idea of race and the practice of racism and other related forms of domination such as sexism, classism and so on thus have their origin, at least in part, in the efforts of a certain group of Europeans who sought to provide a justification for the establishment and maintenance of particular practices of distribution which favored themselves, and the subjugation of so-called 'different' others upon which these forms of distribution depended (Miles, 1993; Omni & Winant, 1986; Shohat & Stam, 1994). These ideas and their associated practices have evolved over the years, becoming entrenched in various attitudes, discourses and institutional practices, many of which have become taken for granted.

A linchpin of racist discourse involves the differential distribution of value. Establishing hierarchies and associating certain groups with negative characteristics requires that certain distinctions be established between these groups. Morely and Robins (1995) use de Saussure's (1974) view of language to clarify this process. For de Saussure, units of language do not naturally reflect their own unique identities. Rather their identities and meanings emerge from the differences in the system of language. Units are defined not by positive content, but by their relations with other terms of the system. In other words these terms become what other terms are not. For example, the meaning of the word 'hot' does not simply refer to an isolated and unique phenomenon, that of 'heat'. The term 'hot' cannot stand alone. Rather, we can really only understand what 'hot' means when we contrast it with its binary opposite, 'cold'. It is the particular relationship between the two and with other related terms such as 'warm', 'cool' and so following that provides those who use the term 'hot' with its meaning. The notion of 'hot' without any opposite or related terms will make little sense. In the same manner, the identities of groups are constituted through their relationships with one another. European culture, for example, is constituted precisely through its distinctions from, and oppositions to, American, Asian, Islamic and other cultures. European culture is what the others are not. It is also important to note here that identity is as much about exclusion as inclusion. Socially constructed boundaries separate those who belong from those who do not (Morely & Robins, 1995).

Said (1978) provides an illustration of how this process works in his account of how the idea of 'the West' came to be. He questions the notion that there are geographical spaces with indigenous, radically 'different' inhabitants who can be defined on the basis of some religion, culture or racial essence. Instead he maintains that the idea of the West comes largely from its opposition to the Islamic and Arab world, a world which was perpetually on Europe's doorstep. Conversely the notion of the Orient originates in its opposition to this idea of the West. Both concepts rely on one another. Neither could exist without the other. The construction of this particular opposition became necessary for those in what came to be known as the West as they sought to justify their appropriation of the rest of the world. As part of this initiative they learned to define their own uniqueness against the Other, that is against non-Europeans. On the one hand, the construction of this imaginary Orient helped to give unity and coherence to the idea of the West. On the other, it allowed Westerners to justify their privileges by defining their alleged superior qualities against the inferior characteristics which they attributed to the people of the Orient.

Europeans shaped these sorts of definitions of themselves and others in the context of 'progress' discourses. As early as the 18th century they began to see progress – conceived in general terms as the positive movement from one state of affairs to another – as a good thing. In this regard many children of the so-called Age of Enlightenment devoted themselves to the advancement of humanity toward an imagined state of perfection. In doing so they looked to science and rationality to deliver society from a state dominated by superstition, prejudice and entrenched hierarchies to an 'achieved condition of refinement and order' (Young, 1995). Many of these people believed that science would provide opportunities for men and women to improve their life situations generally by, among other things, expanding their individual liberties, their chances for equality with others and their political democratic arrangements Some thought of progress as a form of what they referred to as 'civilization'. The terms civil and civilized were first employed centuries before by those who sought to make a distinction between people who lived in cities and people who continued to hunt for their livelihood (Young, 1995). To be civilized meant to be a citizen of a walled city, as opposed to the savage or 'wild man' outside, or the more distant roaming barbarian. Those who lived in these agrarian-based cities were thought to be 'cultivated', while hunters were characterized by their lack of 'culture'. Over the centuries the meaning of civilization came to be associated with newer ways of life. People often used the term to distinguish between these emerging and often preferred forms and the more traditional and less desirable life styles. By the 18th and 19th centuries Europeans tended to associate European civilization with progress, and for most, this meant things related to science, rationality and industrialization. On the other hand, those communities and groups who failed to display a kinship with these perspectives and practices were seen as uncivilized.

Civilization designations and the positive and negative characterizations associated with the progress discourses, as we have seen, were not originally restricted to colonial ventures, however. Miles (1993) claims that the civilization process preceded European colonialism. It began within Europe and within nation states as one particular class sought to legitimate a social hierarchy, and with it, a set of dominating relations. The ruling class in feudal Europe and later the so-called bourgeoisie class in industrial Europe sought to protect their privileged positions, in part, by promulgating a view of serfs, peasants and the working class as simpler and more primitive people. In this discourse these people did not deserve the advantages that the upper class enjoyed because they were somehow lesser human beings that the latter. Matthew Arnold's characterization of working class people as having no culture, as being 'raw and uncivilized', and as savages, typifies this view (Young, 1995).

As social conditions moved well beyond the agrarian/hunting divisions, civilization took on different meanings. In time many dimensions to this characterizing process emerged. One of these discourses revolved around the ways in which men and women thought. Elite Europeans and generations that would follow liked to think that their intellectual heritage originated with Hellenic culture, conveniently ignoring the latter's roots in Phoenician and Egyptian societies. From this tradition they saw themselves as the inheritors of the principles of reason (Morely & Robins, 1995). European elites defined their differences from, and superiority over, other groups in terms of this form of reason. While seeing themselves as 'reasonable' and rational, they characterized other groups as irrational and superstitious. One need only look at the triumphs and accomplishments of embodied reason in science and technology, they maintained, to recognize this superiority. But Europeans characterized groups not only by virtue of the way they thought, but also in terms of *what* they thought. An important indicator of difference in this regard was religion. Mistakenly annexing Christianity as their own and ignoring its connections to the Middle East, Europeans set Christianity as a standard measure of worth. They characterized non-Christians as 'heathens', 'savages' and 'poor infidels captivated by the devil', and saw their mission as one that would save these poor heathen souls (Ruchames, 1969). Moreover, they believed that their moral superiority provided them with the right to do as they pleased with these people. Pope Nicholas V's order empowering the King of Portugal 'to despoil and sell into slavery all Moslems, heathens and other foes of Christ' was not untypical of these times (Ruchames, 1969:2).

As ocean travel increased Europeans began to superimpose this value hierarchy on people in distant lands. Large-scale industry started to flex its muscles in Europe and entrepreneurs sent their agents across the seas to explore new ways of increasing profits. Of the strategies that they eventually employed, the one with the most profound legacy centered on moves to decrease the cost of labour. The enslavement of thousands of Africans precipitated considerable effort on the part of the slave-traders and the communities and societies to which they belonged to provide some sort of justification for the cruel subjugation of so many human beings. Perhaps the first sign of efforts to drawn a line between slaves and slavers was a change in the self-identity of Europeans. For example, before the mid 17th century the English generally referred to themselves as 'Christian'. After this time they employed the designations 'English' or 'free'. By 1680 this had changed again, this time to 'white' (Omni & Winant, 1986). The efforts that followed, many by academics, were to bring into currency the concept of race, set the stage for its various meanings, and shape the forms that contemporary racism would eventually assume.

Europeans set about the task of classifying human beings into groups on the basis of phenotypical features. This kind of categorization, according to Miles (1993), was not however a universal feature of human relations. It only began with these European efforts in the 18th century. Nevertheless the idea that certain somatic features – some real, some imagined – stood as natural marks of difference quickly gained currency. Eventually designated by the term 'race', these outward indicators came to express nature, that is, something given and immutable. People at this time began to accept the notion that humanity could be divided into distinct categories by virtue of their physical characteristics, and that these physical attributes were outward indicators of differences lurking underneath. Race was believed to account for a person's temperament, sexuality, intelligence and so on, and in the same vein, for a group's 'culture'. These relationships provided a convenient account for a particular group's already existing social position. In this discourse a certain (racial) group occupied a position at the bottom of the social register because their supposed lack of inherited intelligence or their moral bankruptcy prevented them from improving their life situations.

Scientists also played an important part in legitimizing and circulating racist discourses that specified hierarchies of biological racial categories. In fact Young (1995) goes so far as to say that modern racism was an academic creation. He maintains that so-called scientific ideas on race became so widespread that they worked as an ideology, permeating both consciously and implicitly the fabric of almost all areas of thinking at the time. While many scientists had a role in constructing and circulating discourses about race, I will mention two particularly influential figures. The first is Carolus Linnaeus, whose founding document of taxonomy was published in 1758 (Gould, 1994). The basis for his division was geography. He merely mapped humans on to the four geographical regions of conventional cartography and came up with the following groups – Americanus, Europaeus, Asiaticus and Afer. Nor did he stop at merely identifying each group. He also attempted to characterize the behavior of each. For example, he believed the American was ruled by habit, the European by custom, the Asian by belief and the African by caprice. Still, unlike most other racist classifications at the time, his did not explicitly assign a rank to the identified groups, although one might question the implicit values embedded in his designated behaviors.

Linnaeus' student Johann Friedrich Blumenbach, who according to Gould (1994) developed the most influential of all racial classifications, did, however, explicitly rank his groups of human beings. Blumenbach believed that *homo sapiens* had been created in a single region and had then spread over the globe. In his view diversity arose as groups of people moved out to other climates and topographies from this point of origin and adopted a range of different life styles. In keeping with his model, he then singled out one particular group as being closest to the created ideal and characterized all other groups by relative degrees of departure from this archetypal standard. In other words, he placed one group at the pinnacle and then slotted the others on one of two symmetrical lines of departure away from this ideal and toward greater and greater degeneration. His criterion for identifying this original and ideal group was physical beauty. Not surprisingly, he affirmed his fellow Europeans as the most beautiful, with those from the area of Mount Caucasus as the most comely of all, hence the designation 'Caucasian' (Gould, 1994). One line of departure went through Native North Americans to Asians. The other presented a problem for him, though, if he was to employ Linnaeus' four races, for there was no intermediary group to link Caucasians and what he believed to be the least physically attractive groups on this side – the Africans. To get around this difficulty he was forced to designate Malaysians as a race unto themselves and slot them in between these two groups; all this under the authority of science.

These conceptions of race had spread widely by the end of the 19th century, their circulation facilitated by those Europeans who had most to gain from such discourses. Hall (1997b) maintains that there were at least three major moments when avalanches of popular representations that marked racial difference overran what was to become known as 'the West'. He contends that ideas about 'race' were profoundly shaped by the representations of race that emerged from slave-trade and post-slave societies, from the European scramble for control of colonial territory, markets and raw materials, and from the post-World War II immigration from the Third

World. The exploration and colonization of Africa proved to be fertile ground for an explosion of popular representations. The exploits of the 'great White explorer' in 'darkest Africa' were charted, recorded and illustrated in maps and drawings, captured in the new technology of photography, and circulated in newspapers, diaries, travel writing, official reports and adventure novels. Perhaps the most effective means of circulating these images and their associated discourses, however, was through advertisements and the sale and consumption of various commodities. As commodities and images of European domestic life flowed out to the colonies, raw materials, soon to be converted to commodities, and images of the so-called civilizing mission captured in advertisements and in the commodities themselves, flowed into the homes of Europeans. Images of colonial conquest were immortalized on matchboxes, needle-cases, toothpaste pots, cigarette packets and board-games. Soap advertisements perhaps best symbolized the 'racializing' of the domestic world (Hall, 1997b). Potential consumers were led to believe that particular brands of soap had the power to wash black skin white, remove the soot, grime and dirt of the industrial slums at home, while keeping European bodies clean and pure in the 'racially polluted' contact zones in the colonial Empire.

The slave trade, and in particular, the period of plantation slavery in the United States, also stimulated the circulation of racist images and the discourses that worked through them. Ironically, though, it was not until slavery was seriously challenged by the Abolitionists in the 19th century that the defenders of slavery set about organizing the circulation of racist images in ways that ensured their wide dissemination. In time these discourses found their way into advertisements, paintings, cartoons, children's stories and books of fiction, among other sources. In providing limited alternatives for making sense of race/ethnicity, these discourses drew on the logic of binary oppositions mentioned above and their connection to biology. White civilized people were thought to be naturally inclined towards intellectual development – refinement, learning and knowledge, a belief in reason, the presence of developed institutions, formal government and law, and a 'civilized' restraint in their emotional, sexual and civil life. By contrast, the Black 'races' were believed to display a more instinctual approach to life. Among other things, this discourse sees Blacks openly expressing emotion and feeling, displaying a lack of restraint in sexual and social life, relying on custom and ritual, and neglecting to develop civil institutions (Hall, 1997b).

Despite the obviously unscientific and culturally biased character of these and other taxonomies and their explicit and implicit hierarchies, they would come to dominate everyday perceptions and actions up until the present time, and in doing so, provide the basis for contemporary racism. Even today we live in a world where the biological conception of race, long since discredited (see for example, Gould, 1981, Shreeve, 1994), remains an important presence in common sense. Many people continue to believe and act as if they believe that the world's population is divided into a number of discrete biologically distinguishable groups, each of which displays a differential and natural worth (Miles, 1993).[1] Unfortunately persistent but misguided social scientists (see, for example, Herrnstein & Murray, 1994) who continue to attempt to demonstrate a connection between biology and social behavior do little to dispel these erroneous racist notions. These and other such efforts and beliefs only serve to buttress forms of racism that mask the social and thus political nature of this process and legitimize the privileges of certain individuals and groups. These discourses have proved to be a powerful force in shaping views of race. Many people have looked to them to make sense of race/ethnicity over the years, and undoubtedly will continue to do so in the years to come.

Contemporary Racism

Contemporary racism assumes many forms and shows up in many different situations, practices and discourses. It is just as likely to surface in schools like Suburbia Secondary School as it is in most other public institutions in the Western world. But social scientists have not always agreed on what racism actually is, nor on the manner in which it circulates. Some academics have portrayed racism as an individual or psychological thing, while others have looked on it as a structural or institutional phenomenon. The former (including, among others, Allport, 1954, and Adorno *et al.*, 1950) maintain that racism is an individual thing. It shows up in personality traits, attitudes and their behavioral manifestations. In this view, racists exhibit an irrational and mistaken view of the world. It is a 'few rotten apples' who are thought to be responsible for racist activity (Henriques, 1984). At the other end of the scale, institutional views of racism reject the role of individuals in the process, emphasizing its structurally embedded and determinant character. Proponents of this perspective maintain that the persistent and pervasive nature of racism cannot be explained with reference to the thoughts and deeds of individual men and women. Rather, they believe that racism is located in institutional arrangements that favour certain groups over others. Each of these positions has difficulty in accounting for what the other emphasizes. Liberal individualists have difficulty in acknowledging the social or institutional aspects of racism, while the more radical 'structuralists' have trouble with incorporating the acts of individual men and women into their schemes.

More recent approaches tend to acknowledge the legitimacy of at least part of both these perspectives. Rizvi (1993), for instance, while maintaining that 'individual' approaches cannot account for how individuals come to develop prejudices, nevertheless concedes that accounts of racism must make room for the intentional actions of men and women. On the other hand, while pointing out that the institutional school of thought fails to acknowledge the complex and complicated associations of individuals and groups, he recognizes the value of its emphasis on the systemic and persistent nature of racism. West (1994) also sees value in acknowledging both the 'behavioral' and 'structural' nature of racism. He maintains that 'structures and behavior are inseparable, that institutions and values go hand in hand. How people act and live are shaped – though in no way dictated or determined – by the larger circumstances in which they find themselves' (West, 1994:18). Shoshat and Stam (1994:23) characterize racism in a similar way:

> Racism, then, is both individual and systemic, interwoven into the fabric both of the psyche and of the social system, at once grindingly quotidian and maddeningly abstract. It is not merely an attitudinal issue, but a historically contingent institutional and discursive apparatus linked to the drastically unequal distribution of resources and opportunities, the unfair apportioning of justice, wealth, pleasure, and pain. It is less an error in logic than an abuse of power, less about 'attitudes' than about the deferring of hopes and the destruction of lives.

Suburbia Secondary School displays both sides of racism, the behavioral and the structural. Racism shows up in the thoughts, words and deeds of individual students and educators and at the same time is embedded in more enduring structural patterns. At times racist discourse and practice is obvious. In other instances it is more subtle. Racist discourse circulates regularly in both teacher and student 'jokes', for example. Depending on the nature of the joke, it can be either subtle or blatant. Racist discourse also circulates in offhanded comments. In one instance a teacher called up a type of 'animalist' discourse to make sense of certain kind of music that he associated with a particular group of people. Natasha remembers the incident: 'After gym we're allowed to play music and just hang around. So me and my friend Kevin were listening to this reggae tape that he'd bought. The gym teacher goes, "How can you listen to that baboon music?"'

Racist discourse may also surface in the classroom. Ronda recalls a time when her business teacher drew a strong connection between people from Africa and AIDS. And racism surfaces in more 'non-discursive' practices. The following incident represents perhaps the most blatant kind of racist behavior, behavior which the victim in this case maintains is *not* the norm in this school. Here he lucidly captures the incident, which ironically took place at a religious service in the school chapel.

Someone behind me nudges me forward. 'Hurry up, you Paki. You're going too slow.' *Stop. Rewind.* I'd like to say that again. *Play.* 'Hurry up, you packy, you're going too slow.' The beast inside of me closes his eyes, bites his teeth, clenches his fists and takes a deep breath inside to cool the fire and rage. Almost instantly I feel my body detach from my soul in an attempt to hide the pain. One more step. I put the stupid piece of cardboard-like bread in my mouth [*his attitude toward the act of receiving communion stands in marked contrast to the reverential attitude he had before he was accosted*] and go back to my seat. I sit down and pretend to pray. As my wonderful new friends file in the bench behind me, I think to myself, 'Is that all you've got? Please, that's nothing. I can handle that. No problem.' I rest back in my bench. It's not over.

Someone grabs a hold of my bench and starts shaking it back and forth. I feel all the parts of my body shake along with the bench, not because of pain or fear, but by simple laws of motion. 'No problem,' I think to myself. 'I've had to go through worse.' Then a voice. 'Look at his head jiggle, guys. Look at the packy's head jiggle.' The only comeback in my head I can think about is, 'Guys, I'm South American. I am not from Pakistan.' But this voice remains in my head. Then an orgasmic groan comes from behind. 'Guys look. The packy's coming. Look, he's coming.' Quite clever, fellas. That's original. *That's* never happened to me before. Then they stop. All along, I have not even managed to turn around. So I do; I say nothing, and turn back. 'Oooooh! He looked at me!!' comes the retort from behind, followed by a succession of shaking my bench and continuous orgasmic groans. Then a tap on my shoulder. 'Hey buddy, can you stop moving your bench?' 'Don't touch me,' I reply. Twenty seconds later I get up and leave.

So there it is. That's one of the not-so-great days of my life. I've had worse, so don't worry, my friends. I can handle it and I don't need sympathy.

Although many students and teachers maintain that racism surfaces from time to time in the school, they see these occurrences as exceptions rather than the rule. Even the young man who experienced the above assault maintains that the school itself is not 'racist'. Not all students see this situation in this way, however. Many African Canadians, in contrast to most other groups, believe that the school is indeed 'racist', only the way in which they view racism differs from that of many other students and most teachers. Instead of seeing racism as something which is embodied in intentional and obvious individual acts, as do many of their teachers and fellow students, many African Canadians believe that they are penalized by a *system* that is in itself racist in character. Michael, for example, feels that racism is part of a system that provides advantages for some, while keeping 'minorities' down. Michael's insights hint at a view that sees racism as something that extends far beyond individual acts, something that is as much part of what is not said or done as of what is spoken or acted out. Maria is another student who feels the effect of these systemic racist patterns. She believes that she has to work twice as hard as other students in order to do as well as them.

Thus racism circulates through the actions of individuals as they take up positions in historically formed discourses and engage in patterns of social practices. Men and women draw on these discourses to help them make sense of the world about them and to assist them in planning their future actions. In this regard racist discourses provide ways for people to make sense of various tones of skin color in ways that work against non-White people. Indeed color is an important part of racist discourse. Dei (1996a) maintains that we must be careful not to deny the saliency of skin color. Although racism involves more than skin color, it nevertheless revolves around the binary opposition of Black and White, or rather White and non-White. Fiske (1996) goes so far as to say that racism originates with 'Whiteness'. He does not equate Whiteness with skin color *per se*, although this concept is closely associated with it. He prefers to see Whiteness as something other than an essential category or a fixed point; Whiteness is a 'space of positions', a strategic, flexible and privileged location from which to view and to keep 'others' at a distance. From this privileged space both viewer and viewed are constituted from the norms of Whiteness. Whiteness has been able to survive for two reasons. First, it has an ability to define, monitor and police the boundary between itself and others and to control movement across these same boundaries. Its flexibility allows it a whole series of possible relationships without sacrificing its superiority. Because its space is strategic and not essential, this allows for movement in and out. In certain circumstances non-Whites can be included, and in others, Whites excluded. For example, Fiske notes that on occasion 'today's women', however White-skinned, can be excluded, while South Korean shop-owners in Los Angeles, for instance, were included during the riots there, if only temporarily. Despite this flexibility, he nevertheless cautions that we must not forget that people with White skin have massively disproportionate access to the power base of their privileged space:

> Whiteness uses skin color as an identity card by which to see where its interests may best be promoted and its rewards distributed. Whiteness may not be coterminous with white skin but white skins embody it best. Whites would not have constructed the invisible and exclusive space of Whiteness if most people with their skin color could not benefit from occupying it. Fiske (1996:49)

The other reason that Whiteness has survived is because of its ability to escape detection and any accompanying interrogation. Its key strategy is to avoid explicit presence. One of its methods is to draw lines around the identities of others, but never inward towards itself. By drawing attention to others, it deflects attention away from itself. This is particularly useful when searching for the causes of social upheavals. In attributing blame for the Los Angeles riots, for example, the media and conservative politicians focused on the actions of a small number of African Americans. They saw the devastation as the responsibility of these deviant individuals, while virtually ignoring the conditions that prompted the latter to act as they did, conditions that can be traceable at least in part to efforts to ensure White privilege.

At Suburbia skin color and its related physical traits serve perhaps more than any other characteristics to mark students. As will become evident in the next chapter, teachers often adjust their expectations of students on the basis of the latter's physical appearance. Students too engage in this practice. The racist students above believed the young man from South America was from Pakistan primarily on the basis of his outward appearance. However, although white skin generally works in favor of those who have it, Whiteness and the advantages that accompany it do not always coincide with skin color. For some students of African heritage Whiteness goes far beyond the skin level, extending to the ways in which people associate with one another and the way they act. Some of these students may refer to their fellow African Canadians who hang around with White students as being 'Whitewashed' or 'acting White'.

Though racist belief and practice are in many important ways associated with 'Whiteness', they ought not be reduced simply to a Black–White issue. As is evident at Suburbia, advantage and disadvantage are also associated with such things as religion, interactional styles, dress, language, to name only a few. Thus students who display and/or employ these various elements of culture in valued ways are likely to enjoy more opportunities than those who do not. Gillborn (1995) cautions us against oversimplifying what he believes to be a complex phenomenon. He maintains that racism takes shape in complicated relationships that revolve around more than simply a Black–White dichotomy. Rizvi (1993) takes a similar tack. He contends that no universal characterization of racism is possible. This is because racist practice is a historically specific phenomenon, that is, it is perpetually being challenged, interrupted and reconstructed in concrete and frequently unique historically contingent contexts. Specific sets of sometimes unpredictable social relationships provide the conditions that give shape to perpetually evolving racial meanings and categories. In other words, racism can emerges in the messiness of everyday life in new and different shapes. In the light of this reality Gillborn (1995) prefers to characterize racist practice and discourse as a form of plasticity, something rigid and enclosing, yet also fluid and molded. He provides an example of the often complex, contingent and sometimes contradictory character of this phenomenon in a school, illustrating how students of a certain group, while they may mobilize against racism from fellow students, will also engage in playful racist name-calling among themselves. This phenomenon is common at Suburbia. Jake, a teacher, has observed playful racist-name calling. On one of a number of occasions he heard

> two Portuguese kids say to each other, 'You're pork and cheese' or something like this and the other kid said it back to him. And it turns out they're both Portuguese kids and it's more of a kidding thing I think because it didn't escalate to anything else.

The contingent and perpetually evolving nature of racist discourse and practice also means that these will not always easily be recognized for what they are. They may assume a number of forms. Gillborn (1995) speaks of the 'new racism', a cultural rather than a skin-color racism that many people of South Asian heritage experience. These forms of racism revolve around ethnicity and cannot always be reduced to a Black–White level. On the other hand, Hall (1980) refers to 'inferential racism', while Fiske (1996) speaks of 'non-racist racism'. Both here are referring to naturalized representations whose racist premises are largely unquestioned. Distancing itself from crude ideas of biological inferiority, this kind of racism is able to hide in the apparently legitimate discourses of social cohesion and homogeneity associated with patriotism, nationhood and nationalism (Rizvi, 1993). It is possible, as Dei (1996a) tells us, to perpetrate racism without ever mentioning the idea of race at all. Talk about home and homeland, or

Heimat, may serve as an example. Morely and Robins (1995) maintain that appeals to revitalize *Heimat* will depend as much on exclusion as on inclusion, without ever referring directly to a superiority/inferiority continuum. They contend that realizing *Heimat*

> is about conserving fundamentals of culture and identity. And, as such, it is about sustaining cultural boundaries and boundedness. To belong in this way is to protect exclusive and therefore excluding, identities against those who are seen as aliens and foreigners. The 'Other' is always and continuously a threat to the security and integrity of those who share a common home. Xenophobia and fundamentalism are opposite sides of the same coin. For indeed *Heimat*-seeking is a form of fundamentalism. The apostles of purity are always moved by the fear that intermingling with a different culture will inevitably weaken and ruin their own. (Morely & Robins, 1995:89)[2]

The other reason why racism does not always display a straightforward or easily identifiable set of practices and discourses is that it is invariably intertwined with other axes of social organization and oppression (Dei, 1996a; Rizvi, 1993; Shoshat & Stam, 1995). Racism is interconnected with gender, class, age, (dis)ability, sexuality, religion, language, culture, nationality and so on, in a variety of interactive, interlocking, contradictory and mutually reinforcing modes. As a consequence the ways in which individuals can belong to a certain group and experience their position within that group will depend fundamentally on their relationships to other groupings. For example, an individual's class and gender positions will dictate in many respects how they experience racism. And while race may continue to be an important organizing principle, it is by no means a monolithic and ultimately primary determining agent. In some circumstances race may play a major role, while in others it may function in a less vital way. This also means that race, or for that matter, any other axis of oppression may not dictate once and for all advantage and disadvantage. A single individual may act as an oppressor in one context, and be the object of oppression in another.

At Suburbia race, class and gender intersect in many ways. For some students race and gender constitute double axes of disadvantage. Ilda, an African Canadian, is one such student. She believes, as also outlined in Chapter 5, that teacher expectations of her in a class where young women are generally in the minority are lower than they would be for White males. As a consequence even when she does well, the teacher questions whether or not her success has been achieved through legitimate means. Race and class also intersect in ways that penalize students. Jean remembers the time when she went to the school with two of her friends a week before class to see one of her teachers. At the school she met a guidance counselor who thought he would help her out. When his files told him that Jean's friends were from a nearby housing development he advised her against associating with them.

Advantage and disadvantage become that much more complicated when we consider the explosion of differences in the contemporary world. Indeed the seemingly infinite array of differences produced within new production processes (Harvey, 1989; Clegg, 1990), in the media and electronic communications (Morely & Robins, 1995; Ang, 1995), and within the so-called 'culture of consumption' (Featherstone, 1991) carry with them the potential for generating new kinds of subordination and domination. Television, for example, supplies us with an array of information, perspectives, and portrayals in an unlimited range of forms, including documentaries, news programming, commercials, info-commercials, dramas, comedies, and so on. We can tune in to a growing number of available channels to learn about anything from the life cycle of newts to the latest crisis to befall our favorite soap opera character. As consumers, many of us in the Western world have considerable discretion in choosing not only the television programs we watch and as a consequence learn from, but also the goods and services we use. In many ways these choices are tied to the lifestyles we adopt and the identities we take on. The differences associated with these choices inevitably confer advantages on some and penalize others, although the duration of these relationships may vary considerably. Such consumer choices also interact in unique ways with more enduring axes of oppression. Lowe (1995) contends that the new forms of lifestyle consumerism may at times reconfigure racism. People of African heritage, many of whom are in the lower income group, are increasingly vulnerable to slick packaging, marketing and advertising that claim to offer them a way of life they could not reasonably hope to experience in other ways. Producers actively seek to exploit these weaknesses by targeting select groups for marketing of specific commodities, a practice that tends to extend the disadvantages that many of African heritage currently experience.

The consumer choices that the various students and educators at Suburbia make may well confer advantages on some, while penalizing others. As mentioned above, this process does not always work in a uniform or straightforward way. It may depend, for example, on context. Students may choose to dress in a certain way or listen to certain kinds of music that provide them with a sense of identity and self-esteem, while at the same time bringing them together with like-minded individuals. Yet in other situations these same practices may the object of derision. Earlier in the chapter we saw how a teacher referred to the students' reggae music as 'baboon music'. In one context this music provided students with a sense of identity, self-esteem and community, but in another, in the presence of a White authority figure, it became a medium for racist practice. The teacher's employment of an 'animalist' discourse served to devalue not only the music itself and the students who were listening to it, but *all* those might who identify with and listen to it.

A more sensible view of racism, then, is to see it both as an individual and as an institutional or social phenomenon. This position is consistent with the view of discourse outlined in Chapter 3. Thus racist discourse and practice are first and foremost part of a social process. Individual subjects are also implicated, but they do not take centre stage. Instead, in order to make sense of their lives they take up positions offered up to them by already established discourses, and act accordingly. Among other things, these sense-making frameworks encourage them to rate skin color and other observable signs associated with ethnicity as important markers of what lies beneath. Racist practice is not necessarily restricted to anything so obvious, though. Indeed racist discourse and practice have become in many ways more difficult to detect in contemporary times. This is because they are easily entangled in other discourses and practices associated with other axes of oppression, including class, gender, (dis)ability and so on, and with other emerging forms of difference associated with new patterns of consumption.

What is apparent in all of this is that representations of race/ethnicity have not been shaped under conditions of equality. Certain groups have had the upper hand both in constructing and in circulating such discourses. White Europeans were among the first to make popular partic-ular ways of making sense of race/ethnicity. They were motivated to do so because they believed that these discourses worked in their interests, protecting their privileges and power. By circulating ideas that separate people from one another and by attaching values to these distinct groups they were able to justify their oppressive treatment of people from other areas of the world. While these racist representations and the practices associated with them did not simply roll over everything and everyone in their paths, the extreme power differential between Europeans and those whom they colonized meant that the latter did not have the resources to put up much, if any, resistance. While conditions have improved for non-White groups over the years, we all still live pretty much in this colonial shadow, where racist discourse and practice continue to flourish. What is different, at least in some respects, is that there is now greater room to resist racist discourse and practice. This, however, often pertains more to some areas than others. In other words, people can recognize and are prepared to resist certain manifestations of racism more than others. In particular men, women and children often find it easier to recognize and thus to challenge the more obvious and blatant forms of racist discourse and practice than they do the more subtle forms. The last section of this chapter describes student and school resistance to the former at Suburbia. The next chapter will explore one of the more subtle forms of racism.

Resisting Racism at Suburbia

The previous sections were intended to provide a context for understanding racist discourse and practice at Suburbia and the ways in which they confer advantages on some students and disadvantages on others. What we see here are the contemporary manifestations of a process that has evolved over the space of at least 500 years. The examples provided above represent only one facet of an increasingly complicated process. These are the more readily identifiable instances. There are, however, countless less recognizable ways in which racist evaluations of difference work to penalize students. The chapters that follow probe these more subtle forms. For now, I want to concentrate on the more obvious manifestations of racism.

As illustrated above, racist discourse and practice are alive and well at Suburbia. Some of these manifestations of racism are obvious, while others are not quite as evident. Because they are obvious, many students and educators are able to recognize them. What is more, some members of the educational community are willing to take action to challenge them. This can happen when people employ particularly demeaning or obviously malicious discourses or practices. In three of the cases referred to above, students and/or educators objected to what individuals said and did, and actively challenged them. In one instance where the teacher associated AIDS with Africans, one of the students in the class objected strenuously to such an idea.

> So I said, [*in a loud, impassioned voice*] 'You listen, all of us Blacks have African descent. I don't care what you say or who you're talking to, as long as I'm in this class you keep whatever racist comments you have, keep it inside because I'm a different student to deal with. All these other Black kids will sit down and take it. I'm different.'

In the second case, the young women who heard the 'baboon' comment objected immediately. One of them, Janice, was not content with her retort, though, and went on to tell her mother, who reported the matter to the school authorities. As it turned out, Janice was not entirely satisfied with the response she got.

> So I go, 'But wait! I'm not a monkey, OK? My parents came from Jamaica, this is what we listen to!' I told my mom. She called the school and told off the teacher. The next day I got called down to the office. Mr Reilly was laughing, he was laughing in front of my face you know, and he said, 'Oh Marion, don't worry, he really didn't mean it.' And I'm thinking, like, 'It's not a joke, you know.'

School responses to racism are capable of being more satisfying than this, to students and educators alike. In the final case, where the student was accosted at the religious service, the school became involved and took more systematic action. But it was the victimized student who got things started. After the incident he went home and wrote up in detail everything that happened, part of which I presented above. He next approached a staff member with the idea of publicizing what had occurred. He thought that it might be useful if someone read his account over the school intercom. The teacher took his idea to the administration who were hesitant to broadcast the account in this way. Instead they felt that it would be better if it could be passed around to homeroom teachers to read. Eventually they settled on this latter option. As it turned out, most teachers read the student's account. The readings had a substantial impact on many students and educators, and in many classes discussions about racism ensued. A number of students reported that many of their classmates were angry after they learned what had taken place in the chapel and were anxious to take action to prevent this kind of incident from happening again. In fact word of what happened spread well beyond the school. The sister of the victim, who attended another school, came home one day with this story, not realizing that her brother was the one involved.

Conclusion

The ways in which racial/ethnic differences are represented at Suburbia Secondary School are not exclusive to this setting. Indeed the discourses to which students and educators turn to make sense of race/ethnicity have a long history. They have evolved over the centuries as certain Europeans and their descendants sought to justify and thereby protect their privileges. This legitimizing process included the partitioning of groups along racial/ethnic lines and assigning worth in ways that favored Europeans.

The attribution of negative meanings to certain groups and individuals on the basis of perceived racial/ethnic associations, and the disadvantages that accompany these meanings, continue to this day in schools like Suburbia Secondary. Some of these discourses and the practices that flow from them are obvious. Others are not. In the former cases it is easier for educators and students to recognize them and hence mount actions to challenge them. I have illustrated above how students and educators contested such racist discourse and practice. The more subtle forms of racist discourse and practice are not as easy to recognize, nor are they as likely to be challenged, or if challenged, to be successfully contested. The next chapter explores one of these more subtle forms of racism – stereotyping.

Notes

1. Shoshat and Stam (1994) maintain that there are a number of mechanisms associated with racism including (1) a positing of a lack, (2) a mania for hierarchy, (3) a blaming of the victim, (4) a refusal of empathy, (5) a systemic devaluation of life and (6) a discourse of reverse discrimination.
2. Part of this quote is taken from Rushdie (1990).

Chapter 5

Stereotypical Representations

Racism surfaces regularly in most institutions in the Western world, including schools. Suburbia Secondary School is no exception. As we saw in Chapter 4, both students and educators are capable of initiating talk and actions that are quite obviously racist in nature. A key element in this process is the way in which certain groups come to be represented through discourse. Indeed the images that are embedded in the discourses that students and teachers employ to make sense of 'different' and often unfamiliar groups will figure into the ways in which they act with regard to them. If for example these images are obviously negative, as they were in a couple of the cases cited in Chapter 4, then those who employ these discourses will likely act on them accordingly, treating members of these groups in equally negative ways. Students who are the objects of these negative representations and actions have little to gain from them. Indeed they are routinely penalized by them. As a consequence those students who are the object of blatantly racist discourse and practice will not have the same kinds of opportunity in schools as other students do.

Xenophobic behavior, however, represents but one aspect of a systematic and unfair distribution of advantages. While calculated and malicious acts of racial prejudice probably occur in schools more often than we would care to see or admit, they constitute just one (less common) way in which certain students may be placed at a disadvantage. Indeed most teachers are well-meaning human beings who have their students' interests at heart (Nieto, 1992). Even though educators' efforts may at times be misguided, it is hard to believe that more than a relative few would as a matter of course go out of their way to penalize particular students on the basis of their perceived heritage or skin color. This is true of Suburbia Secondary School, where the majority of educators appear to be genuinely concerned with the welfare of most, if not all the students. What is more likely, at Suburbia and elsewhere, is that the taken-for-granted beliefs and practices teachers, administrators and policy-makers hold, and which they employ in their efforts to help students learn, work in systemic ways to inadvertently penalize some of these very students.

One important way in which these taken-for-granted beliefs and practices find systemic expression is through the creation and employment of *stereotypes*. In their efforts to cope with a perpetually evolving and changing world educators and students routinely reach for popular and often unfounded images of groups and situations to help them understand, and act in, both familiar and unfamiliar circumstances (Lee, 1996; Ryan *et al.*, 1995; Ryan, 1996a; Giroux, 1993; Dei, 1996a, 1996b; Elrich, 1994; Solomon, 1992; Boutte & McCormick, 1992). These supposedly neutral images can have a profound effect on educators. Among other influences, they provide the basis for ways in which these people persistently see and interact with certain individuals and groups. Unfortunately these interactions can work against the latter, seriously limiting both their immediate and their long-term opportunities. This chapter explores the process of stereotyping at Suburbia Secondary School. I begin, however, by developing a perspective on the process of stereotyping. I do this by reviewing approaches to the phenomenon, critiquing them, and settling on a notion of stereotypes as forms of competing discourse. This is followed by an account of how various stereotypical representations show up and are contested in the school. Finally, I provide a context for understanding these contests by illustrating how they occur outside of the school. To do this I use selected examples from the mass media.

Stereotypes

The term 'stereotype' has a relatively short history. First coined in the late 18th century to refer to the casting of multiple papier mâché copies of printing type from an original mold, it was based on the Greek words *stereos*, meaning form or solid, and *typos*, meaning the making of an impression (Miller, 1982). The concept of a stereotype was first employed in social science by Walter Lippmann in 1922. Since that time the concept has taken on a number of different forms (Mackie, 1973; Miller, 1982; Henwood *et al.*, 1993). Needless to say, academics do not all agree on its precise features. Even so there are a number of elements that, while not common to all views, remain prominent. These include stereotyping as a (1) generic process of categorization, one that (2) works through 'good' and 'bad' images, which in turn (3) frequently misrepresent the groups which they depict.

One key element in the various concepts of a stereotype is the idea that stereotyping is a process basic to all human beings. Social scientists have used the term to refer to the images through which all individuals categorize the world (Lippmann, 1922; Fishman, 1956; Levine & Campbell, 1972;

Gilman, 1985). From this perspective a stereotype is a crude representation. It is necessarily reductive, generalized by those who employ it as typical of that class of object for which it stands. The process of establishing and employing stereotypes, or, in this view, generalizations, constitutes a vital part of the strategies that men, women and children employ to get on with their lives in a world where they have only a limited knowledge of their surroundings. In order to estimate what we can expect from the situations that we perpetually encounter in our day-to-day lives we are forced to rely on what Schutz (1967) refers to as the 'typifications' that emerge from memories of our past experiences. We reach for these typifications each time we adjust our behavior to suit situations that resemble to a greater or lesser extent situations we either have encountered previously or at least already know something about (Ryan, 1996).

Social scientists have also associated stereotypes with good and bad images. Gilman (1985) associates the creation of these images with individual and group efforts to combat the anxieties that arise with a perceived loss of control. He traces the roots of the distinction between 'good' and 'bad' to the process by which all human beings become individuals. This first occurs as the infant becomes aware that there are things in its immediate environment that are not part of the self. As the child is able to distinguish more and more between the world and the self, it senses that it is not able to control certain aspects of its universe. When children develop into adolescents, and eventually into adults, they learn to minimize the anxiety associated with this lack of control by projecting 'badness' on to that which they cannot control.

Most social scientists, including Gilman (1985), maintain however that stereotyping is not exclusively a 'psychological' or personal phenomenon. They see it as also a social process (Henwood *et al.*, 1993; Shohat & Stam, 1994; Wilson & Gutierez, 1995; Merelman, 1995). This means that we select stereotypical models from the social world in which we live. Indeed every social group has a vocabulary of images for the externalized Other. A product of history and of a culture that perpetuates them, these frequently rich webs of signs and references for difference reflect the particular contexts which give rise to them. They are also intimately associated with a society's communal sense of control over its world. These models are the medium through which the tension between control and its loss within individuals and groups, and the subsequent anxiety that produces, finds expression in the forms of the Other.

'Pathologizing' the Other through negative analogies is one way in which the self can protect itself from its own contradictions and from perceived threats from without. Searching for and degrading differences in skin color and physiognomy, for example, is a common way of responding to perceived threats to individual and group autonomy. So it is not surprising that the qualities assigned to the Other generate patterns that may or may not have any relationship to any other reality. In fact many social scientists (including Allport, 1954; Fishman, 1956; Mackie, 1973 and Miller, 1982) either explicitly state or imply in their work that the stereotypical image characteristically does not accurately represent the group to which it refers. Although some maintain that there may well be a 'kernel of truth' in such images, most concede that they are generally misleading, more often than not in a negative way. As a corrective to these mistaken images, and the first step to generating more positive (and accurate) representations, some social scientists recommend more research into relationships between the images and the groups they depict (Mackie, 1973).

In this view, then, stereotypes provide an essential, if not always benevolent, tool for helping us get on in our daily lives. In assisting us to adjust our behavior to suit the particular circumstances in which we may find ourselves, these crude and often misleading representations serve to reduce the anxiety we may feel over the perceived loss of control that we routinely experience. At the same time they remain part of those patterns of relationships that systematically and unfairly distribute advantages among and between certain groups and individuals.

Stereotypical Images as Discourse

Over the years those who have exposed and analyzed stereotypes, as have a number of the social scientists cited above, have provided us with a valuable service. According to Shohat and Stam (1994) they have played a role in revealing oppressive patterns of prejudice which at first glance may have appeared random or inconsequential; highlighting the psychic devastation of negative portrayals of individuals and groups; and signaling the function of stereotypes as a form of social control. In so doing they have drawn attention to some of the more subtle ways in which racism extends its reach and penalizes certain individuals and groups. Some of these approaches, however, have their limitations. In particular those analyses that revolve around a preoccupation with accuracy and a good vs. bad image approach, exhibit a number of theoretical-political pitfalls.

Shohat and Stam (1994) contend that an exclusive preoccupation with positive and negative images leads to a kind of essentialism. They maintain that those who adopt this approach assume, often implicitly, that the group being portrayed has a real essence and that this invariably benevolent nature is being represented in unflattering and inaccurate ways. In the effort to expose the significance of these frequently misleading images, this approach tends to reduce complex varieties of portrayals to a limited set of reified and ultimately oversimplified categories. Media analysts, for example, may force diverse fictive characters into pre-established classification schemes. For these people, there is a 'piccaninny' behind every Black child performer, a 'mammy' behind every nurturing Black female. Static analyses of this sort do not allow for mutations, often ignoring the historical instability of stereotypes and the language that accompanies them. They fail to register, for example, the ways in which imagery might be shaped by changes in the economy.

A number of these approaches also subscribe to a one-to-one correspondence idea of truth. Unfortunately this view displays a number of weaknesses. First and foremost, by presuming that properly assembled images can capture groups and individuals as they really are, such approaches misread the ways in which individuals and groups are formed. Their proponents may believe, erroneously, that these projected images are merely tools for representing what to all intents and purposes are distinct and self-contained objects (groups or individuals). They fail to realize that there is always an important relationship between these portrayals and the groups and individuals they depict. For instance the social position of a particular group will generally dictate the manner in which that group is portrayed, and these images will in turn have a decisive impact on the group, particularly in terms of how they see themselves and how others see them. As illustrated in Chapter 3, discourses actually 'make' individuals and groups. Characterizations in discourse provide ways for men and women to understand or make sense of themselves and others. They cannot be understood at all without the help of these discourses.

Proponents of traditional stereotype analyses also fail to see how representation is in fact a *political* process. In so failing they often do not recognize how these arenas of representation become, in important ways, sites of contestation. It is here that groups struggle over how they are to be represented, the outcome of which both reflects and dictates their respective fortunes. Given the contested nature of processes of representation, it makes more sense then to abandon the language of accuracy and authenticity and focus instead on discourses and the ways in which they work through the images we encounter. From this angle, visual images and texts do not display inherent or fixed meanings. Meaning emerges instead as the viewer attempts to make sense of what he or she sees, in the dialogue between the viewer and the image. This sense can only occur if and when viewers place their experience into discourse, that is, into available patterns of words, symbols and images.

Discourse should not, however, be equated with language. It is in fact a concept that attempts to combine language and practice, what people do and what they say (Hall, 1997a). What this means is that the sense people make of their experience depends in crucial ways on who is doing the interpreting, what kinds of life experience the interpreters bring to the event, the availability of words, images and practices for making sense, and the social or institutional context in which the interpreters find themselves (Fiske, 1996). It is important to acknowledge in this regard that discourse is also a social practice (Fiske, 1996). As a result, not only should those interested in exploring stereotypes from this perspective look to probe the repertoire of already existing signs and symbols, but they need also be concerned with the continuous process in which sense is made of these symbols and subsequently circulated. Discourses offer men and women 'interpretive packages', a series of central yet perpetually evolving organizing ideas or frames, which become part of the way in which they make sense of what they encounter (Merelman, 1995).

But discourses are not merely media for making sense. They are, as mentioned above, also the means through which power is exercised to promote particular interests. What discourses are made available or prevail at a given time and place will inevitably depend in crucial ways on prevailing power arrangements. These discourses or sense-making frames exert their power, in part, by filtering the ways in which our experience makes sense to us. In this view experience itself does not determine its own sense. Rather, the social power associated with the discursive processes dictates the manner in which the events associated with experience are placed into particular discourses, providing them with one set of meanings as opposed to others. These sets of meanings inevitably favour certain interests at the expense of others. Indeed they play a vital role in filtering the voices that eventually emerge in these discourses. Thus it is that television can offer viewers various interpretive packages for understanding nuclear power, for example, that advance particular interests. Putting a 'progress' spin on this topic provides space for certain voices and interests to be articulated at the expense of others (Merelman, 1995).

Discourse, as emphasized above, need not be seen just as a technique of inequality, but also as a terrain of struggle. Fiske (1996) prefers to see discourse not merely as a tool for advancing certain interests, but also as a field of struggle in which various groups strive to have their voices heard and their discourse events inserted into the politics of everyday life. In other words discourse is not just a technology for repressing, marginalizing and invalidating other voices and discourses. It is also the very medium in which the latter are contested. Such contests often revolve around: (1) struggles to 'accent' a word, to turn the way it is spoken or used to advance certain interests; (2) struggles over the choice of certain words or images; (3) struggles to recover repressed words or images; (4) struggles to disarticulate or articulate and (5) struggles to gain access to public discourse or media to have one's voice heard (Fiske, 1996). Struggles over how groups are to represent themselves and others occur generally wherever there are cultural issues at stake (Merelman, 1995). They take place routinely in art galleries, recording studios, television meetings, movie studios, newsrooms, local and national legislatures, courtrooms, school board meetings, and of course in the halls and classrooms of schools themselves.

In sum, the construction, use and effects of stereotypes are perhaps best understood not in terms of more or less static, self-contained and misleading images, but through the latter's insertion into historically rooted sense-making practices, that is, discourses. Associating stereotypes with discourses allows us to acknowledge and explore the perpetual and frequently unequal struggle over how groups are portrayed. As forms of discourse, these portrayals constitute at the same time artifacts and social practices, techniques for repression, and perhaps most importantly, the terrain on which struggles over representation occur. It is here that individual and group anxieties over control find expression, where various interests vie for supremacy, where some voices are heard and others muffled, and where advantages and opportunities are distributed and eventually acted upon.

This chapter now explores how individuals at Suburbia Secondary School make sense of different others and how they use this sense in their interactions with these others. It looks at how the prevailing stereotypical discourses are reflected in the ways people talk about these different others and in the manner in which they act toward them.

Recognizing Difference at Suburbia

The process of making sense of differences first entails that those making such sense notice certain things about their environment that they identify as 'different'. The first aspect that the majority of Suburbia's teachers, students, and parents point to as 'different' is other people in the school community. They consistently speak about the wide variety of differences that characterizes the student population. They refer to the myriad of religions, languages, skin colors, heritages, home countries, interactional preferences, values and so on associated with these students as 'cultural differences'. For most teachers these cultural differences are at the forefront of their thoughts. This is because many of these mostly Anglo teachers have only in recent years encountered so many children who bring with them cultural proclivities that the teachers believe may affect the way the children interact and learn in the classroom. Susan, for example, says with respect to the student population, 'There's plenty of diversity, that's for sure.'

One consequence of this high level of diversity is that many teachers know little about many of their students. Frequently they misidentify them. Margaret says, with reference to her students, 'They're not just Chinese or whatever. They're Indian. I'll see their last name and I won't be able to tell what it is. Portuguese or Pakistani or whatever.' Students are conscious of not only teachers', but also fellow students' inability to correctly identify them. Juanita, who is from South America, points out that she has been mistakenly identified at one time or another as someone from Asia, China, Portugal, Italy and the Philippines. Unless a student's heritage is obvious, many teachers and students will not know their ethnic origin. This is particularly true in the case of South Americans, some Eastern Europeans, Latin Americans, and the wide range of Asian students. In fact identifying a student's heritage may not always mean that much for those interested in understanding their students. This is because there can be such a wide variation within even those groups perceived to be homogeneous in make-up. Erroneous assumptions of homogeneity or mistaken identifications can upset students. Katherine, a student of African heritage, is annoyed when others assume that she is Jamaican. She says, 'Once people think you're Black, they think you're Jamaican ... I don't know if that is a real basis of being upset, but it hurt[s] me.'

One of the consequences of this high level of diversity is that many members of this school community are often forced to rely on sources other than direct personal experience to make sense of those whom they see as different others. Norman, for example, who was born in Eastern Europe, maintains that many of the people who emigrated from this area rely on movies for their knowledge of certain groups of people. He says, 'A lot of the stereotypes are from movies 'cos they see the movies but they [*people from his home country*] don't see [the people] that get stereotyped.' But even when direct experience plays a role in shaping understandings of groups and individuals, it is always placed within the dominant sense-making frames that circulate in and around the wider social milieu. In what forms then do these discourses show up in the school?

Dominant Stereotypical Discourses at Suburbia

Educators and students make sense of what they see as distinct groups in many ways. Some of these patterns, however, take precedence over others. They find expression in the ways in which students and teachers talk about others and in the ways in which they interact with them. Some of these discourses include such ideas as: Croatians have a lot to say about themselves and their country; they are all nationalistic and sexist; Filipino kids seldom talk about their culture and thus are not necessarily proud of it; Polish kids are quiet and reserved; and Portuguese students are not troublemakers. While these discourses circulate freely, there are others that have an even greater impact on how teachers and students perceive and react to certain groups. By this I mean that in conversations with teachers and students, they emerged much more frequently than the above understandings. These include the supposed physical and intellectual abilities of students of African and Oriental heritage.

The first and most powerful is the idea that students of African heritage, particularly males, possess unique physical abilities and will not hesitate to employ them when they see fit. Many students and teachers make sense of the talk and actions of these students by believing that their social practices merely reflect their inherently violent natures. Teachers and students alike react in one of two ways. The first is to respond in an overly aggressive manner. It is generally only a few teachers who adopt this path, however. Riley is one of them. He says:

> There's generally a segment of the Black students that I stereotype and they bring that on themselves. I'm very open in the beginning and they bring that upon themselves, where they have a major chip on their shoulder and everything that's done to them is done in discrimination. And that kind of student I treat differently lots of times, and that is the student that I'll go out of my way to discipline.

A more common reaction among teachers, however, is to do quite the opposite. Most teachers will go out of their way to avoid students of African heritage, particularly in the halls of the school. This is because many of them are intimidated by these young people. Gilby, a teacher, says that 'a lot of teachers are afraid to deal with certain groups of students …Teachers … won't walk through the main office or the main hallway in the morning.' Paul, another teacher, gives his view:

The Black kids, they are effusive, as people, you know they are very verbal. They have got lots to communicate about, they dance around the place. They are very active, dancing is interesting, like they will stand in the forum downstairs, and they will dance, and this intimidates people, this intimidates some people. Like teachers, some teachers will come along and say, 'Can you get out of here please? I don't want you doing that.' You know if you are dancing, or you have your voice raised, or you are doing, you know or you bang the dominoes down hard in the cafeteria, that intimidates lot of teachers, because to them, it means no discipline. It means that they are likely to do anything at any time. It intimidates a lot of teachers.

Marabel is one of those teachers who do not like to be placed in a potentially confrontational situation with male students of African heritage. She is clearly intimidated not only by their manner, but also by their apparent size. She says:

There's some people, some Africans that sit in the north-west corner [of the cafeteria] and they always have on – you know, they're not allowed to wear jackets and hats but always have them on. So I always have to go over and tell them to take it off. And they're big, too, I guess that's the thing. It's not even that they're African, it's that they're big whereas the little Chinese and Filipinos are so small: It's no big deal to say, 'Put your sweater on', whereas these guys are big and I just find that they're always, that they don't want to pay attention.

Teachers are not the only ones intimidated by African students. Some students are also afraid of them. Roger, for example, maintains, 'If anyone's afraid of a group it is probably the Blacks, 'cos they see them as the loudest and most rebellious.'

Associated with this discourse is a belief that there is a relationship between African heritage and sporting prowess. A number of people to whom we talked either believed that Blacks were all naturally good at sports or cited incidents that illustrated such a belief. Frances, an African female, admits that she tires of people who ask her about this apparent connection. She recalls one such incident:

I went to a school track meet with my friend and there just happened to be a lot of Black people on the team. They all had to try out. And this White girl asked me, 'How come Black people are so good at sports?' I said, 'I don't know.' I passed it on to somebody else to answer.

African students may actually be the subject of recruiting efforts. Jason, an African male, contends that certain staff wanted him to play football because they believed he had the natural skills to play the game. He says:

> When I first came here – you know, you come to school to do what you have to do – I didn't want to join up for any sports. But for three months I kept being harassed by the teachers and the teachers kept on saying, 'Oh yeah, you know, you're Black, you can play sports; you know, what's wrong with you?' ... Like they do what they have to do to get you on the team if you're a good sportsman. But I didn't want to play any sports and they just kept harassing me. Then finally they got the hint.

While many in the school community have much to say about African students' physical attributes, they have far less to say about what they believe to be their intellectual capabilities. Although teachers do not explicitly state that African students as a group are less able academically than other groups, this belief is implied in much of their talk. For one thing they never allude to them when citing gifted groups, and when they do talk about them it is to single out individuals, as if these are an exception to the rule. Students do not hesitate to draw attention to the unfair treatment they believe they receive from teachers who hold such beliefs about their academic ability. They consistently refer to the consequences of these unduly low expectations. Ilda, a young Black woman, says:

> At the beginning of the semester, in school, when they hand out papers or anything ... to the rest of the people in the class, like tests, they sort of look [at others] like 'You're going to do well', but when they hand it to me it's like: 'Oh God, why bother?' And then when they see the marks they're like surprised. And they start questioning people around you, like, 'Were you hiding your paper?', and then they make a big fuss about it. 'Now, you have to cover your paper to make sure nobody is cheating off of you.' Just because of that. Then, 'Why did you cheat?'

Students find these expectations may place undue hardships on them, particularly if they are determined to do well in school. Maria, for example, believes that she has to exert considerably more effort than do most students to overcome some of these barriers. She says, 'You have to work twice as hard as every other kid in your class [to do well]. It shouldn't be that way.'

On the other hand, both teachers and students alike believe that Asian and Chinese students are the most gifted intellectually. Jillian, a teacher, believes that Oriental students are superior students, and she looks forward to their presence in her classroom. She says:

> The Chinese, the Japanese they all sit together and they're at the front. They're very bright, very bright. Brilliant. Which is wonderful. And then there is another boy that sits in the front, Ivan, who is right in the front too. And Theresa, and it is kind of neat how they all come to the front and do such hard work as they really are. So in that sense it is sort of, you can't label them but you know that. When I saw my class list I said 'Holy cow!' I saw all the Chans and they are such hard workers that they set a good example for everybody.

But teachers are not the only ones to believe that Oriental students are gifted intellectually. Students are also apt to believe this. Students may also believe that such a belief leads to differential treatment. Billy, for example, says:

> If anyone thinks that a group is the smartest, it's the East Asians or the Orientals, because they've come from the Asian countries. So they're smarter. So they might see the whole group as being smarter ... If a teacher will get a paper from, say, a White student or a Black student and then get a paper from an Oriental student, and supposing it was a class regarding math or anything like that, they might be exactly the same, but they might generally favour, there might be a bias in the teacher's mind that the Oriental might be better.

Not all Chinese students may agree with such a generalization. One young Chinese woman, for example, worries that because she is not able to speak English very well, teachers will think she cannot excel at math, something which she believes she can do. Teachers, too, notice that some of these students struggle with some of their subjects. Others, particularly parents, note that high expectations may unduly penalize them.

Not all members of Suburbia's community make sense of African and Asian students in these stereotypical ways. But because so many base their practice on these understandings, their actions end up marginalizing discourses that represent these groups in other ways. In particular such views often override the manner in which members of these targeted groups see or make sense of themselves, as is evident in the above portrayals. William, a student of African heritage, addresses this matter directly. He is frustrated with the ways in which teachers and authority figures respond to him and his friends. He recognizes that others are 'scared' of them but believes they feel this way because they do not 'know how Black people act'. What he is saying here is that the ways in which he and his friends understand themselves do not get a reasonable hearing among other (more powerful) groups. Other groups have different perceptions of his group and it is these perceptions that generally dominate in interaction. To be sure, the prevailing portrayal of these young people as threatening is not one that acknowledges in any meaningful way the views of the very people being depicted. Unfortunately for William and many others whose voices are not acknowledged in the dominant discourses, these sense-making practices often place them at a disadvantage, depriving them of many of the opportunities that other students may have.

Race/Ethnicity and Media Discourse

Though students and educators struggle over various discourses in school, they do so only within certain limits. This is because the grounds for their struggles have in many ways been determined by prevailing conditions that transcend the school setting. In other words, wider struggles that go beyond what happens in schools will dictate what discourses are available for students and teachers to draw on and which of these carries the most weight. We have already seen in Chapter 4 how certain discourses that favored White interests came to take precedence over others that potentially threatened their privileged position. In what follows I describe how the contemporary mass media circulate meanings, including those associated with the physical/intellectual discourses mentioned above, and show how certain groups and interests have come to dominate this process. I do this in the hope that readers will come to understand the manner in which these discourses circulate and the ways in which they provide the basis for the meanings that prevail in school.

The manner in which discourses circulate has changed dramatically over the past few centuries. From word of mouth in exclusively face-to-face interactions to a multitude of impersonal print and electronic media, the communication of discourses has taken dramatic strides. These changes have a number of consequences for the ways in which discourses are created, circulated and taken up, in schools and elsewhere. The first is the ease, speed and range of circulation. Media technology makes it possible to transmit messages faster, in a manner that is easily accessible, and to a wider range of recipients than ever before. Most men, women and children, regardless of where they live, are now part of the television, newspaper and cinema worlds that encroach on their lives. For example, people who live in the First World spend considerable time watching television, viewing movies at the theatre or in their home, interacting with electronic games such as Nintendo, surfing the Internet, and sending and receiving facsimiles and Email. In 1987 almost 100% of Canadian households had a television, 50% had two sets, 45% had video players, while 68% enjoyed the choice that they received from their cable subscriptions (Young, 1989). In 1994 Canadians averaged 22.7 hours in front of the television over the course of a week. Teens watched less, at 17.1 hours per week (Statistics Canada, 1994). 'No place on earth is a safe haven from modern media' (Morgan, 1995:54). A second change revolves around the impact of these mediated discourses. Because they are so pervasive, they have a powerful effect on all who are exposed to them. Educators and students, like most other people in this day and age, are not exempt from these influences. The ways in which they see one another in schools are, at least in some respects, tied to these pervasive media discourses (Morgan, 1995).

In a media-dominated world, according to Wilson and Gutierez (1995), all of us depend on the media of communication to portray and define those things we personally have not experienced for ourselves. Through radio, television, movies, newspapers and magazines we learn not only about others, but also about ourselves. In the absence of alternate portrayals, what we see, hear and experience through the media easily becomes reality for us. For example, many of the images of the American people whom Europeans referred to as 'Indians' have been shaped in large measure by movie, television and novel portrayals. The media can also influence the ways in which groups and individuals understand themselves. Fitzgerald (1991) goes so far as to say that the media can actually alter group identities. He points to the New Zealand Cook Islanders who he maintains rely on media images to 'find out who they are'. In this case the media have created new forms of Cook Island culture. Cook Islanders learn about being a Cook Islander by watching television when they move to New Zealand, rather than by socializing with fellow Islanders.

The power of the media in creating and circulating these discourses lies, in part, in their massive production of available imagery. Those wishing to project images of one group or another need only dip into this river of representations for a particularly pleasing (or unpleasing) mix of symbols that makes groups instantly recognizable to others (Merelman, 1995). Traditionally the mass media have looked to shorthand ways or short cuts as literary or dramatic devices that will quickly bring to the audience's collective consciousness a character's anticipated value system or behavioral expectations. These shorthand symbols are useful because they allow entertainment and news media to capsulize complex personalities and issues in a shortened character or term. By supplying a few key symbols of an already familiar discourse, media enable the audience to assess a character or make sense of a situation in short order, place them neatly into a category, as for example hero or villain, thus saving the media source from having to elaborate on this particular discourse or provide additional information. Because they allow for such useful short cuts, these devices have become the basis for mass entertainment and literary fare (Wilson & Gutierez, 1995). These short cuts and the underlying discourses which they represent show up regularly in media portrayals of racial/ethnic issues and groups. They have evolved over time, and tend to find expression in different ways in different media, but even so, the physical/intellectual theme remains prominent.

The projected audience has also had a substantial influence on the way media productions have been put together. Those who create these packages have always taken care to construct a product that will appeal to the people they envision as consumers. One of the ways in which producers can ensure the attractiveness of their creation is to design it from a perspective with which the targeted audience can identify. Thus those who wrote novels in 19th-century America worked to make their books attractive to their White European audience by writing them from a position which the latter could not only identify with, but also find pleasing. When non-Whites did happen to cross the pages of these novels, they were depicted in a way that made the White audience feel good about being who they were and doing what they did. As a consequence, novelists routinely depicted 'Indians', for example, as bloodthirsty savages who deserved to be slaughtered by the righteous White man (Wilson & Gutierez, 1995).

Early movie producers followed much the same logic in their films. They routinely employed shorthand portrayals of people of color, depicting them as intellectually and morally inferior. Included in these portrayals of Blacks were the servile 'Tom', the harmless eye-popping 'coon', the fat 'mammy', the sleazy 'mulatto', and the 'buck', a brutal hypersexualized menacing Black man (Shohat & Stam, 1994). Wilson & Gutierez (1995) maintain that film people at this time capitalized on audience insecurity by using negative shorthand racial portrayals to bolster audience self-esteem and reinforce racial attitudes. The first 40 years of American cinema reflected White Americans' fear of the 'threat' that non-White cultures represented to White social values. The release of *Birth of a Nation* in 1915 marked the beginning of an institutionalization of negative portrayals that would endure in film for decades. In capitalizing on White fear film-makers of the time profited financially by giving the masses what they wanted.

Changing attitudes, protests from groups dissatisfied with media portrayals, and a growing awareness on the part of media producers that racial/ethnic groups represented a growing and potentially profitable market, prompted these media people to alter their approach to the portrayal of such groups. Over time some, but not all, media productions softened their negative depictions. In the 1990s, for example, television sitcom portrayals of African Americans as part of the middle class are common. Not all media forms treat Blacks in this somewhat more benevolent way, however. Merelman (1995) contends that while comedies and soap operas may present Blacks as middle class, broadcast j̖urnalism only emphasizes the problems of the underclass. It offers viewers an endless parade of broken families, drug users, violent young males and teenage gangs. Over the years news media have moved in stages, from excluding racial/ethnic groups and issues to coverage that featured threatening, confrontational, stereotypical and multiracial images (Wilson & Gutierez, 1995). Through all of this the media has served up ways of making sense of Blacks through a discourse of fear, painting non-Whites as a threat to the social order. Although such coverage may no longer be filled with racial epitaphs, it is still generally filtered through a White perspective, skewed to middle-class attitudes, and geared towards simultaneously raising and massaging the fears of the latter.

Recent media coverage of the Los Angeles riots and of the O.J. Simpson trial, together with 'reality-based' police shows, tap into this same discourse, calling up threatening images of the Black male. Pat Buchanan's description of the LA turmoil as 'an orgy of rioting, arson, murder and lynching' provide a perspective, appealing to a White conservative man, for making sense of what was happening in South Central LA by attributing it to the young Black male sexual body out of control (Fiske, 1996). Constant media concern that the riot would spread to White LA gave voice to this same discourse of fear. The image of the Black male criminal also played a prominent role in media coverage of the O.J. Simpson trial. According to Fiske (1996), the image of O.J. in handcuffs fits easily into this figuring. So too did the police mug shot of O.J. that was featured on the cover of *Time* and *Newsweek*. *Time*, however, was not content with the ability of the mug shot as initially received to tap into the criminalized meaning of blackness on its own, and consequently doctored the image, darkening O.J.'s skin by several shades. The result was that O.J. was barely recognizable when he graced the cover of *Time*. What was recognizable was the more familiar figure of the Black male criminal. Finally, 'reality-based' police shows bring graphic images of young Black male drug dealers getting busted by narcotics officers into homes in North America and elsewhere on a nightly basis. The young Black male and the negative images associated with drugs, violence and criminality figure prominently in the media's version of the 'war on drugs', despite the facts that 76% of users are White and that those who control the drug trade are generally located in suburban and not urban inner city areas (Andersen, 1995).

> Fear has been the cornerstone of TV crime dramas, and the 'reality-based' shows have taken that tendency to extremes by adding a racial component. In addition to the racial coding of villains, television images of Black criminality intensified during the 1980s and 1990s ... In contemporary programming, however, when the issue of race is embedded within the traditional genre formulation (which holds that crime is caused by individual motivations) and when those individuals are predominately Black (as seen on television today), the resulting equation concludes that Blacks must simply be more violent than Whites. (Andersen, 1995:204)

Controlling Media Discourse

Despite the fact that discourse remains a contested terrain, certain discourses routinely dominate mediated communications. One reason for these apparently unequal struggles revolves around the fact that, in this case, White groups have had the power to control most aspects of the creation and circulation of these discourses, allowing voices that favour their interests to emerge, while at the same time smothering other competing voices and interests. Not only are the vast majority of media operations owned or sponsored by Whites, but most of the people who work in these outlets are also White. Unfortunately opportunities for non-Whites to start up their own outlets appear even slimmer today, with the media moguls attempting to cover all bases by spreading themselves over a variety of media forms. The advantage here goes to the larger (already White-owned) corporations that have the capital base to spread their investments across several technologies and to enter into alliances of convenience. Most communities of color will find themselves priced out of these technological advances, able to participate in discursive struggles at only the most basic levels (Wilson & Gutierez, 1995).

Understandably non-Whites who work in these industries also face considerable obstacles as they seek to have their voices and perspectives acknowledged. One reason for this is that there are fewer of them than there are of their White co-workers. Although the motion picture and television entertainment industries have recently increased their hiring of non-Whites to the approximate percentage of the general population, other outlets such as broadcasters and particularly newsrooms have not approached these kinds of numbers (Wilson & Gutierez, 1995). A more formidable obstacle than numbers, however, is the pressures that these people feel from their colleagues. A common complaint of non-White journalists working in mainstream newsrooms, for example, is that they are forced to see their profession from a White perspective. While these men and women may not believe that their colleagues and superiors are overtly racist, they nevertheless feel that they are, at the very least, insensitive and ignorant. In this regard non-White reporters routinely experience the pressure of unwritten policies that encourage them to approach their stories from 'angles' that are defined in terms of the dominant cultural perspective. This pressure may exert itself in forms such as content observation, informal conversations and editing by superiors.

Editing can have an acute effect on what eventually reaches the television news screen. It can be a particularly effective means of preventing discourses that favor non-White voices from entering the mainstream media. Fiske (1996) provides a useful illustration. He recounts how two Black reporters from a CBS Milwaukee affiliate were frustrated in their attempts to provide a more balanced account of the Los Angeles riot. In their compilation of a news segment that was to recount the events of the second day, they sought to include footage of a White woman looting designer clothes. The two had come across her as she was in the act of placing the pillaged goods into the trunk of her Mercedes. But while most of their footage was aired, the portion which featured this woman never appeared on the evening news. It was cut by the White producer. Because most viewers could not experience this and other events at first hand, their understanding of what was happening in South Central Los Angeles was largely determined by the plethora of images of young Black youths on the rampage, and the absence of scenes like those above that failed to make the final program.

Just because certain images appear on a television screen, or in a newspaper account, does not mean that audiences automatically interpret or accept them in one intended way. Consumers of media fare do not passively imbibe media cultural forms (Sholle, 1995; Ang, 1995). Not all men, women and children buy into the idea, often projected in the media, that Blacks are violent, unintelligent people, for example. Neither, however, do they have the freedom to accept or interpret media images in limitless ways.[1] In other words, spectatorship is on one level open and polymorphous, and on the other, structured and determined (Shohat & Stam, 1994). Indeed there are powerful constraints and incentives for audiences to make sense of these images in particular ways. The images accompany wider social relationships that provide the framework for media–audience interactions. Media outlets will tap into already existing and sometimes widely circulating discourses with which most consumers will be at least partially familiar, like the above notion about the physical and intellectual abilities of Blacks, and will often present segments of them in ways that invite viewers, readers or listeners to make sense of what they see or hear in certain prefigured ways.[2] Rewards often accompany these invitations. Media discourse, for instance, often presents recipients with opportunities to play with the process of self-constitution, to continuously remake themselves in ways that are distinctly pleasurable (Poster, 1995). Media productions are inevitably structured so that it is more gratifying for the audience to make sense in one way than in another.[3] Thus viewers may well derive more satisfaction from a television show if they identify with a perspective that makes sense of the combative Black figures on the screen by attributing responsibility for their actions to these supposedly inherently violent individuals, rather than to a society that systematically oppresses them.

Even though these spectator positions can be resisted or rejected outright, Wilson and Gutierez (1995) maintain that certain portrayals tend to reinforce rather than change audience attitudes, that is, fortify already existing dominant discourses. Media generate their greatest effects when they are used in a manner that reinforces and channels attitudes and opinions that are consistent with the psychological make-up of people and the structure of their group identification. For example, negative media portrayals and news coverage of non-White groups and issues tend to reinforce racist attitudes in those members of an audience who already have them. On the other hand, research also shows that bigots watching television programs that ridicule bigotry often interpret these offerings in ways that reinforce pre-existing beliefs. One such study that surveyed reactions to the 1970s sitcom *All in the Family* showed that more than 60% of the respondents liked or admired the bigoted Archie more than the liberal-minded Mike. It also revealed that 40% felt that Archie 'won' at the end of the show, 46% saw Mike as the one who was made fun of, and 35% saw nothing wrong with Archie's use of racial slurs (Vidmar & Rokeach, in Wilson & Gutierez, 1995). However, the media have their greatest impact on those not well integrated into media discourse. They especially affect the marginalized, children and non-Whites, particularly through their presentations of the latter. Most vulnerable of all to media seduction are perhaps minority children (Wilson & Gutierez, 1995).

Conclusion

While racism surfaces in obvious and easily recognizable ways at Suburbia and elsewhere, it also takes on forms that make it more difficult to recognize. One of the more subtle ways in which racism circulates is through stereotypes. Frequently depicted as oversimplified, mistaken, negative and taken-for-granted images of groups of people, stereotypes were thought to routinely penalize those individuals and groups at whom they were directed. This view of stereotypes has over the years been useful in exposing the often subtle ways in which groups of people can be disadvantaged, but it also displays a number of limitations. Among other drawbacks, its insistence on producing both accurate and positive images of marginalized groups misreads the ways in which these groups come to be characterized, overlooks the diversity within groups and in doing so, limits the political possibilities of such an approach. A more useful way to look at these simplified and often negative depictions is in terms of discourse. Rather than see them as self-contained inaccurate images, those wishing to challenge such portrayals would do well to study the discourses that work through them. Employing a discursive lens helps us come to terms with the ways in which meaning is constructed and sense made and how power operates in and through this process. Of course discourse, as illustrated above, is not just a technique of power, but also the terrain on which struggles over meaning and practice occur.

At Suburbia a number of stereotypical discourses circulate with regularity. The most prevalent ones revolve around the physical/intellectual abilities of students of African and Asian heritage. The talk and action of both students and educators reveal a belief that students of African heritage possess superior and potentially threatening physical capabilities, but simultaneously lack the intellectual capacities to do as well as other students. On the other hand many also believe that Asian students are more able academically than most other students. These beliefs carry with them consequences for those at whom they are directed, placing students who fit into these categories at a disadvantage. Of course these prevailing discourses are not the only ones to circulate in the school, but they do take precedence over others by virtue of the fact that their adherents are more powerful and numerous.

The fact that these particular discourses prevail at Suburbia is not just due to what happens within the walls of the school. They are in crucial ways the product of contests won and lost outside the walls of the school. Chapter 4 indicated how unequal relationships of power over the centuries enabled certain groups to construct and circulate discourses that worked in their interests and against the interests of marginalized groups. This process continues unabated today, although the representations may not be so blatantly negative. One important channel for their contemporary construction and circulation is through the mass media. These exert their power in at least two ways. Firstly, they can provide incentives for viewers or readers to make sense of their images or texts in certain ways by encouraging them to reach for certain discourses, as with the TV viewer who derives pleasure from identifying with a perspective that makes sense of the Blacks fighting on the screen by laying the blame for their behavior on them, rather than on society. Secondly, the discourses that prevail in the mass media depend in crucial ways on who controls these institutions. The fact that most major media outlets are owned and operated by Whites means that the prevalent discourses tend to favour White rather than non-White interests.

As we have seen, stereotypical, demeaning and racist images and the discourses that work through them show up in the everyday characterizations of teachers and students. We shall find they are also evident in curriculum resources. The next chapter explores representations of race/ethnicity in curriculum materials.

Notes

1. Sholle (1995) notes that those who oppose the notion that what is encoded in the object is not necessarily decoded by the subject often base their views on a number of erroneous assumptions including, among others, a dichotomy of passive/active associated with the production of meaning and the belief that one can read the effect of cultural forms by examining the conscious spoken actions of the audience.

2. In the language of semiotics, producers of media, media productions and audiences are linked by codes – rule governed systems of signs, whose rules and conventions are shared among members of a culture (Fiske, 1996).

3. Media employ various techniques to help them do this. Television producers, for example, will employ particular kinds of music, camera angles, dialogue, casting, lighting, make-up, settings and so on, in their efforts to regulate sympathies, extract tears, and excite glands.

Chapter 6
Representations of Race/Ethnicity in Curriculum Resources

One of the most obvious ways in which race/ethnicity is represented at Suburbia, as it is in most other schools, is in the curriculum. These representations perhaps find their most acute expression in the materials that teachers employ in their classrooms. At Suburbia Secondary School, as elsewhere, teachers depend heavily on resource materials to get their messages across to students. Most use standardized textbooks, books, other forms of printed material and on occasion, films, to convey to their charges the content associated with their subject of specialization. Public school teachers cannot, however, employ any such material they wish. Instead whatever they use must in most cases be sanctioned by the government, approved by the school district, and be chosen by their respective departmental units. Once curriculum materials, usually books, have been approved, schools generally supply them and expect students to come to class prepared to use them. At one point, for example, the English department at Suburbia decided that Harper Lee's *To Kill a Mockingbird* would be included in the Grade 9 English syllabus. They were able to choose it because it was sanctioned by the government and the school district. The school supplied students with the book and the latter were expected to come to class ready to explore it in whatever way their respective teachers felt appropriate.

Given the range of choice teachers have, most do their best to make the available curriculum materials relevant to the diverse student population. The wide variation in students, and a history of curricula geared toward Anglo students, however, makes such a task a difficult one. One Suburbia teacher finds that not only may students have difficulty relating some standard curriculum offerings to their own experience, but that they may also have difficulty with their actual meaning. Leigh, for example, maintains that many, if not most of her students have difficulty understanding some of the terminology in one of Shakespeare's works that is often included in the curriculum. She notes that an exception is the one student in the class from the British Isles. Referring to the piece, Leigh says:

116

We teach it as an intro. to Shakespeare and that's why we feel that it is very useful. But the problem being the slang in it, such as 'make a beck' being a stream. It's old English terms that don't really apply and the kids have no idea and they get mad. 'Why can't we just call it a stream? If it's a stream, it's a stream, call it that.' And the fact that it's England that we're dealing with here and hardly anybody has a background that relates to England. For me, I know a lot of that slang, just because it's used in my home. Warren lived in England for a while and he knows. And you see that he loves it, he likes this novel [by Shakespeare] because he has the background.

Leigh also makes reference to another common offering. She wonders how some of the students will be able 'to catch the subtleties [of one of the characters] and her well-developed vocabulary'. She feels this other piece is interesting, but is not sure how relevant a story about a prep school for rich White boys can be for many of her students. She believes, however, that the key to this or any other offering is to find a 'hook' to bring the students into the story. She says:

You have to find a hook. I think the first time I taught a separate piece it was just 'Ough', I don't think anybody liked it. I didn't like it. The second time it was like, 'Oh, I see, hook them with Gene', because there's a character Gene in there who's about 16 and doesn't really understand himself all that well. So if you can hook them in that sense, it doesn't matter what color he is as long as the kid is going through some similar problems that they are. But sometimes you just think, 'Couldn't we find something a little bit more relevant to what's going on instead of the old stuff?'

Finding a 'hook' for all students is not always an easy thing to do at Suburbia. This is because many students have difficulty identifying with the situations and individuals represented in curriculum materials. Some students perceive different things in the materials from what their teachers see, while others may simply reject the messages or images that they perceive, whether or not these perceptions coincide with those of their teachers. Many students, for example, have difficulty understanding Shakespeare in the same way that their Anglo teachers do. On the other hand, students may simply reject what they perceive to be an author's message or image in curriculum materials. At Suburbia a number of students of African heritage took issue with Harper Lee's characterization of African Americans in *To Kill a Mockingbird*. While they more or less agreed with teachers and other students on the basic 'facts' of Lee's description, the two factions differed in the connotative meanings that they attached to the description. For teachers and some White students reading the novel was pleasurable and therefore worthwhile. For many of the African Canadian students the reading was a painful experience.

Understanding what these and other materials and the individuals and groups depicted in them mean to students requires that those interested go beyond the material. This is because the meaning of something like a narrative or a film clip emerges not exclusively from the text or image, but from the complex relationships that are part of the context within which they are apprehended. In the case of texts, for example, what gets produced as 'knowledge', that is, what students (and teachers) eventually see as meaningful, is the end result of a series of activities that include the social organization of text industries, the activities of text producers, and the interaction between the text and the reader (Wexler, 1992). The meaning of the texts is also intimately intertwined with the ways in which historically produced discourses work through these processes. In the end the sense that students, teachers, trustees, editors and textbook writers make of texts, and ultimately of certain groups and individuals, will depend in important ways on the discursive frameworks that are available to them at the time.

As illustrated previously, these discursive frameworks are not simply imposed on students or teachers. It is just not the case that students have no choice but to understand the world about them exclusively through so-called dominant sense-making schemes. Rather, these schemes and the accompanying understandings are always contested. In this respect these sense-making or discursive frameworks are not only the outcomes of struggles, but also the terrain on which wider contests between various groups, interests, perspectives, views, values and so on play themselves out. Men, women and children, in schools and out, perpetually struggle over what discourses and their associated meanings will prevail in the classrooms. Like most other schools, Suburbia is not immune to this process. Contests routinely occur over the sense teachers and students make of their subject material and the world around them.

In the case of *To Kill a Mockingbird*, the African Canadian students who objected so vehemently to Lee's description took action in an attempt to keep certain meanings out of the classroom. In this chapter I attempt to provide an understanding of the process of representation as it played itself out in Suburbia over Lee's novel. This first requires an account of the methods by which race/ethnicity has been represented in curriculum materials over the years, the reasons behind these methods, and their effects. To shed light on these things I provide background on curriculum knowledge generally, and on the colonial and post-colonial curriculum.

Next I outline a perspective on the process of sense-making as well as the struggle over meaning. This leads into an account of how students come to understand *To Kill a Mockingbird*, and the struggle over meaning associated with it.

Curriculum Materials and Knowledge

Curriculum plays a key role in the process of representation in all schools. It does this, at least in part, by establishing the parameters for what is to be regarded as acceptable knowledge in the classroom. School communities employ the curriculum to select and organize from the vast universe of possible knowledge the traditions and visions of reality they deem to be worth transmitting to students. By including what they believe to be the more important forms of knowledge and omitting knowledge of lesser importance, these communities seek to restrict students' range of possible interpretations and ultimately to shape their view of the world about them.

Curriculum resources play a vital part in this process. Perhaps the most important of these resources is the textbook. Curriculum scholars consistently emphasize the power of these books. Klein (1985), Sleeter and Grant (1991) and Apple (1985) all believe that the textbook is the main medium for information for all students. It is *the* major conveyer of the curriculum, and has been for many years – over 500 years, according to Sleeter and Grant. Only the teacher, the blackboard and other writing materials are found as universally as the text. Apple goes so far as to say that the curriculum is defined not by the course of study but by the standardized grade level specific text, and that 75% of time in the classroom and 90% of time spent at home is with textbooks.

The power of the textbook derives not just from the fact that it is used so extensively. It is also very influential because of the character of the knowledge that is supposedly contained in it. Most textbook knowledge assumes a unique authority. In other words, many who are exposed to these books take it for granted that the information that they dispense depicts things as they really are. Textbooks are supposed to tell the truth. Anyon (1979) maintains that history texts in the United States are assumed to provide an account of the past that is objective. These books supposedly make available to students unbiased information which they can use to interpret contemporary events. Such accounts, Anyon (1979) contends, are thought to serve the interests of all equally, presumed not to favor some at the expense of others.

Readers regard textbook knowledge as truthful for several reasons. One is the institutional character of these books. Because they are officially sanctioned by organizations, members of these organizations who use them tend to regard them as, for the most part, reliable (Klein, 1985). Klein also contends that the character of the printed word itself carries a substantial potential to influence the reader, especially the younger reader. She maintains that students being introduced to a topic about which they know little are generally compelled to regard the text version of knowledge as the truth.

Texts can also work in more subtle ways. For example, though students might recognize pieces of fiction as merely stories, they will still in all probability unwittingly absorb the attitudes of the authors. This subtlety extends to the value that textbooks place on certain knowledge. By including some forms of knowledge and excluding others, these books have the power to signal, often in indirect ways, what knowledge is 'worth knowing'. Thus despite what some educators and students may believe, curriculum knowledge is not, nor was it ever, objective or neutral. Over the last couple of decades scholars have increasingly questioned claims about the truthful, objective and neutral character of curriculum knowledge and of the resource materials, including texts and films, that teachers employ in their classrooms. Their argument is that curriculum resources are social products of their time (Anyon, 1979). As a result they are always somebody's version of what constitutes important knowledge. The very selection process, where choices are made about what to include or not to include, will always favor some groups and interests over others.

In other words, therefore, curriculum materials work as part of a *political* process. Among other effects, they promote and sustain political ideologies through the careful presentation of human images. Texts and films, for example, play a part in portraying and establishing approved perceptions of various groups of people and defining relationships between and among these groups. By overtly and covertly creating images of self-doubt and self-belief, these resources can contribute to attitudes that make it easier for some groups to justify the unequal treatment of others (Mangan, 1993).

The Colonial Curriculum

The need felt by dominant groups to justify unfair treatment through school curricula has been with us for some time now. The roots of this need can be traced to European colonial enterprises. Over five centuries ago Europeans set sail from their native shores in a determined effort to improve their lot. While they managed to reap benefits for their respective countries, these acquired advantages came at the expense of those lands and people they encountered in their travels. In order to improve their respective economic positions, Europeans systematically assumed ownership of the lands they set foot on and authority over the people who lived in them. They set about exploiting the resources they found in these lands, employing the necessary strategies to ensure the success of their efforts, including the cruel subjugation and enslavement of the indigenous people. Force was a key ingredient in these strategies. Europeans frequently called on the military to ensure that they had their way with the native people they encountered, both to establish themselves and to sustain their rule.

But force was not the only tool the colonial powers relied upon in these enterprises. They also depended heavily on knowledge, particularly in the task of sustaining their dominance for the long run. Indeed soldiers shared their lodgings with scholars who brought with them their epistemological models, representative symbols and alien forms of knowledge (Mangan, 1993). This was all part of a process in which Europeans treated other lands and peoples as adventures in learning. In their efforts to make over the world in their own image, their inquiry-centered field trips were designed to construct an encyclopedic mastery of the globe (Willinsky, 1994). At the heart of this enterprise, though, was the task of controlling the local populations over which they now assumed authority. With this aim in mind, Europeans organized knowledge into patterns and set up institutions to pass it along to the colonized men, women and children in systematic ways. Thus formal education became a key ingredient in the maintenance of European domination over foreign lands and people.

Europeans used the education systems they introduced to the colonized in particular ways. They designed them first and foremost to create images to sustain their dominance. Towards this end colonizers employed the curriculum and curricular materials, including books, to tap the potential of image construction for shaping the cultural consciousness, not only of the colonized but of the colonizers themselves as well. It was through the schools that Europeans sought to establish appropriate verbal images in order to induct all men, women and children into a new symbolic universe. They needed to monopolize discourse, to ensure that linguistic traffic traveled in one direction only. The introduction of literacy was an important strategy here. It provided people with independent access to this symbolic universe, and at the same time, removed them from the enclosed world of the oral tradition (Mangan, 1993).

Colonizers creatively manipulated the symbols that they transmitted to the colonized to achieve these ends. Among other strategies, they made the most of metaphors, similes and allegories to penetrate the consciousness of colonizer and colonized alike. One of the most enduring images revolved around a Manichean allegory: 'A field of diverse yet interchangeable oppositions between black and white, good and evil, superiority and inferiority' (Mangan, 1993:8). The colonized were routinely depicted as inferior, ignorant, barbarous, evil, immoral, while the colonized assumed superior, intelligent, civilized, good and moral characters. The respective characterizations were intimately linked. The more negative the portrayal of the colonized, the more positive the characterization of the colonizer. The higher the heights that European superiority reached, the lower the depths to which indigenous inferiority sank. This dichotomy applied to all colonized people equally, from Ireland to Indonesia. As Mangan (1993:22) maintains, these common imperial stereotypes were so uniform that they might as well have been cut from the same pastry-cutter.

> Metaphorically speaking, an imperial printing plate with a well-defined picture existed with identical copies in wide circulation throughout the empire: an inferior native and a superior European. A shared imperial ideology transmitted throughout a common culture by means *inter alia* of a general education system produced remarkably consistent image projection over space and time. This is not to deny ideological variation, regional emphasis, sectional difference, individual deviance or collective resistance, but it is to reassert the general existence of a firmly held set of images, if necessary, independent of fact, extraordinarily resistant to change, easy to assimilate, sustained with certainty and potent in effect, which served important ethnocentric purposes.

The images that were routinely filtered through the education systems thus served a vital function in sustaining the colonizers' dominance. Their purpose was to legitimize the superiority of European rule by providing explanations of relationships, descriptions of group capacities and patterns of expected behavior. If, for example, Europeans could demonstrate that the native people's supposed barbarism was irrevocably and deeply ingrained, then colonial attempts to control behavior, 'civilize' populations and exploit resources could be easily rationalized. These messages were directed at the colonizer as well as at the colonized. The latter would be more likely to acquiesce to their inferior position if they accepted the colonizers' denigration/exhalation statements.

The education of the colonizers in these matters was just as important. Mangan (1993) maintains that the symbolism embedded in school curricula and texts allowed Europeans to construct bulwarks against a possible sense of guilt produced by the disjunction of their colonial activities on the one hand, and their domestic practices on the other. These conflicting moralities had to be rationalized for rulers for, as Mangan (1993) contends, they could not afford to be moral cripples. Such a state would destroy their much needed confidence to control. In order to avoid this cognitive dissonance, preserve self-esteem, rationalize control, and justify their colonial policies, Europeans therefore made a concerted effort to institutionalize, in schools and other organizations, racial discourses that were discriminatory, prejudicial and biased.

The portrayal of India and the people of the Indian subcontinent in 19th-century and early 20th-century British textbooks typifies these kinds of efforts. Castle (1993) provides a useful overview of the image of India in British history texts of this time. He maintains that this image emerges in these texts through both what is included and what is omitted, through general observations of the conditions in India, the assessment of individual figures and comparisons between British character and actions and those of the 'alien'. Castle maintains that the image thus produced was both ethnocentric and racist. It enhanced the superiority of Great Britain while at the same time assuming that critical differences between British and Indian people were due to inherited biology and not environment. These racist themes were in turn used to explain and justify the past and current relationship between the two groups of people.

Towards this end, these texts employed two effective strategies. The first was to describe what their authors believed to be India's prevailing conditions. They consistently conveyed the impression that this part of the world was a cacophony of people in anarchy. The texts describe an India in a state of lawlessness and confusion, with a population ravaged by constant war between its constituent states. India was presented as a nation whose native power structure was incompetent and illegitimate and whose people were exploited masses crushed by greed and military ambitions (Castle, 1993). In fact readers who accepted what these texts had to say would be hard pressed to characterize this part of the world as a nation at all, at least by European standards. Moreover it was precisely this disorder which would lead student readers to see a need for intervention, thereby justifying the imposition of foreign control.

The texts also singled out individuals for attention. It mattered little whether these people were of British or Indian heritage. Britons were routinely characterized as heroes, and Indians, particularly those who resisted British rule, as villains. Even those British individuals who somehow strayed in obvious ways from virtue were spared the worst. Castle (1993) maintains that the excesses of the British were often blamed on Indians. The latter were thought to have tempted them with riches, dragged them into a sea of unwanted intrigue and undermined their British character. In the case of Robert Clive and Warren Hastings, for example, texts produced images of immoral, dangerous, untrustworthy Indians who somehow soiled reputations and caused these good men to end their days in alienation.

Texts also targeted Indian leaders, particularly those who resisted the British. They painted one resistor, Siraj-u-dowlah, for example, in characteristic unflattering ways. He was portrayed as 'weak, cruel, debauched, effeminate, despotic, stormy, treacherous, vicious and monstrous' (Castle, 1993:31). And he was discredited not merely for his opposition to Britain, but also for characteristics which were seen as particularly Indian – the potential for treacherous cruelty, emotional and moral laxity, a lack of manliness, and a disregard for the value of human life. These and other like images did little to engender any sympathy in young Britons for the Indian population, however much this might be being exploited by British profiteers, but they did go a long way towards justifying the expansion of the British Empire and reasserting the strength of the British national character.[1]

While educators at home presented young Britons with textbooks that contained Empire-friendly images, educators in the colonial territories abroad sought to use texts with similar messages, convinced that it was important to deliver these ideas both to ex-patriot Europeans and to the indigenous people they colonized. In Canada (Prentice, 1977), New Zealand (McGeorge, 1993) and Australia (Firth & Darlington, 1993), educators routinely adopted texts that were either officially approved in Britain or were sympathetic to the ideals of colonization. Of course officials in these countries (Barman *et al.*, 1986; McGeorge, 1993; Firth & Darlington, 1993) and in other areas around the world such as India (Ghosh, 1993), Kenya (Natsoulas & Natsoulas, 1993) and Uganda (Okath, 1993) also believed that it was vital that the indigenous people receive such messages. By painting a positive picture of Britain and its activities and a negative image of the indigenous populations themselves, they hoped to inculcate a deference for the former and to dissuade the latter from any resistant political activity, while at the same time preparing a few of them to enter the lower levels of government administration and private industry.

Post-Colonial Curriculum Materials

Despite the fact that the European practice of imperialism and colonialism has long since fallen by the wayside, its remnants continue to exert a powerful influence on textbook images. In Britain, Mangan (1993) claims that not only the texts, but also teaching manuals and Board of Education handbooks of the 1890s found astonishing shelf-lives that lasted into the 1960s. And although most of them are now out of circulation, many educators who are still around were nevertheless reared on these documents.

Texts began to change during the 1960s and 1970s. These changes, according to Sleeter and Grant (1991) were brought on, at least in part, by the protest movements of the time. Most scholars agree that the changes were generally of a positive nature, but many of them feel that textual representations of non-White groups still have a long way to go. O'Neil (1984) maintains that in the 10 years prior to the early 1980s the overall depiction of Natives improved somewhat. Whately (1988) recognizes improvements in representations of racial and ethnic groups generally in sexuality texts. One of the changes that Sleeter and Grant (1991) notice is that the texts published between 1980 and 1988 in the United States contain more people of different colors and more members of minority groups. They also note, however, that overall treatment of diversity has not improved a great deal over the 15 years prior to 1988. They claim that although some texts have improved, in specific and limited ways, there are few accounts of interaction between groups or of race relations, and few opportunities for readers to acquire an understanding of these issues. Instead the dominant image remains of a harmonious blending of different colors of people, dominated by Whites, suggesting that everyone is happy with the current arrangements. More recent studies of portrayals of Africa report a mix of results (Pahl, 1995; Wilson, 1995). While many texts have moved away from uniquely negative or unrealistic portrayals, some still lag behind. In a number of texts, for example, Egypt is not considered part of Africa.

Various reviews of the texts published between 1960 and 1980 in Canada and the United States reveal consistent patterns in the depictions of various groups. In Canada McDiarmid and Pratt (1971) reviewed 125 social studies texts approved for use in Ontario between the years of 1960 and 1968. They found that Whites were consistently shown in a more favorable light than non-White people. Sleeter and Grant (1991) discover similar attitudes among text writers in the United States from 1980 to 1988. They maintain that Whites dominate these texts. They are given the greatest amount of attention and the widest variety of roles. Sleeter and Grant observe that prevalent story lines allow Whites to be the centre of attention by ignoring the role of other groups or placing them in the story only during periods of time of concern to Whites. The differences in treatment between Whites and other groups varies depending on the group.

The groups that received the poorest treatment were Native people and people of African heritage. In Canada, McDiarmid and Pratt (1971) reviewed a number of texts that evaluated Blacks negatively. They maintain that Africans are shown as often aggressive, subordinate to Whites, in the slave trade, and engaged in mostly manual labour. In the United States Sleeter and Grant (1991) find that Blacks are featured much less often than Whites. They also maintain that Blacks are shown in limited roles, that there is little sense of contemporary Black life, and that there are only sketchy accounts of Black history. Although texts have generally improved in their treatment of Blacks there is still a considerable distance to go. And though current negativity is more subtle than it once was there are still the occasional blatant racist references. Walker (1993) says that a textbook published as recently as 1970 announced: 'Most negroes can be classified as barbarians.'

Native people have received the poorest treatment of perhaps any group in Canada and the United States. Studies by McDiarmid and Pratt (1971), Lewis (1987) and Moore (1992) all maintain that Native people are consistently treated unfavorably in Canadian texts and readers. McDiarmid and Pratt (1971), in the earliest survey of the three, found that Native people were consistently portrayed as primitive, unskilled, aggressive and hostile. Lewis (1987) in a later study discovered that four images associated with Native people in children's picture books – Native as warrior, White man as hero, nature and animal images, and Natives as willing servants – combined to generate overall negative images. The most recent study, by Moore (1992), concludes that texts still retain images that portray Native people in a negative way, despite claims that these books contain only bias-free material. Studies in the United States reveal a similar treatment of Native people. Vogel (1968) contends that over the years four types of discriminatory attitudes have characterized approaches to Native people in American history texts: obliteration, disembodiment, defamation and disparagement. A later study indicated that Native people are treated mainly as historical figures (Sleeter & Grant, 1991).

What becomes clear in these reviews is that while portrayals of non-White groups in textbooks have improved somewhat over the years, their treatment still pales in comparison to that of Whites. In some texts these portrayals are more subtle, but they remain negative. It must nevertheless be conceded that writers of these texts have made efforts to change the way they write about the various groups in recent years. This is not the case with all materials that teachers use in the classroom. Educators regularly employ material that has not changed since it was originally written. They use it because of what they believe to be its inherent capacity to enlighten all students. Many refer to such works as 'classics'. Educators will include *The Merchant of Venice* in the curriculum, for example, because they believe that all students have much to gain from exposure to it, but in doing so they sometimes overlook or ignore the obvious and enduring racist portrayals it contains. Other more recent publications that have taken on the 'classic' classification also find their way into English classes. At Suburbia *To Kill a Mockingbird*, published in 1960, features prominently in the curriculum. While some may believe that it sets up readers to oppose racism, others, including Black students, may take issue with the images presented in this book. This is discussed in more detail below.

Visual images contained in many of these books and in educational films also represent race/ethnicity in powerful ways. In fact visual images can have a longer-lasting impact on students than textual materials (Whately, 1988). The most influential representations of this sort are still or moving photographs. These will have more of an impact on a viewer than, say, a drawing because they are generally seen as objective representations of reality rather than artists' creations. Such photographic images can also be particularly influential in representing groups to which individuals belong, especially when there is little diversity in the images, as in the case of non-White groups (Whately, 1988). This means that viewers will be more likely to believe that a person of African heritage featured in an image represents all people of African heritage than they would be to see a single White person standing for all White people. Photographs are also capable of presenting impressions in ways that texts are not. For example the facts that 95% of the Native people in the books that McDiarmid and Pratt (1971) reviewed were shown either in traditional dress or poorly clothed, and that none was seen in a skilled or professional occupation, send powerful messages to those who observe these photographs.

Educational films can generate influential images as well, through both the visual and the textual media they employ. Like many of the texts mentioned above, films may carry unflattering images of non-White groups. Walker (1993) reviewed the educational films on Africa available in what was generally regarded as a model school district in the United States. This school district had a large multi-ethnic, mostly African

American population, and prided itself on its sensitivity to issues of ethnic pluralism and cultural diversity. Walker found, however, that with very few, notable exceptions, the information that accompanied the images was 'inaccurate, pejorative, and misleading'. Among other concepts these films presented colonization as positive, Whites for what they did *for* rather than *to* Africa, and treated 'Africa' as an undifferentiated unit. They also failed to mention the African fight against European aggression, ignored the existence of well-educated Africans who prefer to maintain indigenous values, and paid scant attention to indigenous life or else portrayed it in a negative way. Ten years later Walker returned to re-examine this same district's film holdings and found that there were no significant changes, despite the fact that she had brought her earlier findings to the attention of board officials.

Making Sense of Curriculum Resources

A number of the above scholars may write *as if* the meaning of the curriculum resources which they analyzed resides within these books or films. In other words, they seem to be assuming that texts, for example, contain inherent and enduring meanings that remain essentially the same regardless of who is reading the book and of the time frame in which it is being read. This is of course not the case. These readings are only some among a number of potential readings. Like other reading situations, these ones produce meaning as a consequence of a complex interaction between and among text, reader and social context. Simon (1992) maintains in this regard that neither readers nor texts can be granted virtual identities. Instead, he claims, they are girded on to one another within 'reading formations'. These reading formations are part of the wider, historically determined social, political, economic and institutional arrangements that provide the conditions for the possible ways in which symbolic practices can be organized and employed. In other words, socially circulating discourses or sense-making frameworks provide the 'interpretive schema' that set limits and provide possibilities for ways in which text writers, editors, educators and students can comprehend what is, or will be, written in a text.

Simon (1992) illustrates in a useful way how discursive frameworks play a central role in the interpretation of text. To do this he describes the conditions surrounding the positive reception of a Yiddish production of *The Merchant of Venice* in early 20th-century New York. He remembers that he was at first puzzled when he read of its positive reception among a primarily Jewish audience. His perplexity was due to his perception that Shakespeare's portrayal of Jewishness in *The Merchant of Venice* is singularly demeaning. Upon further investigation, however, he came to understand how a particular and prominent discourse at the time provided the conditions that allowed for a portrayal of Shakespeare that met with the approval of a Jewish audience. Simon maintains that around the turn of the century many Jewish people in New York were caught up in a Yiddish cultural revolution that stimulated Jewish pride. He contends that it was this discourse which articulated the revolution that made it possible for the Yiddish troupe to portray Shylock as a hero rather than as a villain, and for the audience to understand this portrayal as one that engendered pride rather than shame. Simon concludes that the positive reception that he initially read about became possible because of the way in which the prominent discourse associated with the Yiddish cultural revolution of the time provided a framework for both actors and audience to interpret Shakespeare in a way that put a positive, rather than a negative spin on Jewishness.

So the meanings students take away from the classroom depend on the sense that they make of texts, including the believability of all the various possible interpretations. The individual (yet social) self plays an important part in this process. The discourses that find their way into reading situations provide a frame of reference for readers, who will use them to define not only who they themselves are, but also their relationships with others and with the physical world about them (Simon, 1992). It is with reference to these discourses that students are continually constructing and reconstructing themselves and their relationships to others. In addition, how students see themselves will play an important part not only in how they make sense of textual materials, but also, having made sense, in whether they will accept or reject these meanings. Readers bring with them their own classed, raced, gendered and sexual biographies which predispose them to perceive certain symbols in particular ways and to accept or reject them accordingly (Apple & Christian-Smith, 1991). Philip (1988:110) outlines how readers necessarily complete texts in different ways:

> A text changes depending on the reader, and without the reader the text is, in fact, incomplete; so too without a text, the reader is incomplete. When a Black child reads *Huckleberry Finn* or a Jewish child *The Merchant of Venice*, he or she completes the text differently than a white [or non-Jewish] child would, since the Black or Jewish child brings to bear on the text a completely different experience than a White [or non-Jewish] child. When I, as a Black person, read *Othello*, I complete the text differently than a white Canadian would, since I bring to bear on *Othello* the burden of living in a society with racist underpinnings.

The particular organization of the symbols in the text will also play a part in the ways readers interpret and respond to the text. Not all texts, photographs or films invite the same kinds of reception on the part of readers. Some materials provide more space or room for interpretation, while others attempt to confine the range of possible interpretations. Some texts, for example, are more 'open', while others display a more 'closed' nature (Eco, 1989). The authors of textbooks generally try to work toward the latter condition. This is because they see their task as presenting so-called factual material to students. Towards this end they organize both the form and content of the material in ways that they feel will leave few opportunities for multiple interpretations. More literary works, on the other hand, work in ways that invite a greater range of interpretations. This is because the symbolism commonly employed here does not look to mirror a factual world, but to tap into readers' (sometimes unique) experiences. This is the case in plays like *The Merchant of Venice* or in novels like *To Kill a Mockingbird*. Yet regardless of the nature of the symbols that texts employ, the meaning that readers attribute to these texts will always rely on the discourses the readers themselves bring to the reading encounter. Restricting the range of possible interpretations, as many textbooks attempt to do, is possible only because their writers are able to tap into prevalent discourses or ways of making sense.

Despite the authoritative nature of text, student readers may not automatically accept the meanings they attribute to the educational material to which they are exposed. Although they may come to an agreement with teachers and fellow students regarding a text's denotative descriptive meanings, this does not always mean that they will endorse them, particularly in cases where the sense they perceive in this material does not coincide with the sense they make of their own life situations. A student may be very unwilling to go along with an account of the world that does not match his or her experience. Readers may also be reluctant to endorse a text's connotative meanings if doing so implicates them in unflattering or painful ways. Students may be unlikely to endorse views that paint negative images of them or those with whom they are associated. Simon (1992) remembers attempting to distance himself from Shakespeare's portrayal of Shylock and his daughter in *The Merchant of Venice* when he was a student. Acceptance of the going interpretation of the two characters proved all the more difficult for him because at this time he was participating in a ceremony designed to produce just the opposite effect – to reinforce and integrate his own Jewish identity.

Resisting or rejecting meanings are not the only possible responses to classroom materials. Given the authoritative nature of texts, students (and teachers) are perhaps more likely to go along with the agreed meanings, or failing that, attempt to negotiate them. Whatever meanings prevail, however, will be the result of a struggle. These struggles may be obvious or subtle. They may occur in the classroom or at a distance from the classroom. Or the unproblematic embrace of certain meanings may be the consequence of struggles that occurred many years ago.

The Struggle over Meaning

Curriculum knowledge is never entirely neutral, objective or factual. Apple and Christian-Smith (1991) believe that it is naive to think of it in these terms. It is more useful to acknowledge that the curriculum and the materials associated with it screen out certain ideas and realms of knowledge and predispose students to think in certain ways, to consider certain possibilities, questions and actions rather than others (Sleeter & Grant, 1991). Yet curriculum materials do not simply represent or mirror dominant beliefs and interests in a straightforward way. Apple and Christian-Smith (1991) maintain that these ideas are not imposed in an unmediated and coercive manner. They are instead always the products of intense conflicts and negotiations. In other words, the meanings that students take away from the classroom are always contested and contestable. The struggles associated with these contests, however, involve wider clashes of interest over what symbolic representations of the world and society will be transmitted to the young. While students and teachers may regularly contest textual meanings and their legitimacy, this often represents no more than the final stage in a wider and more complex struggle over discourse. But because curriculum resources embody these more universal discourses or sense-making frameworks, they, like these discourses, are also in important ways sites for these struggles.

Struggles over resource materials, such as texts and films, commonly spill out of the classroom and into the world beyond. In fact the more obvious struggles are perhaps those that occur in the community and beyond. This is because the construction and production of curriculum materials can be a long and complex process, one that is always influenced by any number of conditions associated with current circumstances. One of the realities of textbook production is that it is big business and, as Apple and Christian-Smith (1991) and Anyon (1979) reveal, dominated by major publishing conglomerates. As a result it is profit, the bottom line, that determines what books are published and for how long. In pursuing profit, however, publishers have to pay close attention to those who make the decision to endorse or purchase the books. In some regions it is formal groups who make the decisions that will influence which books a large number of students will read. In the United States nearly half of the states have textbook adoption committees that determine what books will be purchased for schools. Publishing companies devote considerable effort to making their texts appealing to the larger states of California, Texas and Florida (Apple & Christian-Smith, 1991). As part of their attempts to appease what are often dissenting factions, avoid alienating pressure groups, and appeal to as many potential customers as possible, these companies routinely exercise self-censorship. They generally take few risks. The result is that texts are often dull, routine, intellectually 'freckless' accounts that are remarkably resistant to change (Ornstein, 1992).

While publishing companies look to publish books that are acceptable to everyone, this is not always possible. In fact over the past couple of decades conflicts over published texts have increased. Conflicts over many issues, including race/ethnicity, between and among parents' groups, taxpayers, various community groups, educators and politicians continue to surface in ever greater numbers in such forums as PTA meetings, newspaper editorials, school board meetings and even in the courts. Indeed more and more curriculum materials are being submitted to courts and public commissions for judgments about their appropriateness for classroom consumption. In the United States 244 censorship incidents were reported in 39 states in 1990. These figures were up 75% from the previous three years and 150% over seven years (Ornstein, 1992).

Struggles over what texts or curriculum materials will be adopted at the district or school level can be intense. The California textbook controversy in some ways typifies the escalating battles over what discourses are deemed appropriate to enter the classroom. As with many other states in North America, the State Board of Education in California relies on an advisory board to recommend textbooks and other curriculum materials. Local schools and districts tend to use these materials because they can use state funds to buy them. In 1990 the advisory body recommended history textbooks that some believed contained 'egregious racial stereotyping, inaccuracies, distortions, omissions, justifications and trivialization of unethical and inhumane social practices, including racial slavery' (King, 1992:322). State Department of Education officials and the publisher of the textbook series were quick to take action in support of the recommended texts, launching a massive public relations campaign which King (1992:322) maintains, 'shaped public opinion and distorted the issues surrounding this controversial adoption'. As part of this campaign, proponents of the texts denounced critics on national and local television shows, claiming, for example, that the critics' position would encourage 'tribal warfare' and that the favored texts were 'multicultural' in nature, despite the fact that they were only moderately so.

Critics of the texts were also busy. Academics and community activists were among those who wrote letters and conducted protests, making their point that, among other faults, these texts did not measure up to established state standards. A number of tense public hearings ensued, according to King (1992). Armed guards were present, people attended in unprecedented numbers, and as expected, those concerned express a wide variety of opinions. As well as all this the Black Caucus of the state legislature made a direct appeal to the Board of Education to postpone their decision. In spite of all the protest, the Board voted to adopt one K-8 series and an additional Grade 8 history text. The battle did not end there, however. Parents and school board members in at least five communities refused to buy the books. Others agreed to buy the books only if they were accompanied by supplemental material for teaching about specific racial/ethnic groups and cultural diversity. And yet other communities continued to protest their districts' decision to purchase the texts.

Teaching *To Kill a Mockingbird*

Not all contests over meaning occur outside of the school. Battles over classroom discourse may also take place within schools. This was the case at Suburbia where a number of students of African heritage objected to the inclusion of Harper Lee's *To Kill a Mockingbird*. Lee's novel has for a number of years been included in Suburbia's English curriculum. It revolves around the experiences of three White children who live in a small southern United States community in the 1930s. These young people encounter a number of situations that shape their understanding of the world about them. One of the most significant of these is the trial of an African American man charged with the rape of a White woman. What makes this significant for the children is that the father of two of the children accepts the task of defending the man. We see the trial unfold through the eyes of the children, and with it, the state of race relationships and racism in the community.

The meaning that teachers and students attribute to Lee's text varies considerably. This is not to say that many will disagree over Lee's general denotative descriptions of what is happening in Maycomb. Most teachers and students will probably concur on these accounts. What is at issue is not the question of whether all parties can come to an agreement on the denotative details. The important matter here is the significance of these 'facts' for the individuals who read them: the connotative meanings. What is immediately apparent at Suburbia is that the story means different things to individuals associated with one particular group from what it signifies to other students and to most teachers. Many students of African heritage find the experience of taking up *To Kill a Mockingbird* in class a troubling one. This stands in marked contrast to a number of teachers and students. Margaret, a teacher, maintains that the novel is 'a classic' and that her students 'really loved it'. She remembers that at the beginning of the year a number of students were asking her whether they were going to study *To Kill a Mockingbird*.

Yet students of African heritage were almost unanimous in their condemnation of the book. They had little use for it, and wanted it eliminated from the curriculum altogether. Bob, for example, recalls taking up the book in his Grade 9 English class. He remembers, with some discomfort, the way in which his fellow classmates would scrutinize him at the time. He says, 'When I was in Grade 9 we had to read this *To Kill a Mockingbird*. The reaction from kids, right, they look straight at you. They always look at you and you feel like ... But they keep looking at you.' Another young women said, 'I was like shrinking. I felt like leaving the class, I was so angry.' Chris notes that his teacher didn't handle certain parts as well as he feels she might have. He says that when the words 'colored people' come up the teacher 'goes nuts. Like I'm going to jump up and kill her every time she says "colored people".' Jocelyn had perhaps the strongest reaction. When they came to certain passages in the book, she said, 'I cried.'

These different reactions can be attributed to the different experiences that the respective parties bring to the reading situation. Indeed those who have consistently been on the short end of racist acts will probably react quite differently to negative depiction of people of their heritage from those who are more likely to be on the other end of these kinds of encounter. While some White readers may not approve of the treatment Blacks receive in the book, they may nevertheless take comfort in the fact that the central characters also disapprove of it. It is quite easy, then, for them to see an antiracist message in the book. It is also easy for White readers to distance themselves from the racist attitudes displayed in the novel. They can conclude with little effort that these were things that occurred in the southern United States long ago, and that could not, and do not, take place in contemporary multicultural Canada. This is not always the case for students of African heritage. They are likely to identify with the people in the novel who are the objects of racism and the derision associated with it.

At the root of these different responses is the strategy of the author to write for a particular audience. Harper Lee, a White woman, clearly anticipates that her readers will be White. This is evident in the perspective that she features in the novel. Readers see the story unfold through the eyes of a young White girl, Scout. The novel revolves around the activities of Scout and her companions; the things that are deemed important enough to be included in the book are those things that these young people find interesting. Lee also takes care to ensure that the values that emerge are those that will be acceptable to a White audience. For example, she justifies the worth of her characters in ways that she believes will not offend her anticipated (White) audience (Klein, 1985).

Lee's theme of self-discovery exerts a substantial influence on how the various situations and characters are presented. She expends considerable effort in the novel illustrating how the children come to understand themselves and the world about them. Their growing up, maturing, and the learning they experience in the process, assume centre stage. Consequently the issues, events and characters that they encounter are merely props that allow Lee to best demonstrate her theme. These props include the racism in the community, the trial, and issues of social justice. These issues take centre stage for a while, in so far as they constitute a curiosity and hence a learning experience for the children, and then, as the children move on with their lives, recede. Because they are only props for the more central theme of self-discovery, readers will get very little sense of the history or an understanding of why race relationships came to be this way. We are presented only with the state of these relationships as they existed in the 1930s, and this in a way that best complements the central thesis. Unfortunately the narrative provides us with little opportunity to comprehend why White people would have come to treat African Americans in such a shameful way.

An important strategy that Lee employs here is to present the world through the eyes of the children. This means that readers are treated to a child's pristine, naive view of community events. The world is revealed to the children, and hence to the reader, warts and all. As part of this strategy, the props for the children's learning experiences – the events and the people that are part of them – become objects of curiosity to be studied and learned from. In attempting to make these objects 'strange' Lee, like her colonial predecessors, falls into the trap of emphasizing their exotic side. For example (p.192) she describes Tom, the accused, as 'a black-velvet

Negro, not shiny, but black velvet. The whites of his eyes shone in his face, and when he spoke we saw the whites of his teeth.' Here she might as well have been describing a strange and fascinating animal or toy rather than a human being. Note the similarities between Lee's description and a mid 19th-century colonial geography text that describes the native people of New Guinea as 'savages'. Referring to a typical native, it goes on to say: 'Although he is straight and agile, [he] is not attractive in appearance. His frizzled hair seems to grow in tufts, standing out above his head like a great mop, his lips are thick, and his nose flat and broad' (Firth & Darlington, 1993:85).

A further consequence of Lee's strategy for probing the children's self-discovery is that she presents the African Americans in the study not just in an exotic way, but also in an explicitly negative manner. The first references to them in the book are very negative. They are referred to here and throughout the book as 'niggers' and those who are seen to side with them, like Atticus Finch, Scout's father, are labeled 'nigger lovers'. Even our hero Atticus, who seemingly will have nothing to do with racist attitudes, maintains, 'There is nothing more sickening to me than a low-grade man who will take advantage of a Negro's ignorance', implying that ignorance is common among Blacks. Another side to this negative portrayal is the way that Lee refers to the Black community. With few exceptions they are depicted as a faceless group, waiting to go into the courtroom, watching the court proceedings or simply the subject of conversation. We only get to meet a few who belong to this community – Calpurnia the maid, who is presented in a subservient role; Tom, the accused; his wife, whom we are encouraged to pity; one of Calpurnia's fellow church-goers who is depicted as someone most people would not like; and the reverend Sykes. The only one of these people we really get to know, however, is Calpurnia. We end up knowing little about Tom and the others.

Although the author sets the reader up to reject negative portrayals of African Americans, she nevertheless provides a less than comfortable reading experience for students of African heritage, as illustrated above. Reading *To Kill a Mockingbird* can be an awkward, if not painful affair for these students. This will not be the first time that many of these students will have encountered this pain. This is because most of them will have already come across these demeaning discourses. Indeed they are perpetually exposed to sense-making practices, in the media, in popular culture, in personal encounters, and in institutional settings like schools, that place people of African heritage in demeaning positions. But not only do these discourses implicate people of African heritage of both past and present, they also provide a template for each of these students to define themselves and their place in the world. When the African Americans in the southern town in the 1930s are derided, so are they. When the Blacks of Maycomb are referred to as 'niggers', this also becomes part of the mantle that students of African heritage at Suburbia must bear. And they must do so not just in private but in public, in front of their classmates and teachers.

Reading *To Kill a Mockingbird* without appropriate guidance may do little to assist African Canadian students at Suburbia to develop a positive sense of themselves, something with which they and other students of African heritage constantly struggle. Walker (1993) for one is not optimistic about the chances for African Americans of developing a positive self-image. She wonders what chance these children have of acquiring even a neutral, as opposed to clearly negative impression of their own heritage, and hence of themselves and their role in the United States and global society, when they are so deeply affected by the barrage of negative images of Africa and people of African descent propagated by both commercial and educational media. Nevertheless Rashid (in Walker, 1993:14) believes that there are good reasons for developing a positive identification with one's ethnic roots. She says:

> For African children … a sense of pride and identification with one's ethnic roots is a vital prerequisite for coping with the racism and classism that permeate this society … When young African American children feel positive about themselves and their ethnic heritage, positive feelings about school and community are the next logical steps.

The connection that individuals make between negative portrayals in books and students in the class may sometimes be implicit. At times, however, it may be made more explicit. Klein (1985) recounts the experience of a Jamaican student. The following is an excerpt from her essay *My Schooling in England.*

> My first real embarrassing moment came about in this … class. The teacher read a book called *The Little Piccaninny* which I thought was ridiculous. It put across a picture of little Black girls being really dim and stupid. She looked at me and said, 'We have a little Piccaninny in our class, haven't we?' I was very upset as I felt I was thought of as this little girl. (Klein, 1985:26)

Like the students at Suburbia, students in other situations have been forced to acknowledge the word 'nigger' in class. As at Suburbia these experiences have also proven painful for students of African heritage.

Watts (in Klein, 1985:26), for example, describes a situation in England where a student of African heritage must read a section of Poe's *The Gold Bug* in front of the class. The student remembers:

> Then there's this word 'nigger' that's going to be read out loud by somebody in just a few minutes. And there's me, the only one of me in the whole class ... There must be at least two whole pages sprinkled with 'massa' and 'nigger'. When it comes to my turn to stand up and read ... If I don't draw that same stupid part! Jupiter's part. The 'nigger' part! Me!

Negative references of this sort do little to motivate students who are in some way implicated in these portrayals. When students encounter books that present the group with which they are associated, and by implication themselves, in unflattering ways, then they will be less willing to engage such material. This is painfully evident among the students of African heritage at Suburbia. It is also the case in other contexts. Klein (1985), for example, notes how student borrowers of *My Mate Shofiq* 'slung back' the book at the librarian, dismissing it as 'a load of rubbish'. Even though the book was designed to probe racism in a meaningful way, the presentation of racist images at the beginning was enough to lose Black readers on the way. Allen (1995) found that the Black students in his study rejected any illustrations that portrayed Black characters in less than realistic fashion: in unusual or unfamiliar clothes, with bare feet; that used dark colors, contained unfamiliar backgrounds or settings, or situations that were unfamiliar or in conflict with their reality. When they came across books with any of these attributes, they lost their motivation to read and avoided or refused to read them.

At Suburbia a distaste for *To Kill a Mockingbird* prompted a number of students of African heritage to protest its use in the classroom. They demanded that this particular novel be dropped from the curriculum. The students brought their concerns to teachers, to the English department and to the administration. The students were not the only ones to question the appropriateness of the book. At least one teacher was not happy that it was part of the curriculum, considering that so many students found it so offensive. Her feelings, however, did not play much of a part in the ensuing battle, which proved to be remarkably brief. The English department met, considered the students' concerns, and collectively decided to retain the novel as part of the curriculum, dismissing the students' feelings on this matter out of hand. Apparently most of them believed that because *To Kill a Mockingbird* was a 'classic', all students must have much to gain from it.

With this decision they ensured that the meanings they attributed to the book – which quite obviously differed from those of the students – would prevail. Not only would it guarantee that these demeaning discourses enter the classroom, but their mediation of these discourses in their role as teachers would also provide their interpretations of the book with increasing legitimacy.

Conclusion

Both students and teachers perpetually contest the meanings that are attributed to race/ethnicity in curriculum materials. They do so, however, in the context of wider struggles over meaning and practice. Indeed both students and educators make sense of these materials in the shadow of curriculum materials that historically looked to justify European colonialism. In that context curricular resources played an important part in the production and circulation of discourses that explained and attempted to legitimize the inhumane treatment of thousands of men, women and children around the world. Such discourses continue to circulate today through contemporary curriculum materials, although they may operate in more subtle ways. But these discourses and the various readings associated with them do not simply impose themselves on students and educators. Rather they are contested and contestable. Both educators and community members regularly challenge and resist many of these discourses. The California controversy and the struggle over *To Kill a Mockingbird* at Suburbia represent just two instances of such challenges. These struggles are not always even, though, for the odds are often stacked against discourses that work in the interests of marginalized and non-White groups. The upside of this is that because these representations are human constructions, and are thus contestable, there is ultimately hope for supplanting racist and demeaning discourses with alternate ones that favour the marginalized. This is explored further in Chapter 9.

Notes

1. Ironically, as Castle (1993) points out, the authors of these texts probably knew no more of India than they represented. Their own knowledge of the British Empire probably rested on the ethnocentric history that they themselves had studied. Even so, the pictures of India that they painted passed into a lasting public consciousness. Indeed these texts continued to legitimate a view of India and her people that long outlived the needs of the Empire. Reprinted for decades afterward, they continued to make an impression on students and the general public in Great Britain for generations to come.

Chapter 7

Representing Oneself: Student Communities and Student Identities

Representation works in other ways at Suburbia Secondary School. Aside from generating means for teachers and students to make sense of texts, images, and the actions and talk of others, it is also an important part of how these people make sense of themselves. Indeed the ways in which students represent themselves to others will become part of the way they see themselves, that is, who they are and what they stand for. Students become themselves as they perpetually identify with elements in their respective symbolic environments. The clothing they choose to wear, the music to which they listen, the languages and discourses that they use are all meant to serve as signs that communicate to others their identity and their beliefs. This process of identification and the accompanying tactics of representation involve another phenomenon: they simultaneously bring some individuals together and set others apart from one another. In this regard student heritage plays a part. This is apparent at Suburbia, where the casual observer may notice that students seem to congregate in groups according to their respective heritages. Besides their heritage, various groups may also stand out by virtue of their choice of clothing, music and language.

This chapter explores the process of student identity and identification and the consequences this has for the ways in which students associate with one another. I approach this chapter slightly differently from the previous two. In those chapters, as well as in the one that follows, I illustrate the way in which the processes associated with representation distribute advantages and opportunities in an unequal way; in this chapter, I highlight the process of representation and its power to allocate these advantages in a more roundabout way. I begin by highlighting an issue that surfaces regularly in situations where there is a great deal of (racial/ethnic) diversity – the degree to which groups (should) associate with group members and/or mix with other groups and individuals. This is an issue that concerns social commentators and scientists as well as students and educators at Suburbia Secondary School. To shed light on this phenomenon, I first describe the manner in which groups of students at Suburbia associate with one another. I then appeal to the concept of identity, and in particular, the ways in which students seek to represent themselves, to explain these patterns of association. This is where the distribution of advantages enters the picture. I conclude that it is our contemporary anonymous, uncaring and debilitating global culture that prompts students to construct identities and represent themselves in ways that sometimes bring them together with like-minded individuals and set them apart from others. In their attempts to 'be somebody', to establish themselves as individuals of worth in a world that routinely devalues them, students select images from their cultural environment and take them on as their own. Representing oneself in such ways is often not accomplished without a struggle. At Suburbia students routinely struggle with school authorities over how they represent themselves, including dress, music and language. Before I address these points, however, I attempt to set the stage for this account by citing two dissenting views on contemporary diversity and community.

Contemporary Heterogeneity and Community

Many social scientists and observers of the current social condition frequently draw our attention to its heterogeneous nature. They are quick to point to the apparently wide variation in beliefs, world views, lifestyles, art forms, and institutional arrangements that men, women and children hold, practice and labor under. Some, like Anderson (1990), go so far as to distinguish this state of affairs as 'pluralism with a vengeance'. Not all social observers would characterize this heterogeneity in the same way. Some social scientists and activists celebrate new opportunities for previously marginalized groups to step out from the shadow of domination and have their voices and views heard. Others are considerably less enthusiastic about this situation. Members of this latter group tend to employ the term 'fragmentation' rather than 'plurality', 'heterogeneity' or 'opportunity' in their analyses, and they look on with alarm as they see the chances for unity, uniformity and monolithic forms of community slipping away. Drucker (1993) for instance prefers to look at the emergence of previously silenced voices and social movements as a divisive form of tribalism. He highlights the destructive side of this, citing conflicts in the former Soviet Union and Yugoslavia as examples.

According to these scholars the United States is not immune from the global dangers of fragmentation. They see these movements eating away at the fabric of North American society as well. Bloom (1987) and Hirsch

(1987), for example, express their alarm at the divisive nature of US school curricula that recognize the legitimacy of a range of cultural views and perspectives. They reject this so-called 'cancerous relativism' and opt instead for a universal curriculum that has its roots firmly planted in Western civilization. Others see a threat from what they refer to as the 'cult of ethnicity'. Schlesinger (1991), for one, believes that the 'recent apotheosis of ethnicity' will leave the United States 'a society fragmented into ethnic groups'. He maintains that 'the cult of ethnicity exaggerates differences, intensifies resentments and antagonisms, drives deeper the awful wedges between races and nationalities' (p. 58). He fears that if th´ United States continues to embrace this trend it will never be able to realize George Washington's goal of one people, one nation. Such a course risks instead 'the disintegration of the national community, apartheid, Balkanization and tribalization'.

Similar fears have surfaced in Canada. Bissoondath (1994), for example, is concerned first and foremost about the impact that Canada's Multicul-turalism Act is having, and will have, on the country. Like Schlesinger, he fears that extending to various groups greater space to live their lives as they see fit encourages unhealthy divisions and threatens national unity. Bissoondath (1994:43) criticizes the Act for failing to mention 'unity or oneness of vision'. Its provisions, he claims, 'seem aimed instead at encour-aging division, at ensuring that the various ethnic groups whose interests it espouses discover no compelling reason to blur the distinctions among them.' He believes that policies of this nature will prompt members of these ethnic groups to erect impenetrable boundaries around themselves and retreat to what will become ethnic ghettos. Because these efforts tend to 'eradicate the centre', eroding that which might be held in common, they provide the conditions for setting different groups against one another.

> In stressing the differences between groups, in failing to emphasize that this is a country with its own traditions, ideals and attitudes that demand respect and adherence, that policy has instead aided in a hard-ening of hatreds. Canada, for groups with resentments aroused and scores yet unsettled, is just another battleground. (Bissoondath, 1994:43)

It is tempting simply to dismiss these claims outright. Diversity has been with us in one form or another for some time now, and has never been seen as the 'problem' that Schlesinger, Bissoondath and others believe it to be. Those interested in these matters might just as easily explore the conditions that prompt these individuals to isolate diversity of this nature as a problem, something that I address later. For now, however, I propose to explore the substance of these claims. I want to inquire into patterns of relationships between and among groups of different heritages in Suburbia Secondary School. In particular I am interested in the ways in which students in this school associate with one another, and the conditions that might prompt them to interact in this way.

Student Association in Suburbia

How do students associate with one another in the school setting? The cafeteria provides a good place to begin to answer this question. Many students tend to congregate on the basis of heritage at lunch-time. Walking into the cafeteria one cannot help but notice that certain groups stick to certain areas or sit at particular tables. In one corner students of African heritage play dominoes at a table while a much larger group watches the action or mills around conversing casually with one another in this same general area. At another table Chinese students talk, and work on what appear to be school-related activities. Filipino students play cards in another area, and so on. In the cafeteria, in the halls and to a lesser extent in classrooms it is evident that many students choose as their friends young men and women of similar heritages. Some groups tend to stick together more than others in this school. A number of Chinese students, for instance, prefer to socialize with students who have emigrated from China or Hong Kong and seldom associate with those of different backgrounds, given the option. Students of African heritage mix with those who do not share their background, but tend to socialize primarily with students of similar backgrounds. Students of many other heritages, including Portuguese, Italian, Filipino and Polish, also tend to associate with those of the same heritage.

It would be a mistake, however, to assume that students do not mix with others who are different from themselves or that the groups of which they count themselves members are stable. In fact, most students in the school had friends who had emigrated from different countries from themselves or were from different traditions. Indeed a closer look at the cafeteria reveals that there is a good deal of mixing. In the classrooms, too, student conversations are not restricted exclusively to teacher/student interactions or to interaction with those from similar backgrounds. Both casual and more systematic observations and conversations reveal that most students communicate and/or associate with different others on a regular basis. Boundaries are often tenuous and fluid, and groups themselves may crisscross a number of categories. Students may associate not only on the basis of heritage, gender, or social class, but also on the basis of the music, fashion or particular lifestyles which they prefer. One group of students in

Suburbia, for example, combined elements of their heritage and music. Some students of African heritage identified with the West Indian part of this by adopting reggae music – a type of music made popular in the West Indies – as their own. The music and their heritage, together with a number of lifestyle and fashion choices, set them apart, both from other student groups and, especially, from the adults who ran the school.

Other students circulate regularly between and among groups of students. For example, two students from South America counted as their friends students from a wide range of groups and heritages. These students were open to a range of different perspectives, avoided aligning themselves rigidly with particular groups, views or practices, and occasionally employed practices which some used to set themselves apart from others (such as music), to gain entry to groups. In this respect, they displayed what appeared to be flexible identities. They might just as easily have seen themselves as Canadians, rather than as South Americans, depending on the situation.

How easy or difficult is it to interact with fellow students? Associating with different others, like integrating into the school community generally, is not always an easy thing to do. Indeed those who attempt it must overcome a number of formidable barriers. The most obvious is language. Many students who are new to the country are fluent in their home language, but frequently experience difficulty with English. As a result many of them find it difficult to communicate with others who do not speak their native tongue. Naturally many of these young men and women would prefer to be with those with whom they can communicate. Many students are also drawn to those of similar background because of their common experiences. Conversely, they may be reluctant to approach different others because they lack this common ground. Marcia ,who is from a South American country, finds many 'Canadians' unapproachable or 'cold'. Students' peers exert considerable pressure on them to stay within their groups and to avoid others who are not part of the group. Those who do stay within stand to inherit certain rewards such as status, esteem, and friendship; individuals who stray from what some of their fellow students believe to be their appropriate peer group may be subject to penalties. Agnes, for example, an Anglo of European background, has been called a 'whigger' by White students for associating with students of African heritage. Similarly, students of African heritage have referred to Jean, a young woman of African heritage, as 'whitewashed' for 'acting White'. Most students in the school are cautious about whom they associate with and whom they approach. Veteran students will sometimes advise new students, on the basis of their racial heritage, whom they should or should not associate with and where they ought to sit and hang out. Beatrice, for example, a young woman of African heritage, remembers her first few days at the school:

> When I first came here, people weren't too friendly towards me because I hung on to this White girl. And she was saying to me, 'Oh well, maybe you really shouldn't sit with me at lunch because the Black people might say this and say that.' And when I was walking around the hall, some people went 'Pshhhh'.

How do school staff, parents and students feel about apparent divisions among and between groups of students? Generally speaking, the staff look with disfavor on the tendency for groups of students to isolate themselves from other groups and from the school community. They do so for a number of reasons. First they fear a potential for conflict between members of different groups. Although not common, the administration has had to deal with incidents of violence between groups of students. On at least one occasion the school administration was forced to call in the police, who subsequently laid charges. Teachers see a number of benefits in integrating students into other groups and into the general school population. They support strategies that will accomplish this end because they believe it is pedagogically sound, helps communication between students, breaks down isolationist tendencies, cuts down on group antagonism, helps teachers get to know students, and allows students to reap the benefits from participating in a larger school and community milieu. Parents also support associations of this sort. While students generally valued their peer associations, some felt a need for students to get together. One saw 'nationalism' as a threat to school efforts and wished instead that the school could develop more of a 'school spirit'. Another believed, 'A Black community and a White community ... have to come together as one. We have to show everybody that we can do it.'

In what follows I employ the concept of identity in an attempt to understand how and why students associate in this and other similar schools in the ways that they do.

Student Identity

Identity is closely associated with what people do and say. Who young men and women are, who they learn to be, are allowed to be, or mean to be, is reflected in the people with whom they associate and the kinds of activity in which they participate. Loyalty to certain people and practices will go hand in hand with the kinds of people students believe themselves to be. But identity is not just about uniformity or sameness. Rather, according to Hall (1991b:49) identity is always established across differences. He claims that the idea that identity has to do with people 'that look the same, feel the same, call themselves the same is nonsense.' Instead as a process and a narrative it is always told from the position of the Other. For example, he maintains that to be English is to know yourself in relation to the French, Russians and so on: you are what they are not. For Hall, identity achieves its positive through the narrow eye of the negative.

> Identity means, or connotes, the process of identification, of saying that this here is the same as that, or we are the same together, in this respect. But something we have learnt from the whole discussion of identifica-tion ... is the degree to which that structure of identification is always constructed through ambivalence. Always constructed through split-ting. Splitting between that which one is, and that which is the Other. (Hall, 1991b:47)

In the final analysis the manner in which students perceive themselves, and where, when and with whom they identify, will define the borders of their existence and their place in the world. In this regard, identity and identification prescribe the boundaries of group membership, bringing individuals together and setting them apart from others. As a consequence, identity can, in many important ways, be associated with the choices students make to affiliate with certain students and to do certain things, while avoiding others.

The construction of identity is not, however, an individual or exclu-sively personal thing. Selves are neither made nor changed in isolation (Britzman *et al.*, 1993). Rather the process of identity formation is dialogical in nature (Taylor, 1991). Who we are and what we become is tied very closely to the social circumstances in which we find ourselves. Our interac-tions with others whom we may or may not know, as well as a range of other phenomena in our social milieu, shape in fundamental ways who we think we are and whom and what we identify with. The dialogical nature of this process has a number of consequences. The most obvious is that we are not left to define ourselves as we see fit (Peshkin, 1991). In other words, as Hudak (1993) observes, we simply cannot be anything that we wish. Although men and women do have a role in constructing their identities, they do so within limited and limiting social parameters. What is more, these parameters are not something the individual invents. They are patterns we find in our culture and which are proposed, suggested and imposed on us by our culture, society and social group. Indeed these patterns can generate what Giroux (1991:248) refers to as 'cultural borders'. He maintains that these borders are 'historically constructed and socially organized with maps of rules and regulations that serve to either limit or enable particular identities, individual capacities and social forms.' Individual groups are also not responsible for the generation of group identities. Grossberg (1993) contends that the 'structures of identity' do not belong to particular subject groups. How groups see themselves and what they do to maintain their identities rest in considerable measure with social arrangements that are in many respects beyond their control.

These social practices both offer and subscribe social positions and their accompanying identities for men, women and children. We take up these positions in spaces that are socially established. It follows then that identity is neither a fixed nor a coherent quality, as many social scientists believed at one time. Rather our identities shift with the circumstances in which we find ourselves. Who we are will depend on whom we are with, what we are doing at the time, where we are and so on. Moreover, as Hall (1991b:57) contends, these identities may be contradictory, cross-cut one another and locate us differently at different times:

> All of us are composed of multiple social identities, not of one. We are all complexly constructed through different categories, of different antagonisms, and these may have the effect of locating us socially in multiple positions of marginality and subordination, but which do not yet operate on us in exactly the same way.

The locations in which we may find ourselves are always endowed with social value. Grossberg (1993) prefers to look at the process of identity construction and the allocation of value associated with it 'spatially and machinically'. He proposes that there are three systematic processes involved. The first is the production of subjectivity, a universally endowed value. Everyone experiences the world, and as a consequence, comes to knowledge about themselves and their world. Subjectivity in turn is closely associated with a second process which produces differentially-valued subject positions. Subjectivity and the subjects associated with this subjectivity are always located at particular positions within this stratified space, which both enables and constrains the possibilities of experience. Finally Grossberg (1993) speaks of a territorializing machine which distributes subject positions in space. This third related process provides the parameters for where and when individuals can stop and place themselves. It 'maps out the sorts of places people can occupy and how they can occupy them. It maps how much room people have to move, and where and how they can move' (Grossberg, 1993:100).

The point Grossberg makes here is that the social relationships in which men, women and children are entangled determine in important ways not only the kinds of identities they will assume, but also the particular value associated with these identities. Miles (1993) makes this same point with respect to group identity and worth. He maintains that the construction of naturalized difference creates a naturalized hierarchy of acceptability and belonging. Moreover, a context of relative scarcity facilitates the identification of certain social strata among 'subordinate classes.'

Identity and Representation

Because our identities depend so much on social conditions, the type of interactions in which we engage and the sorts of social phenomena we encounter will shape the kinds of people we will be. In this respect, the concept of representation takes on a particularly important role. Hall (1991b) contends that identity is always a kind of representation. How we represent ourselves to others and the kinds of representations or images with which we identify will become part of our identities. Explanations and theories about identity and 'groupness' have traditionally revolved around a preoccupation with face-to-face interaction. Identity, some scholars believed, depended first and foremost on the reactions of those one came in contact with. Socialization into the conventions associated with religion or language, for example, occurred most often in a family, extended family, or (local) community context. Taylor (1991) notes the importance of another's recognition in this process. He contends that 'identity crucially depends on my dialogical relations with others ... It is negotiated through dialogue, partly overtly, partly internal, with others' (p. 34). Because identities were thought to be fostered in these more or less bounded social fields, those who supported this view inevitably characterized identity as something that was coherent, continuous and fixed. Contemporary media culture has changed all this, however. No longer do we depend exclusively on those with whom we interact on a face-to-face basis to shape who we are. The images associated with this media culture now play an increasingly important role. Indeed the systems of representation and production of images and associated discourses, perhaps in ways at least as powerful as our personal interactions with others, offer positions for us to occupy. Moreover, these images and the discourses that work through them have taken centre stage in our contemporary world. Tierney (1993:6), for example, maintains that

> we have become a society where social identity is formed through the mass media. The multiplicity of images that cascade in upon us defeat

any suggestion that a reality exists or can even be known: instead, a hyperreality has taken hold, where multiple significations occur simultaneously. We can no longer relate our understanding of the self to the images we see, but instead we have become images ourselves, created by complex social and cultural forces.

Like everyone else, students are exposed to this image-producing process, leading Giroux (1993:115) to grant representation a pivotal role in the production of identities and particular sets of social practices. Citing Simon (1992), he acknowledges that students 'inhabit a photocentric, aural, and television culture in which the proliferation of photographic and electronically produced images and sounds serve to actively produce knowledge and identities within particular sets of ideological and social practices.' By granting the concept of representation a formative and not merely an expressive place in the constitution of social and political life, he acknowledge that difference and identity are associated with questions of power, politics, history and culture. Giroux (1993) is suggesting here that representation is much more than a random process. He points to its systemic and persistent nature. In fact he goes on to refer to 'machineries of representation' that 'work to actively produce common-sense notions of identity and difference [and] actively structure the conditions of existence' (Giroux, 1993:116). Hall (1991b) also emphasizes the systematic nature of representation, referring to the role of 'regimes of representation' and pointing to the need to understand the relations associated with these regimes. Understanding them, however, requires an understanding of the new global culture and its relationship to local cultures and practices. The images and discourses associated with this global culture routinely transcend the boundaries which at one time marked off families, local communities and nation states from the rest of the world.

The Global

The process of representation has taken on a more important role in our contemporary society because of this move towards globalization. We now live in a world where men, women and children engage in social interactions that as a matter of routine transcend local and national borders. Technological accomplishments have now made it possible for us to overcome what were once spatial and temporal barriers in ways that allow us to receive and send communications of all sorts to and from most parts of the world. These interactions may be carried on just as easily in economic, financial, cultural, political or military realms (Smart, 1993). Appadurai (1990) characterizes these interactions as 'global cultural flows'. He contends that today people, including immigrants, tourists, refugees, exiles and guest workers, can travel to and from most countries in the world with relative ease; multinational corporations and government agencies move mechanical and informational technology across previously impervious boundaries; currency markets, national stock exchanges and commodity speculations move megamonies through national turnstiles at blinding speed; newspapers, magazines, television and film distribute images and information to a growing number of audiences around the world; and ideologically saturated images carry state or counter-state world views. Particularly important to the process of representation here are the images and accompanying discourses that are produced and transmitted in the media. They bypass borders easily, work in powerful and often subtle ways, and may have very little to do with 'national' identities. Hall (1991a:27) contends that

> in cultural terms, the new kind of globalization has to do with a new form of global mass culture, very different from ... the cultural identities associated with the nation state in an earlier phase. Global mass culture is dominated by the modern means of cultural production, dominated by the image which crosses and recrosses linguistic frontiers much more rapidly and more easily, and which speaks across languages in a much more immediate way. It is dominated by all the ways in which the visual and graphic arts have entered directly into the reconstitution of popular life, of entertainment and of leisure. It is dominated by television and by film, and by the image, imagery, and styles of mass advertising.

Featherstone (1991) understands this culture as transnational in nature, a third culture, so to speak, that is oriented beyond national boundaries. Unlike more local varieties, this new media culture does not have roots in any particular community or tradition, although there is little question that most dominant forms flow from the United States (Morely & Robins, 1995).[1] According to Smith (1990:177) 'today's emerging global culture is tied to no place or period. It is context-less, a true *mélange* of disparate components drawn from everywhere and nowhere, borne upon the modern chariots of global telecommunications systems.' Anonymity is only one aspect of this new global culture, which Wexler (1992:111) contends is also characterized by what he refers to as a 'social emptiness'. By this he means that images have replaced 'reciprocal, caring, emotionally full, mutually identifying social interaction'. Men, women and children no longer interact in personally satisfying and supportive ways, as he implies they once did. Along with this anonymity and emptiness, global culture transmits other sets of values, some partially hidden, others not. Although these transmissions are often designed to create desires (and values) in their audiences, those who consume such images may not recognize these traits in themselves or in their immediate communities.

These globally oriented regimes of representation do not, however, transmit global, or at least universally agreed values. Rather they are oriented toward particular world views and support particular interests. This is in part due, as Giroux (1993) points out, to the fact that the images and discourses associated with these regimes of representation are part of corporate-controlled strategies to compete in increasingly competitive transnational economies.[2] In many respects the images we encounter are designed to motivate us to buy a certain product, subscribe to a particular view of the world, or to adopt specific ways of doing things. They endeavor to do this in part by organizing discourses in ways that manipulate viewers, readers and listeners. For example, in order to make sense of an electronic image the viewer may temporarily have to align him- or herself with a particular position (Ellsworth, 1993). To achieve this, producers employ a range of aesthetic conventions to appeal to the viewers' feelings. In other words, they may offer a viewing position that makes pleasurable a particular position, routinely tapping into the hopes, desires and fears of the viewer in the process. The positions which consumers or students are encouraged to take up, however, inevitably inflect knowledge with meanings that support particular gender, class and racial/ethnic interests. In educational documentaries that Ellsworth (1993) analyzed, the narrator speaks from a position of knowledge as a man who is White, middle-class, able-bodied, heterosexual, Christian and a scientist. In taking up these positions in this discourse (in this case, one of paternalism) students are expected to identify with a way of making sense of the world that both supports and legitimizes mythical norms that reflect the above interests. Media images also valorize qualities associated with these interests, such as masculinity, femininity, youthfulness and sexuality (Denzin, 1991). Although readers, listeners and viewers are induced to desire these traits, most will find that they frequently do not measure up.

Control of these images reflects these same interests. Marginalized groups do not generally have control over the images that turn up in the electronic media, in newspapers and magazines, and in school textbooks. Indeed McLaren (1995) maintains that most marginalized groups simply do not have the resources to generate their own images. McCarthy (1993a), for example, notes that during and after the Los Angeles riots Hispanic and African Americans did not have access to the media in ways that would have allowed them to tell their side of the story. The result was that the world was presented with images of this event from a perspective that did not necessarily coincide with that of these two groups. He also notes that starker treatments of the marginal abound in popular film culture in the United States. In films such as *Rambo, Red Dawn* and *Aliens* thousands of alien people die on the screen in seconds and entire cultures are wiped out. McCarthy (1993) contends that similar treatment of marginal groups occurs in school, where texts and films are based on media discourse that saturates popular culture with negative images of the Third World. Drawing on Said (1978) and citing examples from various texts used in the United States, McCarthy (1993:296) observes that

> Western scholars arbitrarily draw a line of demarcation between 'East and 'West', 'West' and 'non-West', the 'North' and the 'South', the 'first world' and the 'third world'. This arbitrary line of demarcation is stabilized by the constant production and reproduction of attributions, differences, desires and capacities that separate the West from the non-West. The West is rational. The third world is not. The West is democratic. The third world is not. The West is virtuous, moral and on the side of good and right. The third world is vicious, immoral and on the side of evil.

McCarthy (1993) says that the electronic media images generated over the Persian Gulf conflict merely exploited these dichotomies. These images were arranged in such a way as to help viewers in many countries around the world separate the cause of the allies of the West from that of the bad guys of the East – a case of the Crusades all over again.

The Local

While this global culture has a powerful effect on men, women and children, it does not simply roll over everything in systematic fashion, creating similarity as it does so (Hall 1991b). Images do not descend upon mute and passive populations on whose *tabulae rasae* they inscribe themselves (Smith, 1990). Indeed, the increasing diversity we see about us seems to indicate that something a little more complex is going on. Hall (1991a) acknowledges this complexity. He contends that globalization has two faces – the global and the local. What men and women do and how they see themselves depends very much on how they *receive* and *interpret* this global culture at the local level (Smart, 1993). One common local response to global anonymity and complexity is for all of us, men, women and children, to reach for our roots. Hall (1991a:35) maintains that in doing so we hope that identities will come our way, since these are thought to be stable, still points in a confusing and quickly changing world.

It is a respect for local roots which is brought to bear against the anonymous, impersonal world of the globalized forces which we do not understand. 'I can't speak of the world but I can speak of my village. I can speak of my neighbourhood. I can speak of my community.' The face-to-face communities that are knowable, that are locatable, can give them a place. One knows what the voices are. One knows what the faces are. The recreation, the reconstruction of imaginary, knowable places in the face of the global post-modern which has, as it were, destroyed the identities of specific places, absorbed them into this post-modern flux of diversity. So one understands the moment when people reach for those groundings.

Anonymity, as we have seen, is just one aspect of this global culture. There are other sides to the images and messages that we encounter. For example, students may reach for their immediate communities, often peer groups, for the caring and emotional support that Wexler (1992) believes is absent from their interactions with the wider (adult) society. Peer groups and their associated identities offer many young men and women forums for establishing a self that compensates for these social absences. Successful friendship groups enable them to affirm themselves in ways that other social groupings do not. Many students may also find that not only are they excluded from these cultural representations, but they and their communities are devalued and even threatened by them. This marginalization and potential annihilation, according to Smith (1990), drives people to preserve an identity and with it, a sense of 'collective dignity'. In response to marginalization certain groups may sometimes revert to forging oppositional identities. Ogbu (1992) notes that what he refers to as 'involuntary' minority groups – African, Aboriginal and Hispanic groups in the United States – adopt such a strategy. These groups tend to construct a collective identity in opposition to the dominant group as a reaction to the experience of oppression. Ogbu contends that the formation of a collective oppositional identity system is usually accompanied by the evolution of an oppositional cultural system or cultural frame of reference that contains mechanisms for maintaining and protecting the group's social identity. In these situations, identity formation is constructed and expressed through representation, that is, the construction of difference, and negotiated in the public sphere (Pinar, 1993).

High-school students may find themselves marginalized in other dimensions besides race. Gender and social class represent two of the more obvious structures of domination. Often taken for granted here, though, are the inequalities that revolve around age. Adolescents generally do not enjoy the same range of opportunities or choices as adults do, despite the fact that they may be exposed to the same persuasive media discourses as adults are. In school, for example, adults routinely set the parameters for behavior in the class and out, and students are expected to abide by these conventions, even though their compliance may not conform to images of men and women that are valorized in the media. The point here is that conventions that revolve around not only race/ethnicity but also gender, social class and age combine to marginalize these young people and provide grounds for the construction of oppositional identities (see, for example, Willis, 1977; McRobbie, 1978; Eitzen, 1992; Wexler, 1992). The construction of these identities may however involve much more than just efforts to connect with local or 'ethnic' roots, important as these may some-times be. In fact for some young men and women ethnicity and/or race may actually play a relatively minor role in identity and as an organizing principle. Heath and McLaughlin (1993) maintain that the inner-city youth to whom they talked believed that ethnicity seemed more often a label assigned to them by outsiders than an indication of what they believed to be their real sense of self. For these young people, ethnicity was important only as it functioned within a host of embedded identities – son, student, Baptist, gangbanger, athlete, immigrant, younger sister – that could get someone somewhere in the immediate community. In addition to this, ethnicity took on a particularly fluid character in the inner city. In the hybridity that characterized urban institutions, it was perpetually being reinterpreted and reinvented within the multicultural contexts of schools, housing projects, community organizations and social life.

Whether student identities may be rooted in a desire to find comfort in a confusing and anonymous world, to compensate for an emotional void, or to establish collective and individual dignity, they will always constitute more than a knee-jerk reaction to the global. Hall (1991b:62) maintains that the global is in fact the 'self-presentation of the dominant particular'. In other words, the global has a way of localizing and naturalizing itself. Cosmopolitan cultural forms articulate with, and give expression to identi-ties and circumstances at the national, regional and local levels (Smart, 1993). Appadurai (1990) puts yet another spin on this phenomenon. He contends that just as quickly as forces from various metropolises are brought in they tend to become *indigenized* in one way or another. Music, armaments, advertising techniques, language hegemonies and clothing styles are absorbed into local political and cultural economies and repatri-ated. Men, women, and children at the local level both consciously and unconsciously ingest the discourses that travel along the global communications highway, combine these images with the resources at hand, and selectively adopt them as their own.[3]

Patterns of consumption play a key role here. In fact Friedman (1990:324) maintains that self-identification and consumption are inextricably linked. According to him, consumption in this day and age is part of a more general strategy or sets of strategies for the establishment and/or maintenance of selfhood.

> Every social and cultural movement is a consumer or at least must define itself in relation to the world of goods as a non-consumer. Consumption within the bounds of the world system is always a consumption of identity, canalized by a negotiation between self-definition and the array of possibilities offered by the capitalist market. The old saying, 'you are what you eat', once a characterization of a vulgar ecological view of humanity, is strikingly accurate when it is understood as a thoroughly social act. For eating is an act of self-identification, as is all consumption.

At Suburbia students work at 'becoming somebody'. Students want to be somebody (Wexler, 1992), to find a place for themselves in placeless times (Morely & Robins, 1995). They want a real and presentable self, anchored in the verifying eyes of the friends they come to school to meet. Part of this work involves colonizing the images that saturate the world about them, trying them out, and eventually letting go of some of these icons while adopting others as their own. In their attempts to compensate for an anonymous, uncaring and debilitating world, young men and women become part of what these images signify (see also Corson, 1998).

Struggling for Identity at Suburbia

Forging an identity is not always an easy or straightforward matter. Indeed students must often struggle to have representations of themselves accepted or recognized by others. These struggles are generally the result of the nature of the identity that many students choose to assume. In their quest to make their mark, to ensure that they are recognized as someone of worth in an anonymous and debilitating world, young people may take on oppositional identities. For some, oppositional identities and the sometimes profane representations that accompany them are a way of resisting this debilitating culture and in the process acquiring recognition and worth – if not from the authorities, then from their comrades. Schools, however, do not usually condone activities, discourses or images that deviate from their generally conservative principles. As institutions that are geared to socialize students into the prevailing culture, they look to ensure compliance to norms that promote rather than subvert the status quo. What results is often a struggle between students and school authorities over the ways in which students represent themselves to others.

In a number of ways Suburbia Secondary School sanctions the norms of anonymity associated with contemporary culture. Merely enforcing school rules that apply to everyone equally encourages students to become part of an eventually undifferentiated mass of humanity. One of the specific ways in which Suburbia does this is through the dress code. School authorities require students to abide by a strict dress code. They expect males to wear grey dress pants, dress shoes, a white shirt, and a school sweater. Females can wear either the dress pants or plaid skirts of a specified length. The school staff strictly enforce this code. There are no exceptions to it. If students are found to deviate from the rules they are told to make the appropriate changes, even if it means going home. Like any rules, however, there is some room for interpretation, and students constantly test these various lines of interpretation in their perpetual quests to establish their identities. What results is a constant struggle over which items of clothing students can wear to represent themselves. The following excerpt from my field notes represents a typical student encounter with school authorities.

Uniforms seem to be the object of concern now that the warm weather has arrived and the guidelines for uniforms have changed slightly. I was sitting in the office when one of the secretaries brought three students along to see one of the vice-principals. One was a young woman who obviously had never been sent to the office of an administrator for disciplinary reasons. She appeared to be a little nervous. She was wearing, at least at first glance, the appropriate uniform – white shirt, grey slacks and black 'dressy' shoes. However, when she lifted up the bottom of her pants, it was obvious that the shoes were boots (boots were defined as having eight lace-up holes or more). But they were considered OK when worn with pants. The staff member speculated that the teacher who sent the student down had probably seen her lacing up her footwear, assumed she was wearing the wrong shoes, and sent her down to the office. He told her that she was free to go, but warned her that she could wear her boots only with slacks and not with a dress. The next candidate, a young man, insisted that he was not sure what counted as appropriate footwear. He was wearing a brown semi-construction boot, which the staff member said was not acceptable.

Not being sure about proper wear he asked whether my shoes were acceptable, to which the staff member replied 'yes' … [and] ended by saying that shoes were appropriate if they were 'dress shoes' that could be worn with a suit. He then offered to bring in a pair of his old dress shoes for him but the boy declined the offer. He told the young man that he was OK for today but would have to come with the proper footwear tomorrow.

These scenes are typical of what happens every day at Suburbia as students attempt to represent themselves in ways that depart from standard school-approved ways of dressing. Constant supervision regularly turns up those who represent themselves in ways that are too individualistic for the school authorities. In many cases resistance to dress norms is short-lived, as violators are sent to administrators who judge the nature of the violation and direct students to do what they must to conform to these norms. Despite the strict guidelines for dress, however, students continually find ways to express their individuality and group connections, and in some cases to flout the rules. There is some room for variation in footwear and some groups of students prefer some styles of shoe over others. Some students even identify themselves with others through their shoelaces. For others, jewelry is something that they use to represent themselves. Perhaps the most obvious way that students have found to differentiate one student or group of students from others at Suburbia, given the fairly rigid guidelines, is not through what they wear but how they wear it. The manner in which students wear their school uniforms can serve two purposes. First it can immediately identify a student with a particular group of like-minded students. Second, it can display a certain defiance of the enforced anonymity.

Bob is one student who uses his manner of dress to identify himself with others as well as to illustrate his resistance to the school dress code without really violating it. I captured the following description in my field notes.

Bob comes as close as any student I have seen in the school to flouting the school's dress code. He does wear the standard white shirt and grey flannel pants, but the manner in which he does suggests a certain irreverence. His shirt is a golf shirt, undone at the neck. A blue tee-shirt is visible below this outer wear. He wears a gold chain around his neck. His shirt-tail is out. At one point I look over and see his shirt partially tucked into his colorful pink briefs clearly visible above pants that ride very low on his hips. One wonders how it is that these trousers do not fall down to his ankles. His high-cut black shoes are not laced up and the bottoms of his pants are tucked partially into his footwear. He can't help but drag his shoes as he walks.

Dress is not the only area in which students struggle to represent themselves. They also do so through the music they prefer. This is not always an easy thing to achieve in the school environment. Most educators, including those at Suburbia, feel that playing and listening to music is not always conducive to teaching and learning, particularly within certain contexts, like classrooms. Nevertheless students do find ways to play and have their music heard. Some of these are actually sanctioned by school authorities. Even in these situations, students find that they have to struggle for what they want. Sue, a student of African heritage, remembers with some bitterness the difficulties that she and some of her friends had playing their music in the cafeteria.

> We were playing – the Black people, you know where the Black people sit in the cafeteria? – they had a little ghetto-blaster and they were playing reggae, right? It wasn't bothering anybody. No one was saying, 'Oh, you know, whatnot.' And the teacher, the day after, the next day, he said, 'Well there'll be no music in the cafeteria and whatnot.' Mind you, that was from a little ghetto-blaster … Well, the reason why they said no music in the cafeteria was because it disturbed the classes adjacent to the cafeteria. Mind you, they had the system on playing hot rock sort of music in the whole system in the cafeteria. Now, what I would like to know is how a little ghetto-blaster is going to disrupt the classes and a big system like that isn't going to? That sort of hit me, you know. And again, in the morning they usually play country music, and last month was Black history month and once again they put it to reggae. They turned it down really low, whereas country music would be high.

Students also struggle over the language they use to represent themselves. Educators do not always approve student languages that do not resemble standard English. More will be said of this in the next chapter. And beyond the struggles associated with dress, music and language, students may find they must sometimes struggle with the school authorities with whom they associate. There are times when educators voice their disapproval over the company that students may keep, even though efforts to separate students may not meet with much success. Janice, for example, remembers:

> I was in Mr Jones' office one day because I'd swore in front of a teacher. He called me into his office and he goes, 'I don't know where you get

your ignorant attitude. Maybe you get it from the Black people you hang around with?'

Conclusion

One can speculate on the motives of those like Bloom, Hirsch, Schlesinger and Bissoondath, cited earlier in the chapter, who express alarm at what they see as the increasing fragmentation of the communities and societies in which they live. One reason for such trepidation may well rest with perceived threats to the writers' security, although this reasoning would not necessarily apply in the same way to Bissoondath who emigrated from Trinidad to Canada as a young man. It may well be that those who have had for years the luxury of going about their business with the assurance that their world views were, and would always be, the natural and predominant ones, are not ready for challenges from individuals and groups whose views and life ways were not previously recognized, valued or permitted. The perceived uniformity, as well as the power and privilege that once accompanied this dominance appears, at least in some small measure, to be evaporating now that some of these previously marginalized groups have found platforms from which to speak and be heard. Giroux (1993) contends that charges of fragmentation are but one of a number of strategies on the part of the privileged to regain this lost turf. Wallace (1993:253), on the other hand, reveals that perceptions of *recent* disorder can come from but one sector of society. Referring to *New York Times* critic Richard Bernstein's (1990) charge of a 'society in disarray' she asks:

> When has American society ever been in order for people of color and people of sensitivity, for those who are visibly and invisibly other? For the poor, the gay, the women, the children, the disabled, the elderly, the not-White? 'Society' is now in disarray for Bernstein only because he, and those of his cast of mind, have been forced to recognize that they are not the only ones on this planet, that they are, in fact, a distinct although not yet endangered 'minority'.

Are associations of men, women and children increasingly withdrawing into groups of like-minded people, erecting boundaries between themselves and others, cutting themselves off from the rest of the world? The answer is a paradoxical yes and no. On the one hand, we have all been brought closer together over the last few decades. New communications technologies, for example, have created a 'global village' (McLuhan, 1973) in which we can now rub shoulders in both a figurative and a literal sense with people from virtually every part of the Earth. On the other hand, men and women may react to this global culture in ways that involve some sort of retreat. Indeed a search for meaning, security, caring and dignity in what may often be a confusing, uncaring and debilitating world might well prompt individuals to construct identifies and identifications that set them apart from other individuals and groups. But this process may not be one that is routinely undertaken by all men, women or children, nor is it as straightforward or as uniform as Schlesinger and Bissoondath imply.

This appears to be the case for the young men and women at Suburbia. Although there is considerable evidence here and at other high schools with diverse student bodies (Peshkin, 1991; Brighton, 1994; Verma *et al.*, 1994) that students associate by race or heritage, there were also many instances where students associated with others from different backgrounds. Furthermore, groups (and identities) tended to be fluid and revolved around categories other than heritage, including social class and gender, and interests such as music, fashion and life styles generally. The opportunities to occupy different roles and subject positions are many in an environment this diverse, and some students at Suburbia and in other schools are able to take advantage of them (Peshkin, 1991; Brighton, 1994). One of the students to whom Brighton talked, for example, was willing and able to take advantage of these opportunities. He appeared comfortable with his flexible identity/ies as he moved from group to group.

> I act differently when I'm with a group of guys who are into certain music. I'll take on that attitude that I live and die for this music, you know like a chameleon, you'll change whoever you're with. You don't change your entire personality, but you just change to fit, at least, I do that. There's guys in the group who listen to rap music, so they have the dress and the attitude. It's not that rap defines their attitude, but you know, that whole culture, I would say, that rap culture. When I'm with them, 'cos I listen to just about everything, I do my best to identify with them. (Brighton, 1994:12)

Students do not take on their identities without a struggle, however. School authorities often contest the ways in which students choose to represent themselves. In their efforts to socialize young people into the dominant culture, educators frequently attempt to restrict the ways in which they dress, the music they listen to, and the language they use. Conflicts arise over these issues when students attempt to resist various school conventions in the process of taking on oppositional identities that will provide them with a sense of worth and belonging in an anonymous and often debilitating contemporary world. And while school institutions segregate students formally by grade and form, and informally by other means, they will never be completely successful in dictating how they associate with one another.

Notes

1. For example, the United States is the largest exporter of motion pictures and television programming. Beyond this, however, and perhaps more important, is that the form which these media productions follow sets the tone for the viewer around the world. Morely and Robins (1995) maintain that America has written the 'grammar' of television, and in doing so has 'set the frame' for global television programming. It is in response to these and other forms of 'coca-cola-ization' that the European Community has recently made moves to alleviate what it perceives as a threat to its identity (ies).
2. Corporations control both electronic and print media in powerful ways. Providing advertising revenue allows them to influence such things as the plot of a television program, the kinds of feature that a magazine may carry, or the type of coverage that a news program may give a potential news story (Andersen, 1995).
3. In this regard, Morely & Robins (1995) and Ang (1995) argue against a 'hypodermic needle model' of media effects. They both emphasize the variable ways in which different groups can interpret and adopt the meanings associated with media productions.

Chapter 8
Valuing Languages

This chapter explores another aspect of representation and the effects it has on the opportunities of certain groups of students. Instead of examining the content side of this process, as was the case in the previous few chapters, it highlights the primary medium through which educators and students represent the world about them – language. The focus here is not on discourse *per se*, but on the particular language(s) that students and educators use to convey these discourses. As I illustrate in what follows, the manner in which students use, in this case, the English language, will dictate their fortunes. Those who are able to demonstrate a certain degree of skill in speaking and writing standard English will find themselves with more opportunities than those who are either unwilling or incapable of using these forms of English in the required situations. Like the issues associated with meaning, these language issues are always contested. Students, educators and many others associated with education routinely struggle over what languages are to be used in what situations and how they are to be valued. And like the contests over meaning, these struggles are generally not equal. Standard English language use and value invariably have the advantage in these struggles.

At Suburbia, as in any other institution, language plays a role in the process of representation. Because of the highly discursive nature of the activities that go on here, however, language is in fact the primary medium of representation. In this institution, as in all other walks of life, the signs that constitute what we know as language make it possible for us to give shape and meaning to our thoughts and feelings. By standing in for aspects of our experience, these signs allow us to render our consciousness in a public way, and in doing so, to communicate with one another. But this is not simply a one-way process. Language does not just represent existence. It also, in crucial ways, shapes it. This is to say that language plays a key role in constructing values, meaning, selves and the multiple perspectives that accompany them. It is through language that people come to acquire a sense of themselves, their community, and others, and to understand where they fit in the grand scheme of things.

Schools like Suburbia seek to capitalize on the central role of language in learning. Corson (1993) contends that language takes on such a crucial function in schools because the reproduction of social and cultural functions is driven by interpersonal communication. He says that we learn how to perform even the most basic act by observing how others do it, by using and listening to those others as models, by noticing others' reactions to our performance and changing it accordingly. More than this, though, Corson (1998) notes that language is the primary medium through which students make new concepts their own. Students learn as they listen, talk, read and write about new concepts and ideas and relate them to what they already know. But language is much more than just an instrument of communication, or a tool that facilitates through its communicative capacities the intellectual development of students. Language is also a symbol that communicates value to those who are associated with its various networks. Those who participate in language conventions assign worth to language users on the basis of the ways in which they employ these conventions, both in the classroom and out. This attribution of worth does not occur through natural or preordained processes. Rather it is the result of struggles between and among groups who vie to have their various conventions, styles and meanings accepted as legitimate and accorded corresponding value. The results of these struggles are evident in Suburbia and other schools where certain languages and language styles are favored over others, evident in those conventions which are generally employed in the classroom and out, and in the attitudes of students and educators towards the various conventions.

The differential worth assigned to groups and their language conventions has led those in Suburbia's educational community to see language both as a 'problem' and as a 'resource'. Most take for granted the value of the dominant language in this school – English. In an important way, many parents, educators and students see English as a resource, something that when learned will assist students to master the curriculum and improve their life chances. In addition many – but not all – see non-English languages as a problem. Parents, students and educators alike consider students' home languages, non-standard varieties and various accents to be impediments to learning English and subject matter content, as well as barriers to the opportunities that the market has to offer them. There are exceptions, though: not all students view non-English languages and varieties in this way. Some actually see them as resources. They perceive, sometimes implicitly, that home languages and varieties can help them not only rescue a measure of social worth, but also assist them to master an English-based curriculum.

This chapter describes the effects of the process of valuing associated with linguistic representation at Suburbia Secondary School. Towards this end, I first outline the dimensions of language variety at Suburbia. Next I describe how linguistic expressions are valued and the effects that this has on various groups of students. An account of teacher attitudes towards the speaking of non-English languages and non-standard varieties is then followed by a delineation of the origins and development of one form of non-standard English variety spoken at Suburbia – *Patois*.

Language as an Issue at Suburbia

Suburbia's students speak many languages. The extent of this linguistic diversity was made plain by a recent survey which indicated that the student body speaks over 60 different tongues. Language becomes an issue here because the overwhelming majority of teaching/learning interactions occur in just one language: English. School officials expect all students who enroll at Suburbia to be prepared to learn from English-based curriculum materials and to listen to classroom interchanges in the English language. If students are to have any hope of mastering the curriculum they have little choice but to learn English. Some experience more difficulty with this than do others.

Most teachers are on the look-out for students who have difficulty with English, and many are adept at diagnosing problems. Ginger, however, never ceases to be surprised at how little English some of her newer students actually know. She recalls her most recent new arrival:

> One boy, Johnny, he came from Hong Kong a few weeks ago, so he told me. He came into my class and he couldn't understand what I was saying. I was kind of shocked. He couldn't understand what I was saying. I said, 'When did you get here, when did you come here?' He said, 'Friday.' So I'm thinking he meant that he arrived here the Friday before.

While Johnny has managed to overcome some of his problems, at least to the point of being able to deal with course work, other students in this class have not been as successful. Bill continues to experience difficulties. He has told Ginger that he understands everything, but she is sure he 'doesn't understand anything that's difficult.' She has another student from Sri Lanka who is also having problems. Ginger says:

> She's having troubles, but I think it's just the language. She's kind of frustrated because she's working hard and getting 50s and I told her just make this your 'getting used to culture' year ... She asks questions

and she nods and says she understands, but there's always a word in there [that she doesn't understand].

Fred, another teacher, is getting better at recognizing students with language problems. He says that he recognized the difficulties that one of his newest student was experiencing 'right off the bat':

Just as the first time I talked to him, I noticed he was very ... not slow with his English, but you could see that he was always thinking before he was speaking almost to make sure he has the words correctly and he has chosen it in the right form before he starts talking to me. And then I got a memo that he is at ESL and that the first test ... when he did the first test, he came up and asked if he could write it with the ESL class. So I said 'Fine'. But I think his speech is the hardest point right now. The written stuff that he does is fine. Just as I said, he does very well on the test. So I think he can read and write fine. It's just when he tries to speak that he has a little bit of difficulty.

Fred also notes that this particular student, like many of the newer students who come into his classes, exhibits a certain kind of behavior. He appears shy, but will approach him when he experiences difficulties. Fred says:

He does have a little difficulty with the English language so I think that makes him a little bit even shyer in the group. I don't think he's that outgoing type of person. At least he hasn't struck me as [that type]. When he needs help, he'll ask for it. But he doesn't ask for it in front of the group. He will come up to me after class. He'll wait patiently till everyone leaves after class. 'Sir, can I borrow a textbook to take home?' Or, he'll catch me in the hall or he'll knock on the office door. 'Sir, can I borrow a textbook to take home?'

Ragini is perhaps typical of many students who travel from distant lands and end up at Suburbia. She is a recent immigrant to the country and regularly experiences language difficulties. Among other problems she often has trouble understanding fellow students and teachers. Ragini believes that 'Canadians, they speak too fast.' She often has to ask them to repeat themselves, something that she feels uncomfortable doing. She also believes that she has trouble making herself understood. As a result she is sometimes unwilling to speak up or let teachers or other students know that she has not understood what they have said to her.

Mary is also a recent immigrant, but knows even less English than Ragini. This was particularly evident when we talked to her. She had trouble understanding what we were saying and had even more difficulty making herself understood. Unlike Ragini, however, she rarely speaks English, preferring to stay within her own ethnic group and speak to her friends in her native tongue. For her, 'English is the main problem.' She admits that she becomes 'nervous' at the prospect of having to talk to someone in English. Although she is a good student in sciences and math, she worries that teachers will think that because of her language problems she does not have a grasp of the subject matter. Mary believes that the language barrier gets in the way of establishing better relationships with her teachers. She wants to be in a position to talk with teachers more than she is now able. In the country she emigrated from she 'could talk [about] a lot of things [with] the teachers. But here if I don't know how to [talk] to you [in] English, I don't [know] how to explain to you what [I think]. And I think they [*teachers*] haven't got a lot of time for you to explain your feelings.' She wishes that she had a teacher who could speak her language. If this were the case then she feels that she would be able to establish a better relationship with the teacher, who in turn would be able to provide clear explanations of some of the things with which she experiences difficulties.

Language, Power and Value

The fact that English is the language of instruction at Suburbia is not the result of a coincidence or of a naturally occurring process. English is entrenched in its current, obviously secure position as the consequence of an ongoing struggle. In other words, English assumes such a dominant position in this and in many other schools in the Western world because power relationships over the years have favored it over other languages. Teachers and students conduct their interactions in this language not because it is an inherently better language for instruction, but because the various arrangements that are part of the wider social structure have dictated that English be used in this context.

The English language, and the various discourses associated with it in this case, together play a unique role in mediating and shaping the power relationships that are responsible for its current dominant position. One of the ways in which English does this is through the attribution of value. The language that is employed in the classroom works in important ways to establish the worth of various social practices and of the individuals and groups associated with them. It does this in at least two ways. First, language can act as a determiner of worth. Certain arrangements of words have the power to allocate value. Secondly, though, language itself is also a reflection of worth. Educators commonly evaluate students on the basis of how they use language in the classroom. Particular English language discourses can then predispose men and women to believe in their specific worth and consequently to look upon them as important resources. At the same time they also depend on a supportive social context to generate conditions that allow for this attribution of worth. Walsh (1991:32) makes this point, emphasizing as she does so the reality that language is much more than simply a mode of communication.

> Language is more than a mode of communication or a system composed of rules, vocabulary, and meanings; it is an active medium of social practices through which people construct, define, and struggle over meaning in dialogue with and in relation to others. And because language exists within a larger structural context, this practice is, in part, positioned and shaped by the ongoing relations of power that exist between and among individuals. As such language affects as well as reflects the individual reality of its speakers, and the sociohistorical and ideological environment in which these speakers reside.

How can particular arrangements of words or styles of language have the power to assign worth? Of the various historical beliefs about the power of language that Corson (1993) traces, two are relevant here. The first concerns the relationship of language and thought. In the tradition of the 'strong' version of the Sapir-Whorf hypothesis and various Orwellian-like schemes about language (Corson, 1993), this theory posits that language determines thought. Over the years scholars have successfully refuted the more extreme versions of this theory (Lucy, 1992). Nevertheless most agree that language, and the previous dialogues that people have taken part in, although not the ultimate determiners, are in important ways associated with the way they think about things, including their world views and the values to which they subscribe (Corson, 1998). In this regard, language is also an important vehicle for voice. Walsh (1991) maintains that language enables people to fashion a voice, a 'speaking consciousness' that is rooted in their collective histories and lived experiences. Not all languages or discourses are able to do this equally for all people; some will enable, confirm and validate the collective interests and experiences of certain groups, while others will do just the opposite.

Corson (1993, 1995) also refers to the idea that particular patterns of words can carry with them certain powers. He acknowledges the power that great orators of the past and present seem to possess and the ways in which some individuals, including academics, can mystify others with the language that they use. He goes on to point out that the syntax of a language can offer a ready vehicle for capitalizing on power relationships and conveying a highly partisan reality. In this capacity, he maintains that the role of syntax in drawing causal relationships between participants and processes facilitates the designation of the relative status of social actors. It can do this by placing them in different roles in sentences. A writer, for example, can designate individuals as agents, experiencers or objects, or alternatively, as Corson maintains, delete them entirely by using a passive, a transformation or a substitution. In the same way, professional educators can deploy power and worth in the terms they use to describe their students. By assigning students labels such as 'gifted', 'underachiever', 'delinquent', 'disabled', educators are also, in a fairly obvious manner, employing language to differentially allocate worth.

As emphasized above, language is inextricably entangled in a wider social context, and depends on this social context for its power to assign worth. This means that this power does not reside in words alone. Rather anyone who uses language avails him- or herself of a form of power that is part of a social institution. Individuals and their linguistic practices will always bear the trace of these various institutions. This means the power, value and sense of particular linguistic expressions is as much a product of the (often unequal) relationships between and among groups and individuals as it is of the various arrangements of symbols and sounds. The power of language to assign or reflect worth will thus always depend upon who is speaking, when, where, why, and with whom. In this regard institutional frameworks routinely endow particular individuals (and not others) with the power to assign value. Teachers, for example, as illustrated above, are empowered by virtue of their positions in educational settings to assign value to student actions through their linguistic practices. On the other hand, their power to assign value in other institutional settings, such as factories, dentists' offices and courtrooms, will be decidedly less, even when they employ the same language or phrases.

Bourdieu (1991) employs an economic metaphor to capture the role of institutions in the attribution of linguistic worth. He prefers to see the institutional context in terms of markets. Bourdieu believes that linguistic expressions are always produced in particular markets. These markets, in turn, endow certain linguistic products with value. Some products, of course, are valued more highly than others. Those who are able to produce the right expressions will inherit this value and the power that accompanies it. Doing this, however, requires the possession of what Bourdieu refers to as capital. Those endowed with appropriate linguistic capital then will have an ability not only to create the right language forms, but also to understand the norms of language enough to produce the right expression at the right time for that particular linguistic market. Those who are able to do so are best placed to exploit this system of differences to their advantage and to profit from it. While some may enjoy persistent advantages over others in particular markets, the institutional rules that govern these markets are not fixed. All those who participate in them continually contest each others' forms of capital, working, as they do so, either to maintain the current, largely unstated rules or to change them.

Valuing English

Linguistic markets in Western countries usually value the English language over many others. These markets extend to most institutions, including schools. This value may be demonstrated in a number of ways. The mere fact that the language of instruction is English, as it is in Suburbia, will send a message to all about the respective values of other languages. The awareness of this reality inevitably engenders particular attitudes towards all such languages. Teachers can and do make incorrect assessments of students' abilities because they do not or will not always acknowledge that culturally different students often approach literary activities in ways inconsistent with school norms (Corson, 1998). Philips (1983), for example, notes that teachers saw the Native students in her study as disrespectful, misbehaved and uninvolved, rather than simply as users of different language norms. It is not surprising then that minority language users may learn to devalue their heritage language, while the majority English users may come to believe in the inferiority of various minority languages and the superiority of their own (Walsh, 1991). Those whose first language is not English may see their own language as a problem, while viewing English as a resource. Majority language users may adopt this same attitude, as is commonly the case at Suburbia.

Teachers at Suburbia acknowledge the value of the English language. Many take for granted their belief that a facility in the English language will assist students in their studies, and later on in life when they move into the world of work. As a consequence, some object to students speaking their first language if this is not English, not only in the classroom, but also in the halls. Tish's attitude typifies the approach of many teachers at Suburbia. She believes that English should be the language of the classroom, and that all students should speak it when they are in her room. She says, with reference to one group of Chinese students who tend to speak their native language much of the time, 'In the class we speak English and I feel that they should communicate to each other in English.' She has a number of reasons for wanting all students to speak English in class. The first is her concern for order in the classroom. She believes that whispering or talking in students' native tongues can create noise levels that are unacceptable. She says:

> The last week in December I left the class to go and get a review sheet for them and came back, and I didn't know anything was going on. And then at the end of the class some girls came over and said, 'As soon as you left it was like Hong Kong in here. They were just speaking so loud and we couldn't hear anything and they were all speaking in their language.' And I think it's frustrating for them. Maybe that's wrong of them but I don't think it is. I think you should speak the language which is the norm for that area so that everyone can understand. Because at the very first week of school I was thinking: 'I've never had a problem with noise in my class before.' And here there was a little whispering going on and I was thinking: 'Why is this bothering me so much? I've never noticed it.' And I mentioned it to my department head, and he said it's because they're whispering in Cantonese or whatever language, and it's such a high tone that it's distracting.

Another reason Tish has for insisting on spoken English in the classroom is that this will help the non-speakers, she believes, to learn English. Practicing and interacting in English is one of the ways to learn and improve students' use of the language. She rationalizes this as: 'The languages in Canada are English and French, and if you get hired [*for a job after graduation*] you're going to have to speak English or French.' Tish also feels that if students are to learn from other students then anything they say should be understood by everyone else in the class. She maintains, 'If they're going to say something, it should be for the benefit of everyone to understand, especially if they're bright.' Finally Tish believes that certain groups isolate themselves from the rest of the students when they speak their native tongue in the classroom. She feels that using English and separating such groups will help these students integrate with the other students.

The belief of many teachers at Suburbia that speaking English at the expense of their first language in classrooms and in the halls of the school will speed up their learning of English is not something that is supported by research, however. Corson and Lemay (1996), Cummins and Swain (1986), Cummins (1995) and McLaughlin (1986) all maintain that such a practice, particularly with respect to so-called minority groups, will neither enhance English language learning nor will it help students master the curriculum. Intensive exposure in school to the majority language, particularly in the early stages, accompanied by school neglect of the first language, may not only produce low achievement in the majority language, but also mark a decline in mother-tongue proficiency.

Conversely, developing proficiency in the first language, which may include conceptual information and discourse strategies, enhances second language development. What is also important, however, is that the school value the respective mother tongues. In this regard Cummins (1986) maintains that educational success for minority language speakers depends on the extent to which the language and culture of these students are incorporated into the curriculum.

While many students may see the English language as a resource, some may also see their mother tongue in the same light. Not only may mother tongues be important in a social sense; they may also assume a crucial role in students' intellectual development. This may explain, at least in part, the Chinese students' tendency as described above to speak frequently in their native tongue. Goldstein (1997) sheds light on this issue in her study of a group of Cantonese-speaking students in an English-speaking school. She maintains that Cantonese is important to these students in both a social and an academic sense. Students use Cantonese to gain access to friendship groups. Not only are friendship groups important to these students for the usual reasons such as camaraderie, security and so on, but they are also important for academic reasons, in two ways. First, friends are helpful in explaining math concepts to those who, partly because of language difficulties, cannot understand them. Second, friends are important in the role they can play in helping others advocate for marks in cases where students feel the marks they receive aren't appropriate. Ironically students see the use of English in certain contexts as a liability. These Cantonese-speaking students consider their fellow students 'rude' if they speak to them in English, a practice that will in turn jeopardize friendship opportunities.

Differentiating Forms of English

The structure of North American society provides the conditions for the English language to flourish. It does so through markets that value English over other languages. These markets make their presence felt in many schools, including Suburbia. Here parents, educators and students alike acknowledge the value of learning the English language and adopt strategies to facilitate it. But these markets generally favour more than just the English language *per se*. They also adjudicate the *way* in which it is spoken. Variations in syntax and accent are socially marked to the point that even a basic exchange between individuals may reveal these differences, and in so doing give evidence of their respective positions (Corson & Lemay, 1996; Corson, 1993). The result is that not only people trying to learn English who display an accent, but also those who employ various English language varieties, may find themselves at a disadvantage, in schools and elsewhere.

This concern with accent is part of a process in schools that Corson (1993) refers to as the 'ideology of correctness'. Corson points out that schools routinely hold up a standard language as a model of excellence against which all linguistic practices are measured. Speicher and McMahon (1992), on the other hand, trace this preoccupation to the centuries-old affiliation between good grammar and good morals that permeates our attitudes. They maintain that the propagation of such views has been so successful over the years that it persists even among those who routinely depart from this ideal. And while morality may not always enter the equation, those who employ deviant practices will inevitably be marked in unfavorable ways. A number of these individuals may come to accept this inferior status. The consequence is that many who don't speak English perfectly may be troubled by it, and take steps to get rid of these imperfections. Such is the case at Suburbia.

At Suburbia there are those who find themselves in the position of trying to eliminate any trace of 'accent' and others who resent the attitudes some have towards their form of English language. Juanita is one student who is very conscious of her accent. She came to Canada in Grade 3 and over time has acquired enough English language skills to get by both in school and out. Nevertheless her speech still bears the traces of what she believes to be an accent, and she wishes she could eliminate it. She says, 'Sometimes it [_her accent_] bothers me because I want to do better and improve myself in English.' She wants to acquire what she refers to as a 'normal' accent.

Shemina and her parents display a similar attitude. Their arrival in Canada was more recent – they have been in the country only six months. Shemina's parents believe that learning English is 'very important' both for their daughter and themselves. They want their daughter to be 'just like other children' and believe that in order to achieve this they will have to learn how to pronounce words properly and eliminate any traces of accent. Indeed they themselves work very hard on such pronunciation. Shemina's father says, 'We used to pronounce every word. "Tee" and "dee" is "duth" here. We would pronounce that word.' Shemina's mother is particularly concerned with speaking correctly. She has a job as receptionist and as such she feels it is vital for her to learn the language. She wants to eliminate feelings of inferiority that arise in situations where people refuse to talk to her. She maintains, 'I feel inferior because when I talk over the phone some say "I can't understand you. I don't want to talk to you. I want to talk to your supervisor."' Shemina's parents are also worried that she 'won't be able to express herself' well enough to master the technical terms in science. They are concerned because they want their daughter to be able to master the language of science so that she can some day become a doctor. They have considered paying for English language classes for themselves and their daughter, but hope that Shemina can learn the English that she needs at school.

Accents are routinely diminished by the school's language correctness phobia. Yet they can act as a positive source of capital. In a French language high school not too far from Suburbia, Ibrahim (1997) documents the importance that the French language teachers place on accent. He describes the surprise of these teachers when they first hear the Parisian accents of some of the students who have emigrated from East Africa. These teachers are surprised because they do not expect students from this part of the world to be able to speak in an accent that has a higher capital than their own Canadian accent. They also, as a matter of course, make a connection between this highly valued accent and what they believe to be the students' academic abilities. Teachers have questioned, after hearing students speak, whether the general stream is the appropriate one for them.

Accents are not the only aspect of linguistic practice to attract attention. Other variations from the standard ideal that revolve around vocabulary and syntax are also frequently diminished in schools. Those who deviate in their language practices from the standard or ideal variety are routinely marked. According to Toohey (1987) a standard variety is usually defined as that variety of language which is considered appropriate for communication over a wide area. It is commonly used in institutions, radio, television and newspaper, is usually taught in schools and has its norms of accuracy written down. Standard varieties, not by any coincidence, are almost always the mother tongue of the generally powerful educated middle class, who according to Corson (1998) attempt to cement their status in society by using their relatively powerful position to uphold these ideals. Because they have generally been successful in propagating the idea that the status of these ideals is due not to inequalities in power, but to their inherent goodness, many of those who do not or cannot meet these standards are more or less willing to accept the limited opportunities that await them.

The maintenance of the status of the standard language variety generally includes a simultaneous devaluation of non-standard varieties. As part of this process language practices which deviate from the ideal are sometimes wrongly described as 'poor' or 'sloppy', arising from speaker's laziness, lack of education or even perversity (Corson, 1993). The problem for students who do not speak the standard variety is that these negative attitudes affect teacher expectations (Edwards, 1989) and, in turn, student performance. Citing research by Giles and others, Corson (1993) contends that teachers' perceptions of children's non-standard speech produces negative expectations about children's personalities, social backgrounds and academic abilities. He also refers to studies in Great Britain which reveal that the standard variety is rated much more favorably than the non-standard varieties. These and other findings emphasize that it is the attitudes toward the non-standard varieties, rather than the actual differences, that are critical in these negative judgments. This is something I address below.

Negative evaluations of non-standard varieties occur routinely at Suburbia. For instance teachers take a negative view of a non-standard form of English spoken by a number of students from the West Indies which they refer to as *Patois*. Most teachers to whom we talked were aware of *Patois*, but some did not consider it a legitimate language. One teacher referred to it as a type of 'slang'. He said, 'The Black people [*from Trinidad*] speak their own language. Is it *Patois* or something? It's a kind of a slang that they use ... It's almost like it's kind of not recognized in the same class as the English you know.' Another teacher maintains that *Patois* is 'backward-sounding'.

Others disapprove of *Patois* for reasons other than its sub-standard status. Some teachers do not like it when students speak *Patois* because they believe that it has the potential to undermine their control. Ashley, a teacher, maintains that the speaking of a language (which turns out to be *Patois*) with which she is not familiar disrupts the classroom. She says, with reference to one of her Caribbean students, 'He's sort of loud and I guess it's just the language. And he is actually speaking a different language than some. I don't know whether he's speaking some Pakistan language.' Caribbean students may resort to *Patois* in confrontational situations and say things that teachers may not understand. Students may also use it, some claim, to talk about other students 'behind their backs'. One staff member clearly recognizes the loss of control which some teachers may feel in such situations. She says:

> When students are speaking *Patois* to someone who does not understand it, it's totally foreign. For instance, if I'm speaking it to you, you may interpret it as losing control. You don't know what's going on, you don't want them to speak it, 'cos you don't have that control. So I see it as that, from a teacher's perspective, 'If they're speaking that language

I don't know what they're saying, they could be saying, swearing at me, whatever.' So it's a loss of control, power, that kind of stuff. And that's when their [teachers'] back gets up.

Speakers of *Patois*, on the other hand, who are virtually all students, are generally upset with others' attitudes toward their language. They don't like the negative depiction of it, and they resent instances where they are told not to speak it. John, for example, says 'It is a proper language, but I think that the whole system throws a negative connotation on *Patois*.' Joan generally accepts not being able to speak it in the classroom, but becomes very upset when told not to speak *Patois* when she is not in the classroom. She says:

I was speaking *Patois*, myself and a friend. We were speaking *Patois* in the hall and [a teacher] came and told us we shouldn't be speaking. Who is she to tell me when and where I can't speak my language? I'm not in the classroom. When I'm in the classroom I know that I don't speak *Patois*.

At Suburbia, as elsewhere (see, for example, Solomon, 1992) the academic market does not value *Patois*. As a consequence, those who value standard English, as many teachers do, look upon *Patois* not as a resource but as a liability and commonly discourage speakers from using it. While there are no data to point to a relationship between these negative attributions, school success and identity, it is reasonable to assume that here, as in other similar settings, students do not benefit from this attitude. For example, students who speak non-standard varieties of English, including *Patois*, are routinely placed, often inappropriately, in language development or lower-streamed classes (Corson & Lemay, 1996; Anthony, 1998). There is, however, a market where *Patois* is valued. It is obvious that it is a favored form of currency within those peer groups who speak *Patois* here at Suburbia and elsewhere in the region. Both Solomon (1992) and Ibrahim (1997) maintain that various forms of 'Black English' and *Patois* constitute an important part of the identities of members of groups, and are consequently important resources for the speakers in contexts that involve group members.

One of the principal reasons why teachers at Suburbia and elsewhere consistently devalue non-standard English varieties, including *Patois*, is that they accept the idea that these varieties are inherently inferior to the standard variety. This may be the case of a number of reasons. One of these has to do with the fact that people who live in monolingual societies do not always realize the presence of wide variations in language use, attitudes and behavior. They are also probably not aware that everyone makes 'errors' in language use at some time. But as Corson (1993) maintains, many of these errors are not errors at all, but rather varieties of language that preserve their features as regularly as any language. Furthermore, there is no evidence to suggest that any one variety is inherently superior to the next. All languages and varieties are equally adept at communicating necessary information between speakers (Speicher & McMahon, 1992). Most linguists agree that standard varieties are no more linguistically pleasing, accurate, true to tradition or in any sense structurally superior to any other variety. Each is as rule-governed, creative, logica[1] and capable of elegance as the next (Toohey, 1987). All language users develop various forms, styles and language functions that are necessary for them to live their lives in the circumstances in which they find themselves; those linguistic forms that cease to be useful are simply discarded. Thus, whatever disadvantage children experience in schools because of their use of one variety or another, it is not due to the disfunctionality of the language variety, but to the attitudes towards the use of that style or form of language use.

This functional view of language finds support in a number of areas in society, including the courts. Indeed the legal system in the United States has ruled in favor of this view of languages. In Ann Arbor, Michigan parents of African American children brought an action against a school for failing their children (Labov, 1982). The lawsuit alleged that the school had failed the children because it had misidentified them as 'educationally disabled'. The school based this decision, the parents claimed, on the basis of the children's use of an African American non-standard variety of language. After hearing arguments, the court ruled in favour of the parents, maintaining that the children's use of this variety was not in itself an obstacle to their success. It further ruled that teachers' mistaken stereotypical beliefs about this form of language influenced their expectations of students' academic abilities and led them to misjudge the students' potential. These lowered expectations eventually caused these students to fail. In the end the children were deemed deficient in their academic pursuits because their language variety was mistakenly judged to be deficient (Corson, 1993). The courts did not stop at these observations, however. In an attempt to rectify this injustice it also ordered teachers of culturally different children to take some in-service training in sociolinguistics.

Understanding *Patois*

One of the main reasons that teachers look poorly upon *Patois* at Suburbia and elsewhere is that they do not see it as a legitimate language.

Rather many of these people believe that the students who use it are simply using a form of slang or 'broken English' that breaks what they feel to be the proper rules of English language use. This view is partly due to their igno-rance of these particular linguistic practices. What they do not realize is that although *Patois* make take on a number of forms, it displays enduring patterns that have evolved over the space of many years. These language forms, just like any other language variety, have important parts to play in the lives of the people who employ them. Indeed they serve a number of vital communicative and social roles.

Most students who use *Patois* at Suburbia employ Jamaican forms. This is because many of them have either emigrated from Jamaica or have parents who were born there. There are, of course, many similarities with other West Indian forms of *Patois*, a point on which I elaborate below. A form of English Creole, it emerged as a result of European colonial ventures and the contact situations between Europeans and Africans that resulted from these ventures. The development of *Patois* as a form of English came about as West Africans who were subjected to slavery sought to employ a mode of communication that would best serve their very demanding needs at the time. It has evolved since the time of the slave-traders in response to the changing circumstances of the people who have used this variety of English.

Alleyne (1976) contends that Caribbean forms of speech date back to the 15th century, when Europeans were first beginning their expansionist movements. A 'pidgin' form of language was the first mode of communica-tion of this sort to emerge as Portuguese and West African trading partners sought a way of communicating with one another. This pidgin was a simplified form of language. It was used only as a second language by the respective parties for the limited purposes of basic trading or bartering. Because the partners did not require an elaborate system of communica-tion they were able to bridge the gap between their two languages in a way that suited these simple needs by stripping the Portuguese language of its inflection system and other forms of syntax, some of its sounds and much of its vocabulary, while at the same time adding various sound, phrase and sentence patterns of the West Africans. Alleyne (1976) further maintains that when other Europeans entered the slave trade on the west coast of Africa, they began to massively substitute Dutch, French and English terms.

As the circumstances of the contact situation changed over the years new forms of language emerged and developed. Africans of varying linguistic and geographical origins initiated changes in language to cope with varying communicative needs within their own numbers and with Europeans. For example, the fact that many enslaved Africans found themselves face to face with fellow Africans who didn't speak their language forced them to draw on forms of language that would help them communicate with each other. Often forbidden to speak their native languages, many reverted to pidginized forms of the respective European languages. As slavery emerged, then became institutionalized and then outlawed, what started out as elementary forms of pidgin, unstable, structurally restricted, non-native forms of communications between peoples of different cultures, developed into linguistic practices with expanded roles, functions and structures. With increased stability these eventually came to represent the native language of the descendants of those originally involved in the contact situation (Roberts, 1988). Referred to as 'Creoles', these forms of language have developed in a manner typical of most languages (Alleyne, 1976) – from an initial period of instability, to one of greater institutionalization, and finally to a period of local dispersal. As the latter stage took root, the different situations in which the respective Creoles were spoken provided circumstances that nurtured a wide variety of these forms of language throughout the West Indies. To this day, in the West Indies and in other regions of the world where they are spoken, including Canada, West Indian Creoles continue to evolve in concert with the social circumstances in which they are used.

The West Indies have many varieties of English. These forms vary from territory to territory as the result of different historical influences. The variety spoken also depends on who is communicating as well as on the nature and purpose of the communication. Alleyne (1976) attempts to capture this diversity in terms of a continuum that ranges from standard English at one end to Creole at the other. At the latter end there are many West African influences, while at the standard English end there are none. In reality though, Alleyne (1976) alleges, many people speak an intermediate variety as they include or drop any one element of the linguistic register. He also contends that certain groups of people tend to use more forms of one variety than of another. In Jamaica, for example, he says middle-class intellectuals and professionals tend to speak more of the standard English variety, while rural people use more elements of Creole.

The type of language variety will also vary from region to region in the West Indies. This diversity is due to the differences in the respective historical and current circumstances. On one level, colonizers and their successors of different language groups had different kinds of involvement in settlement and development patterns. For example, an open-door policy in Trinidad allowed for the immigration of thousands of French and French Creole-speaking refugees, so that by the middle of the 19th century Trinidad was linguistically and culturally more French than English (Roberts, 1988). But even two different areas under the same influence can display clear differences in language development. The contrast between Jamaica and Barbados provides a good illustration. Even though Jamaica was under British colonial rule and exposed to the English language for over 300 years, the importation of more Africans, particularly during the slave period, and the greater degree of physical remoteness fostered more varieties of language, and more varieties that are more distant from standard English (Roberts, 1988). This stands in contrast to Barbados, where language development proceeded in a more uniform manner.

In order to illustrate the respective influences of the various languages on Creole, I will use the Jamaican example as outlined by Cassidy (1961). In terms of vocabulary, English is by far the largest contributor to Jamaican Creole. At least 90% of words have an English origin. A number of these terms and words, however, exist in altered forms. The smallest contributor is what was once the North American Native language of the area. Long since extinct, its influence is indirect, coming through Spanish and Portuguese, and is limited to names for plants, animals and foods. There are also small French and Oriental influences. The former contribute names for plants and foods as well as some familial terms, while the latter has lent labels for foods and domestic items. Spanish and Portuguese languages have contributed a little more than the previous three sources largely because they were the channels through which much of the lore of the New World flowed to the English. Most of these words are associated with weather, topography, agriculture, slavery, foods, cookery, plants, animals, money and trade. Many of these words and terms have since become obsolete.

The biggest non-English influence on Jamaican Creole is African. Cassidy (1961) estimates that African and quasi-African terms number around 400. Though they are associated with more spheres of life, most terms are affiliated with plants, food, animal life, utensils, music, dancing, superstition, people and their conditions, and greetings and exclamations. The biggest influence of African languages is not necessarily in the area of vocabulary but in pronunciation and grammar. Perhaps the single greatest difference in the former is not in single sounds but their combinations with English sounds. The same is true for grammatical structures. Indeed the grammar of Jamaican Creole reflects a compromise between African and English structures.

Like many other non-standard varieties, West Indian varieties of Creole have historically been poorly regarded. Alleyne (1976:57) says that they have invariably been described as 'inadequate, underdeveloped, illogical, and deprived'. Those who speak the language are 'said to receive little verbal stimulation in their childhood, to hear little well-formed language, and are as a result impoverished in verbal expression', and as a consequence 'cannot speak complete sentences, cannot form concepts or convey logical thought'. Roberts (1988) traces this devaluation back to the time of the slave-traders. He maintains that the colonial slave society successfully circulated the idea that Africans had no language. By the 17th century, when the present-day features of Creole became entrenched, it was easy for Whites, who were always eager to embrace justifications of their inhumane treatment of fellow human beings, to consider it to be 'broken' or 'corrupt' English and evidence of the supposed mental limitations of the slave population. The historian Edward Long (in Craig, 1976:96) for example, writing in 1774, typified the common (White) opinion of the time by asserting that 'the language of the Creoles is bad English larded with the Guinea variety.' This view provided the basis for what was to follow when slavery was eventually outlawed and the colonial powers withdrew. While there have been changes in positive directions in recent years, many continue to see these language varieties not as tongues as functional and viable as any other, but simply as a form of 'broken English' or 'bad English'.

As illustrated above, this negative view of West Indian Creole or *Patois* continues to find its way into the thoughts and practices of teachers who have little knowledge of its history or of its value. This is not necessarily the case for those students at Suburbia and at other schools who use it (Solomon, 1992). Many recognize its value and put it to good use in social situations.

Conclusion

Students and educators at Suburbia and elsewhere in multilingual situations continually struggle over what languages varieties are to be spoken in school. Many students choose to speak their home languages or varieties, while many educators prefer students to speak standard English within the confines of the school. These preferences are the result of the way in which the respective languages are valued. This value system reflects not a language's inherent ability to represent life, but rather a particular configuration of power relations that favour the preferred language. In other words, the reason why some languages are favored over others is because the groups who historically spoke these preferred languages had, and continue to have, more power than those who did not and do not. This is why the English language continues to be the language of choice in North America and why many educators, parents and some students believe that students need to learn English to succeed, not only in school but in life after school. A number of them also believe, erroneously, that the best way to learn English is to speak it in as many situations as possible, often in place of the student's heritage language.

Of course, as was evident above, not all students acknowledge the value of speaking English all the time. A number of them recognize not just the personal and social benefits of speaking their home languages and varieties, but also the possible academic advantages. Because they hold these beliefs, they commonly use their home languages and varieties around the school. This practice, however, runs counter to the beliefs of those educators who feel that students need to speak the standard variety of the English language in as many situations as possible. The result is that educators and students sometimes clash over language practices. One area of conflict occurs with regularity over the use of *Patois* in the classrooms and the halls. Some educators do not see *Patois* as a legitimate language, while others see it as a threat to their authority. As a consequence, these educators attempt to actively curb the use of it, both in their classrooms and in the hallways. Those students who use it, on the other hand, see it as an integral part of their heritage and take issue with educators who attempt to discourage them from using it. What many educators do not realize, though, is that *Patois* displays enduring linguistic patterns that have evolved over the space of many years. These language forms, just like any other language variety, have important parts to play in the lives of the people who employ them. And like any other language, they serve a number of vital communicative and social roles.

Chapter 9

Struggling for Discursive Equality: Contesting Discourses and Finding Voices

The process of representation plays a key role in shaping the way students, parents and educators perceive and react to the differences that they commonly associate with race/ethnicity in schools. Its effects are perhaps more acute today because of recent changes in contemporary social conditions. Among these are the changes in immigration patterns, the proliferation of images and a skepticism toward received information. The shift in immigration patterns is very evident in Suburbia Secondary School, where students identify with over 60 different heritages. Of all the differences in and around the school environment, it is those that both students and educators attribute to race/ethnicity that they notice and react to, far more strongly than they do to the many other kinds of difference. The ways in which they perceive these questions of race/ethnicity are in turn affected by the multitude of images they encounter in the mass media. Students, educators and many in the Western world cannot help but be influenced by the ways in which the print and electronic media portray race/ethnicity. Finally, those in the school community, like most others, may find ample cause to doubt the information they encounter in the media and elsewhere, including what were, at one time, time-honored 'truths'. This latter condition provides opportunities for those wishing to challenge the traditionally dominant views and so-called 'truths' that have consistently disadvantaged some groups.

This book employs the concept of discourse to explore the process of representation. It does so because discourse provides more conceptual and political opportunities than the other alternatives for investigating, and if need be, challenging the representations of race/ethnicity that educators and students employ and act on in schools. One reason for employing this lens is that it revolves around the phenomenon of meaning. It assumes that representations always mean something to people, that is, that men, women and children must always make sense of the signs and symbols that stand in for the things that people intend to represent. Unlike some options, however, the discursive option that I employ here does not assume that meaning resides or inheres in the image or text, or has its source in the heads of individuals. Rather it emerges in the dialogue between people and the signs or symbols they apprehend. This does not mean that representation is an individual thing; the process of representation is fundamentally a social process with a history. In this regard, people must rely on the available and socially-generated sense-making frameworks or discourses to be able to understand their experiences. Indeed they will not be able make sense of their experiences without first placing them within the framework of words, logic, perspectives, metaphors and so on that are associated with some discourse.

Discourse is a form of power. It filters in crucial ways the manner in which people can make sense of their lives. But discourse is not just a technique of power. It is also the terrain on which individuals and groups struggle over meaning. Men, women and children perpetually contest the meanings that they attribute to the signs and symbols that they construct and apprehend. These contests over meaning occur regularly in schools. They are perhaps more obvious in situations where meanings of race/ethnicity are at stake in highly diverse settings like Suburbia Secondary School. Such contests, however, are generally not equal. Some groups – most often those of Anglo/European heritage – generally have the advantage over others when it comes to constructing and circulating meanings that prevail. This dominance is the result of battles over meanings won and lost that transcend this and other school settings and which extend back at least five centuries. Over this time groups of Europeans, and later those of European heritage, worked to protect their privileged positions by using their power to shape and to circulate ways of making sense of race/ethnicity that preserved the advantages they themselves enjoyed, and continue to enjoy. Even today, these same groups continue to exert their influence over discourses by controlling the sources of their production and the technologies that circulate them. For example, those who run the electronic media, like those who own and manage the publishing houses that produce everything from popular magazines, newspapers and school textbooks, are generally of European background, and consequently tend to filter what they produce through perspectives that favor the already dominant groups of Anglo/European heritage. The manner in which they generally do this is to favor discourses that present the latter group in a positive light while simultaneously portraying others negatively.

These struggles and their subsequent outcomes play an important role in the distribution of advantages among students in schools. At Suburbia explicitly negative and obviously racist representations and the practices that flow from them surface from time to time, and when they do so, work against those at whom they are directed. Because they are easily recognized and generally not sanctioned by most students and educators, they stand a reasonable chance of being successfully challenged. The more subtle forms of racist representations and practice, on the other hand, are more likely to go unrecognized and thus uncontested. So-called stereotypical representations, like the notion that Black students are simultaneously gifted physically and handicapped intellectually, surface commonly at Suburbia and influence how both educators and students perceive and relate to these students. These and other discourses that provide the framework for racist readings show up in curriculum resources in addition to other sources like the mass media. Struggles over representations also occur over the ways in which students choose to represent themselves. In their quests 'to be somebody' in an often uncaring, anonymous and debilitating world, students will often contest school rules to forge an identity that sets them apart from some students while simultaneously bringing them together with others. Students can also be placed at a disadvantage by virtue of the way in which they choose to represent themselves. Educators at Suburbia and elsewhere commonly assign worth to students on the basis of the particular language variety they use and the skill with which they are able to employ it. In this case standard English is the preferred medium of communication and those who are not able to demonstrate a certain level of skill in their use of it will not enjoy the same kinds of opportunities as more proficient others.

The struggle over meaning in the classroom at Suburbia is not unique. These kinds of action occur in other schools and in other educational communities. But they involve more than simply battles over signs. Rather, when teachers, students, administrators, trustees, parents and others take action to promote their preferred readings and meanings, they are also taking part in a wider struggle over forms of life, over how people will live their lives (Simon, 1992). What happens in schools in this regard is part of wider struggles that extend far beyond their boundaries. But this doesn't mean that what happens in and around schools cannot in turn influence what happens in other sectors of life. In fact, school communities can be important sites for contesting and eventually changing more universal discourses that work only in the interests of some groups. Challenges of this sort can, in the long run, improve the life situations of marginalized groups. In this regard, those interested in these issues have much to learn from the ways in which processes of representation are implicated in the unequal distribution of advantages and opportunities, both in school and out.

The analysis so far has left us with two important lessons. The first is that the meanings associated with representational processes are human constructions. It is we who are responsible for the sense that we attribute to the signs and symbols that populate the social world. But because we have been the ones to shape these meanings, we can also be the ones to change them. The second consequence of this approach to representation revolves around issues of power versus issues of accuracy. What should be clear by now is that generating representations that work for marginalized groups will involve marshaling practices of power rather than focusing on efforts to generate illusory notions of accuracy. Improving the opportunities of students of marginalized groups requires that we find ways to contest debilitating representations and replace them with those that work in their interests through whatever means they can, and within limits, of course. Holding out for accurate images of marginalized groups will accomplish little, for the sense that people make of these groups is in fundamental ways shaped by the already existing discourses into which people place their experiences of them. Thus it is to these discourses that we must turn; we need to find ways to shape discourses that allow the voices of the marginalized to be heard.

Shohat and Stam (1994) point out that voice is not exactly congruent with discourse. While discourse is institutional, transpersonal and unauthored, voice is personalized. It has authorial accent and intonation, carrying with it the stamp of particular individuals and of groups. Voice resonates with the collective memories, feelings, struggles, experiences and subjectivities unique to particular groups of people as they act in and on the world about them. Bakhtin (1981) prefers to think of this as a 'speaking consciousness'. Individuals or groups do not speak in or with just one voice, however. Rather a voice is always a composite of many often different and sometimes contradictory voices, which in turn both consti- tutes and relays a specific interplay of discourses. Not all discourses are congruent with particular voices, either. Nor are all discourses equally equipped to permit men, women and children to articulate their own voice or voices. For example, racist and colonial discourses generally did not allow the voices of the colonized to be heard. It would have been difficult, if not impossible, for Africans or Native North Americans to confirm or to convey the pain they felt at the hands of Europeans through discourses that sought to justify these same practices. This does not mean that these experiences could not be understood through these sorts of templates, but that they would simply serve to disconfirm this aspect of their experience. Furthermore, whatever voices did emerge would inevitably work not in the interests of these colonized people but rather in the interests of the colonizers.

In what follows I provide a number of suggestions that are designed to help marginalized groups have their voices heard. In order to be heard, students must be able to voice their urges in ways that connect with local and group discourses. To assist in this process, schools need to provide conditions that permit all voices to search for skills and concepts to reconstruct their cultural principles in their own terms (O'Connor, 1989). This quest requires that schools help students and educators recognize, understand, and challenge debilitating and racist discourses and eventually replace them with discourses that allow these voices to be heard. In all of this I acknowledge that doing something about debilitating racial/ethnic discourses that show up in schools requires that those wishing to replace them must target areas that transcend the school. The intent of these strategies is to provide those traditionally marginalized by practices of representation with the same kinds of opportunity both in school and out that more favored others currently enjoy. I target four general areas. The first one is stereotypical discourses. As a way to help educators and students understand and challenge them, I recommend that they look critically at the media. This section overlaps with the next one, curriculum resources, since stereotypical discourses show up in these sources. Here I suggest a number of strategies for dealing with these resources. Next, I address issues associated with identity, and present a number of ways for approaching language issues. Finally I touch on the relationship of knowledge and discourse.

Targeting Stereotypical Discourses

Ensuring that all students enjoy the same kinds of advantage in school and out requires that we attend to some of the more subtle ways in which such advantages are unequally distributed. As I have indicated above, one of the less apparent ways in which this occurs is through the manner in which certain groups are portrayed. Persistent representations of groups can have a powerful effect on how others perceive and interact with them, as well as on how group members see themselves. For example, educators who buy into the widely circulating discourses of Blacks that depict them as naturally unintelligent and violent people are likely to expect most Black students to conform to this portrayal, and this view will inevitably shape the way in which they react to these students. Not surprisingly, many Black students respond in kind to what can often be demeaning treatment. An initial step in doing something about this one-sided process of representation is to see it in terms of competing discourses rather than as simply the projection of inaccurate images. Seen in this way, a resolution to the problem of negative portrayals lies, not in ensuring that representations reflect the way groups 'really are', but in working to allow normally excluded discourses and voices to emerge and compete on equal footing with previously dominant discourses. Because discourse is not merely a technique for oppression, but also a terrain of struggle, those interested in improving the position of marginal people by focusing their efforts on discourse have reason for hope.

A good place to start in this regard is to help students understand the ways in which they and others are implicated in the circulation of mediated discourses, how they might resist oppressive discourses, and how they might join with others to ensure that marginal discourses and voices have a chance to compete in the mainstream media. As Corson (1998:184) suggests, media education is necessarily always a critical enterprise.

Media education is about technology, but is does not stop at the 'how it works' and 'how to operate it' stage. It asks students to think critically about technology, about its cultural and sociological significance, as well as its place in business and science. Media education asks students to look critically at information, regardless of its source or medium. It asks them to see the media as industries whose owners have agendas of their own. It helps students to distinguish between commercial messages, casual communication, and the messages of propagandists. Above all it suggests students recognize that our commonsense judgments are usually filled with prejudice and error, which colors everything that we come in contact with.

A critical approach to discourse and media literacy requires first and foremost that student experience be taken seriously (Sholle & Denske, 1995). Teachers must give students the opportunity to speak from their own experience about such matters as their commitments, their styles of consumption and their investments in the media. This doesn't mean that this experience necessarily be valorized, but that students take the time to critically interrogate it. It is important that they have the chance to reflect on how they invest affectively in the various discourses to which they are exposed and how this investment in implicated in their self-formation. Sholle and Denske (1995) believe that students will be in a better position to understand the complex ways in which they become who they are if they can answer the question, 'Who am I when I see this?' when they watch television, for example. It is also important for them to understand how the sense-making schemes they employ in these various situations both silence and disempower themselves and others.

Students must additionally have the opportunity to develop skills that will allow them to resist the often taken-for-granted dominant discourses embedded in media images and to recognize and extract other more muffled voices. Being able to see through these prevailing discourses, however, requires a certain cultural or political preparation that primes the spectator to read critically. Indeed, disempowered communities can decode dominant programming through a resistant reading only to the extent that their collective life and historical memory have provided an alternative framework of understanding. Shohat and Stam (1994), for example, point out that in the case of the Persian Gulf war, a majority of Americans were unable to interpret the events in ways other than the American administration wished, since they did not have at their disposal any alternative grid to help them out. Few understood much about the legacy of colonialism and its unique complexities in the Middle East. Bringing out the muffled voices in media discourses/images requires then that students be provided with an alternate framework or grid that will give them the opportunity to make sense of what they see, hear or read from a perspective which is different from the prevailing one. One of the many ways in which this might be done is to expose students to the history, including the motivations and interests, behind the development of various discourses.

Making visible dominant, yet often invisible, taken-for-granted discourses behind media portrayals, and recognizing and bringing out other marginalized voices is not always a straightforward matter, particularly for those who have investments in the former.[1] One way to help students in this process is through a technique Shohat and Stam (1994) refer to as 'jujitsu'. By this they mean reversing or turning ordinary ways of looking at things on their head. This often involves using common discourses against domination by redirecting them at the privileged rather than at the marginalized. *Babakiueria* (1988), a film that reverses the position of Europeans and Aborigines in Australia, exemplifies the jujitsu technique. In this case it is the Aborigines who, in colonizing the 'indigenous' White Europeans, employ the various colonial discourses and policies. The effect of the film is to 'make strange' both the cultural practices of European Australians (welfare, sports, recreation, work) and the discourses employed to make sense of them (social science, progress and so forth).

Shohat and Stam (1994) also see a role for a pedagogic jujitsu in the class-room. Here students and teachers would take an active role in snapping Eurocentric texts out of their original context by rereading and rewriting them. They would have the opportunity to 'decanonize' the classics by rescripting them according to an alternative perspective. For example, students might imagine a film from the perspective of a minor subaltern character. Shohat and Stam's (1994) goal here is to turn spectators into 'spect-actors', spectators who retain the power to think and act. Among other things, a pedagogy of this sort could both empower minorities and build on privileged students' minimal experience of 'otherization' to help them imagine alternative subject positions and divergent social desires.

Some teachers at Suburbia already make an effort to critically interro-gate the media in these ways. Doris, for example, is one teacher who takes the time to address the media, and in doing so, looks to equip her students with decoding skills. She usually does this as part of her coverage of current event issues. On one occasion she concentrated on how the media presented the facts related to a recent shooting in the city where the alleged Black perpetrators shot and killed a White woman. She says:

> We talked about the ... murder and how the media really focused on showing those pictures. And another article, an editorial, that showed that a Chinese-Canadian woman had been murdered two years ago. It never made the papers. And so the issue, I felt, was that, well, this hap-pened in a part of [the city] that – you know, it's ethnic, it's Chinese killing each other, so who cares? But with the [murder] it was in the ter-ritory of the people who have power; they go to that restaurant. And so it became to be very much a White–Black issue.

Addressing issues of this sort is not always easy for teachers like Doris to take up in class. Often there is resistance on the part of students. Doris says 'It's difficult to discuss these issues in class because there's really some very inbred prejudices that [surface]. When I try to discuss something like the stereotype in our society of the young Black male, I was just horrified with the barrage of what I got back from some people in the class.' She finds it difficult to get a discussion going at times, and doesn't want to be placed in the position of personally having to take a stance against the views of cer-tain students. She says that next time she tries to bring up similar issues she is going to break the class into small groups. Despite these difficulties, Do-ris says that some of the students have privately expressed their gratitude to her for bringing up things that are important to them.

Developing individual decoding skills constitutes just one step in what must be a much larger strategy geared toward assisting marginal discourses and voices to gain a more secure footing. A possible next move is for students (and teachers) to begin to look for ways to circulate alternate discourses. They can do this themselves by looking for opportunities to introduce different ways of understanding various events and issues in a range of contexts. Talking informally with friends or with others in more formal contexts both in- and outside of the school is one way of expanding the range of such discourses. Students can also join with others to pressure media outlets to include alternative voices in their communications, while at the same time encouraging them to avoid debilitating portrayals of marginal groups and issues. As consumers we all have a certain amount of power at our disposal, and if protesters employ the right strategies consumer-driven media will at least give them a listen. Finally, students can be encouraged to find ways to help media outlets which sponsor alternate perspectives to establish and maintain themselves. While it is becoming increasingly difficult for minority interests to own and operate large-scale communications networks, the move towards catering to an increasingly fragmented market, the growing importance of content and of knowing the audience, does provide some hope for new media that favor racially and culturally diverse groups (Wilson & Gutierez, 1995).

Targeting Curriculum Resources

Curriculum resources, as illustrated above, often contain debilitating racialized discourses that can give rise to racist readings. There is more than one way to approach the task of resisting and replacing such discourses, however. Indeed, the ways in which members of the school community may prefer to go about this task may vary. The students of African heritage at Suburbia, as we have seen, took what they believed to be the best route. In order to ensure that a particular kind of making sense of people of African heritage did not prevail in the classroom, they sought to prevent a book that lent itself to such a reading from entering class. This strategy is one that is recommended by some scholars, and adopted by some state institutions and school districts (Klein, 1985; Government of Ontario, 1980; North York Board of Education, 1985). Those who endorse this approach usually provide educators and institutions with criteria designed to assist them in choosing appropriate curriculum materials. Others believe that excluding materials that may lend themselves to oppressive interpretations in the classroom is not the best way to contest more universal racist discourses (Simon, 1992). These individuals believe instead that providing both teachers and students with opportunities for recognizing, understanding, and challenging certain readings is a better strategy for overturning the discourses associated with these readings.

Those who favor the screening of materials generally provide a list of criteria that they believe all materials should meet. They recommend these sorts of resources because they believe they have the capacity to produce their preferred outcomes. The Government of Ontario (1980), the North York Board of Education (1985) and Klein (1985), for example, all foresee that texts that conform to their criteria will engender in all students a feeling of self-worth, provide them with the opportunity to develop an awareness, understanding and appreciation of any and all different cultural groups, and the capacity to recognize the universality of human experience. They also believe that all students should be able to use these resources. Accordingly, texts capable of producing these conditions would contain accurate and up-dated information, include a balanced treatment of all groups, show a wide variety of people in a wide variety of roles, acknowledge the contributions of all groups, avoid negative and stereotypical portrayals, and provide strong role models for all groups. Occasionally agencies will supply advice for editors. In this regard the Government of Ontario (1980) encourages editors to avoid racial and cultural bias in the use of names, avoid using external characteristics to describe groups, recognize dialects as legitimate languages, and not to employ value-laden terms that present stereotyped, biased or unjustified judgments of various groups.

Not all agree that blocking certain materials from entering the classroom is the best strategy. While Klein (1985) does suggest criteria for identifying racist or inappropriate texts, she also believes that most energy should be directed toward readers and not reading materials. For one thing, the elimination of all books that contain elements of racism or 'bias' is simply not realistic. It is seldom possible to replace all inappropriate books, whether they are part of the curriculum or are just available on the shelves of the school library. Klein (1985) goes on to acknowledge that biased books can be used to a good purpose. Simon (1992) also favors an approach that admits what some might consider inappropriate material into the classroom. He contends that the withdrawal of texts may not be the best way to contest discourses that anchor racist practice. For Simon, interrogating such texts in the classroom may be the better way to contest and overturn the more universal racist discourse and practices that regulate classroom readings.

Allowing racist or biased material into the classroom carries with it considerable risk, however. In particular, it places a substantial burden on the teacher. Not only must teachers be able to recognize potential oppressive discourses, they must also be prepared to employ appropriate strategies that allow students to generate alternate readings that challenge these ways of making sense. If teachers are not able or willing to engage in these sorts of practices then they will be acting as agents for such discourses. Not all scholars believe that teachers are up to such a task. Walker (1993), for example, believes that it is unrealistic to expect most teachers to use, say, poorly constructed films of Africa critically, since these teachers are themselves products of the same educational culture that produced the films, and participants in the very media culture that generates demeaning images of Africa. She also maintains that most teachers believe, erroneously, that this kind of material has already gone through a vigorous screening process. If racist or biased material is to be let into the classroom, then the onus will be on teachers to recognize such material and to help their students challenge it.

Teachers thus have a formidable task ahead of them in educational institutions that do not strictly limit the kind of material that enters the classroom. It is up to them to ensure that oppressive discourse does not prevail in these situations. The first thing that is required of teachers in this regard is that they be *willing* to contest racist (or classist, or sexist, or homophobic) readings. Not all teachers may agree with equity endeavors of this sort, however, and hence may either opt out or engage in resistance activities (Robertson, 1998). Such a commitment also requires time and effort on the part of teachers, something that not all may be prepared to devote to such a project. For those who do support such an approach there are a number of things they can do that will help them and their students contest oppressive discourses. Among other abilities, teachers and students need to be able to: recognize oppressive discourses when they see them; understand their genesis and production; supplant them with alternate ways of making sense; and take action to circulate these alternate discourses, both in the school and outside it.

The first task, to be able to recognize oppressive discourses, is not always as easy as it sounds, particularly for teachers and students of the dominant culture who may take such things for granted. It is comparatively easy for these people to overlook such discourses because they are frequently the benefactors of such ways of making sense, and as a consequence, are not usually portrayed in unflattering or demeaning ways that would attract their attention. This is not always the case for those people who belong to the marginalized groups who are often portrayed in unflattering ways. It is therefore often easier for the marginalized to recognize ethnocentric and racist discourse. This was the case at Suburbia where the students of African heritage were much more sensitive to the racist portrayals in *To Kill a Mockingbird* than were the teachers and other students. Because teachers and students have much to learn from students of marginalized groups, they would be wise to give them plenty of space to voice their opinions on these matters. Klein (1985) feels that teachers should encourage these young people to trust their own judgments in these matters. She cites the case of a seven-year-old Black girl who was able to identify at a glance what she knew from experience to be 'distorted or untrue' in a text.

Teachers also need to be able to understand oppressive discourses and help students to understand them. To do so they will have to acknowledge and explore issues surrounding the presentation, distribution, evaluation and definition of what counts as knowledge in society (Klein, 1985). Such an understanding also requires that teachers and students delve into issues of race and racist discourse and practice, including the historical roots of racism and its connection to authoritative definitions of knowledge. An historical perspective will help students understand, among other things, why African Americans in the southern United States in the 1930s were treated in the manner described in *To Kill a Mockingbird*, and why these descriptions found their way into a novel which is commonly used in high schools in the Western world. Explorations of this sort can help students to understand their place in the world. Simon (1992) contends that a study of an individual's responses to curricular materials can help him or her to understand their position in relation to the various available ways of making sense of society.

Many scholars and institutions provide lists of questions that are designed to stimulate critical exploration and hence critical understanding of curricular materials and the discourses associated with them. Walker (1993:18), for example, provides a useful set of questions for stimulating a critical viewing of films on Africa and the African Diaspora. They are as follows:

- Did you learn about how the people in question see themselves and what they themselves think about their lifestyle?

- How is the information conveyed?

- What do you think was the film-makers' intent in making the film?

- How do the film-makers portray the people in question – respectfully or not? Do you think the people in question would feel that their way of life has been portrayed accurately?

- How is the portrayal done?

- What aspects of life are portrayed?

Once students and teachers come to an understanding of oppressive discourses they will be in a better position to challenge them. Understanding the roots and evolution of these discourses will make it easier for them to question the authority of the printed word and visual images that they encounter in the classroom. With this knowledge, teachers and students will be able to see how authority is conferred on curricular resources by academic disciplines, through social status or by the state which hires professional staff to identify preferred meanings (Simon, 1992). They will also be able to see that the process of canonization of ideas is a matter not of recognizing abstract truth but of assessing how well educational resources function for particular people at particular times (Klein, 1985). In the end, such knowledge will provide both teachers and students with the confidence they need to reject oppressive discourses.

The rejection of certain discourses is not, however, strictly a one-way process. Discourses are not simply discarded, and that is the end of things. Rather, as some ways of making sense are discounted, others emerge to fill the void. It is up to teachers to encourage and help students to articulate these new or alternative ways of understanding. They must make it possible for voices not normally heard to take part in the creation, recreation or modification of discourses in this setting. Among other ways of doing this, they can call on those students of marginalized groups to make sense of texts in ways such students feel are appropriate. This may involve consulting the community. Teachers also need to work to make sure that other students listen to what these students have to say. At Suburbia this would have meant that the students of African heritage would have had an opportunity to express their views on *To Kill a Mockingbird*. Teachers may find in fact that they will themselves have to present students with alternate ways of comprehending the educational resources of interest. Whatever the strategy, however, they will need to ensure that alternate discourse or readings will get a serious hearing in the classroom.

Some teachers at Suburbia have found ways to interrogate racist and demeaning discourses in the curriculum. Naturally, some subjects lend themselves more easily to such an approach than do others. English is one such subject area. English teachers have many opportunities to address stereotyping, among a whole range of other social issues that are important to young people. Janice, an English teacher herself, uses Shakespeare to get her students to look critically at the phenomenon of stereotyping. She likes to focus on *The Merchant of Venice* for these purposes. Janice employs a number of different strategies to heighten students' awareness of stereotyping. One exercise involves a comparison of two actors who portray Shylock. She has the class compare the actors' different interpretations of the role. Now one of these actors is Jewish, and as it happens, his portrayal differs from the other gentile actor's in that it is less stereotypical. Janice presents a view to students that maintains this is so because the Jewish actor has a greater insight into what it means to be Jewish.

Janice also uses a second exercise. Here she gets students to break into groups and to list all stereotypes they encounter in *The Merchant of Venice*. Janice then moves from group to group encouraging, helping and often prodding and challenging students to think a little deeper about the kinds of the things they are saying. She talks about one incident where she challenged one group:

> They went through all the prejudice that Portia had against these people. And so the final part was 'Would you forgive Portia? What do you think about Portia now that she's said all these things?' And, I mean, all five of them, 'Well, that's OK.' I said: 'Pardon me? Wait a minute. You're walking with a friend and she sees somebody and she says, like, "Oh, that person is like a Jew," and looks down her nose. What would you say? Would you let that person say that or would you go, "Hold it; wait a minute"?' And you could see Susan and Sarah went 'Oh no, we'd say something to our friend.' And I said: 'Well, what if she keeps saying things like that over and over again? Are you going to keep saying, "Oh, that's just her"? Or are you suddenly going to decide, "I'm not great friends with this person any more"?' And you could see the wheels turning.

Janice also explores with the students the context for the stereotyping in the story. She does so by investigating the history of relations between Jews and others in Europe, and some of the restrictions that were placed on them, such as being prohibited from owning land. She also points out the direction in which she hopes to move. She says:

> So slowly but surely you're hoping to move from the stereotype to the individual, where Shylock says, 'Here's what they think of me but they're not looking at me, the individual.' And that's one thing, when I

was going around from group to group, I was saying, 'They're taking one brush and doing the broad stroke and just whitewashing everybody the same way. They're not looking at Monsieur Lebon so much as, "Well, French people, I don't like French people." Here's what they tend to do.'

Janice, however, does worry that in drawing students' attention to these kinds of stereotypes that she is actually perpetuating them.

> While we were discussing all the stereotypes that Portia was listing about these people in Period 2, you're just thinking, 'Oh my god, am I telling them things they never knew before, that all French people are sissies?' That kind of thing. There's just that fear that you're educating them how to be ... perpetuating the stereotype ... There's just that little bit of a fear and you're thinking, 'Oh, god ...' and you don't want to sit there giving them that knowing look, like 'Well, don't you understand?' 'Oh, are all Scottish people ...?' I thought it was going to be something about Scottish people are cheap, that's what I thought it was going to be. And I thought, 'That's because that's the stereotype I've learned.' I just thought: 'Jeez, are we just telling them a little bit ...' and I didn't want to be like, 'Oh, I know what they mean', that sort of thing. You feel guilty 'cos you've heard it before. That's one of the questions they do for an essay, 'Does *The Merchant of Venice* perpetuate the stereotypes?' That's one of the essay questions. 'Does it teach you, does it school you in the stereotypical view of Jews and should it be taught in Grade 10?'

Other teachers find ways to use other literature that does not contain obviously racist discourses like those in *The Merchant of Venice*. Bill, for example, addresses the issue of stereotypes when he uses *Harriet's Daughter*, a novel that revolves around the lives of two young immigrant girls of African heritage. In one of his classes he first asks students if they believe that these experiences are a realistic representation. He then launches into a line of questioning on racial stereotypes. He wants students to call out what comes to mind with different groups. 'What about Russians?' he asks. Students think of snow, furry hats, a poor country and the fact that everybody wears boots. Bill then introduces the idea that a lack of experience with and about other countries and cultures leads to stereotypical thinking. 'What about Australians?' he asks. Bill conjures up images of crocodiles, snakes and koalas. 'But this image is not fair,' he says. He then wants to know what students think about the English. He personally does not like some of the stereotypes associated with them, including the fact that many think all English people drink tea, use proper English, English mustard and are 'stiff.' Bill asserts that stereotypes are not true, and sometimes result from a lack of contact.

Once teachers and students make it possible for alternative discourses to emerge in the classroom, they must also find ways to circulate them beyond the classroom and school. One way of doing this is through student- or community-run newsletters or newspapers. In Nova Scotia, for example, students at Cole Harbour District High School, a school that has experienced conflict in the past, put together their own newspaper and circulated it to the communities that feed into the school. In it they confronted racial issues head-on. Among other topics they have taken the mainstream media to task for depicting the Black community in the area in stereotypical fashion as 'economically depressed' (Thorne, 1998). Another strategy for going beyond the classroom is to organize protests of organizations that circulate inappropriate discourse. Klein (1985), for example, cites the case of a group of students who wrote letters to a publisher who had circulated a book that the students found offensive. While the publisher did offer an explanation, he did not offer to change anything. In the meantime under the guidance of their teacher, the students set about making their own book which corrected what they believed to be the disagreeable representations of young people in the offending book.

Schools can develop their own curriculum resources on a larger scale than this. In so doing they can avoid some of the problems that inevitably accompany corporately produced resources, and provide opportunities for various groups to construct materials from their own perspectives. May (1994) describes how Richmond Road School in New Zealand systematically produced their own materials. At this school, curriculum teams were responsible for developing curriculum resources over the course of the year, supervising them, and providing support for staff. The school made sure that Maori and Samoan teachers were spread throughout the teams. One of the things that the teams would do was to explore themes that were associated with the school's various ethnic groups. For instance, over the course of three years the teams developed resources that focused on Maori themes. In year one they emphasized Maori Gods, developed focus topics that included 'creation and origins through mythology', and explored the concept of *mauri* or life force. On the basis of this the science team, for example, developed its resources by exploring science as the realm of Tawhirimatea, the god of winds and storms. Particular topics associated with this included earth science, water, air and weather.

Fostering Identities and Communities

As we have seen, representation plays an important part in the ways students construct their identities. Students routinely adopt any number of images, commodities and discourses in their cultural environments to stand for who they are. In doing this they hope to stake out an identity that is unique, at least to a point, and valued. This is not a natural process, however. Rather, it is in many respects a reaction to what is often perceived as an impersonal, uncaring and debilitating contemporary global culture. In their efforts to 'be somebody' students at Suburbia and elsewhere identify with many of the images they see about them in efforts that may simultaneously bring them together with some people and set them apart from others. For some this may mean the adoption of oppositional identities that cannot be achieved without struggles with authorities. Doing something about this debilitating global culture will involve many of the same tactics referred to in the previous two sections as well as in the ones that will follow. Rather than retrace these same steps, I will instead focus on the various ways in which students associate with one another.

From what we now know about student identities and their accompanying groupings it would seem that certain measures to integrate students into other groups or into the general school culture may well be misplaced. To be sure, efforts to break down or dissolve peer associations and groups would probably act against student interests. These young people, as we have seen, have much to gain from such associations. On the other hand, those students who stick pretty much to one group would probably benefit from associations with other individuals. Also, those who adopt oppositional tactics and identities, if they do not judiciously channel these, may often find themselves deprived of many of the opportunities that other more accommodating students experience. What can be done to facilitate a range of associations and interactions? What probably won't work are efforts to force students together. A number of students at Suburbia insisted that such tactics would definitely not bring different students together. Also misguided are attempts that revolve exclusively around methods to get individual groups to communicate with each other. Such strategies mistakenly attribute blame for communication difficulties to the groups themselves and ignore the global structures and regimes of representation that play a key role in the construction of identities and induce students and others to interact in the ways they do. Any efforts to help students communicate with others must be combined with other strategies that address these structural inequalities.

One of many ways of assisting students to interact with different others might involve efforts to help them construct flexible identities. Those who are able to build a certain amount of flexibility into the ways in which they are able to see themselves, as we have found in the cases above, are more able to identify with wider ranges of different practices, interests and individuals, and as a result are more comfortable associating with a wider variety of students and others. In this vein, Tierney (1993) calls for the reformation of the identities of those involved in the pedagogical process. He recommends that educational institutions engage in 'identity-work' where they provide individuals with the opportunities to understand their own and others' lives through prolonged engagement with the Other. In order to have any effect, however, such strategies would need to address the wider structural realities that shape in fundamental ways these identities.

One starting-point for this task might involve a focus on meaning. Here the pragmatic tradition of Dewey, James, Mead and others provides a useful framework for understanding and dealing with what some see as a world already oversaturated with meaning(s) (Baudrillard, 1983). Those who embrace such an approach would necessarily look for opportunities to both explore the construction and circulation of meanings in, for example, media culture and trace the consequences of these meanings for men and women. Among other options, teachers and students might want to interrogate how the construction of desire, pleasure, fear and fantasy associated with visual media (Ellsworth, 1993) is implicated in the ways in which people see themselves and others. Understanding where they themselves are situated in these power plays would also involve a look at the politics and economics behind these attempts at manipulating potential consumers. Students would gain insight into these global enterprises by exploring how corporations like Nike, for one, are able to pour millions of dollars into glossy ads featuring self-assured celebrities through the employment of what amounts to slave labor in countries like Indonesia (Andersen, 1995). Exercises of this sort would also provide them with the opportunity to learn how they can best exercise their power as consumers.

Analyses of meaning work best when they are accompanied by conditions that allow different voices, traditions and emerging identities not only to exist but to flourish (Giroux, 1991) – the very strategies which Bissoondath (1994) and Schlesinger (1991) condemn. Men, women and children are most likely to be willing to cross boundaries and assume more flexible identities not only when they understand where they fit in the greater scheme of things, but also when they are free from oppression, when what they say, do and believe is not ignored or trivialized. One of the ways in which McCarthy (1993) sees schools accomplishing such a task is through the reformation of knowledge. He feels that schools need to transform the organization and arrangement of knowledge itself in ways that bring the uninstitutionalized experiences of the marginalized to the centre of the curriculum. There are a number of ways in which this can be done. I will mention three here.

The first would make student narratives a valued and integral part of what goes on in the classroom (Giroux, 1991; Drake & Ryan, 1994; Ryan & Drake, 1992). Having students talk about their life experiences provides all students with the opportunity to gain unique insights into a side of life that they may not ordinarily have thought about or understood. It also gives them the chance to identify with at least some aspects of others' lives and experiences. A second strategy involves the introduction of literature (Ryan, 1994b) and forms of drama (Kehoe, 1985) that allow students to experience vicariously the situation of others. Vicarious experiences of this sort provide opportunities for students to pick out aspects of situations or elements of characters with which they can identify. Thirdly, schools can also look for ways to respect the representations that go along with these identities. Aside from honoring fashion and general clothing statements, and languages and discourses preferred by students, educators may want to attend to the music to which they listen. One Suburbia English teacher employs many strategies towards this end. One of these involves featuring student preferences in music. He begins each class by having everyone listen to one student's favorite piece of music. After listening to it, the student may, if he or she wishes, speak to it. After this those who wish to comment may follow up.

However, these strategies must necessarily be accompanied by a critical approach to knowledge. If these tactics are to have any impact, schools and teachers need to equip students with the skills to understand how knowledge gets constructed and the uses to which it is put. Included here would be opportunities to understand the historically contingent nature of the form and content of particular forms of representation (Giroux, 1993), including, as mentioned above, the role of media culture. Unfortunately educational institutions can only do so much to equip students to deal with the realities that exist outside school doors. If any real change is to take place, then educators, students and all those concerned with social justice need to work toward changing these structural inequalities, both in the immediate community and in the national and global arenas.[2]

Valuing Language

As illustrated above, school practices, including those at Suburbia, generally assign differential worth to different forms of linguistic expression. Suburbia's educational community exists as part of a market that values non-English languages and language varieties that depart from standard English less than it does standard English practices. This attribution of worth generates effects that are both social and academic in nature. Speakers of the various languages and language varieties are socially marked by virtue of the language or version of the language which they employ. Those who make use of language practices that differ from standard English will find not only their language practices devalued, but also they themselves, their respective cultures and communities held in lower esteem.

These social consequences are closely related to the academic effects of using language in what amounts to a linguistic market place. Those who employ practices that the market favors tend to do better in school than those whose practices the market does not value. Cummins (1986) provides convincing evidence of this. He maintains that the extent to which school practices reflect a valuing of certain languages and language varieties will dictate how well students perform. Those students whose language and culture is incorporated into the curriculum, and thereby valued, tend to do better than those whose language and culture is either ignored or devalued in school practices. On the other hand, Toohey (1987) maintains that when the form and content of students' oral expression is stigmatized or ignored then reading and writing pose formidable challenges. If what students are given to read in no way touches their experience or expression, if the background knowledge it assumes of the world and language is not theirs, they will have difficulty making sense of print. Furthermore, if what students write about is foreign in content and form to their teachers' then they cannot have a conversation about their work.

The lesson to be learned here is that the mode of expression employed by students is important to their success in school and in life generally. This is so not only because of the technical role linguistic practices play in communication functions, but also because of the status and power they confer on speakers. Thus those interested in helping students, particularly students who do not speak standard English, to succeed in school and life must find ways to value all students' linguistic expressions and the cultural practices that accompany them. The most obvious way to do this is to recognize the respective languages and varieties to the point that they are institutionalized in school practice. Instruction in students' first language or variety is one ideal option. This is so for both social and academic reasons. It signals to all students the importance of the respective form of expression and provides the best means to master a curriculum in a second or third language. Research indicates that this holds both for varieties of the dominant language (Rickford, 1997) and for other languages (Cummins & Swain, 1986).

This option, however, is not always possible. One of the reasons why not revolves around numbers. As is the case at Suburbia, there are often too many students employing many different linguistic forms and too few teachers who either understand or are capable of instruction in the various languages or varieties. For example, only a couple of teachers at Suburbia speak any of 60-odd languages spoken by the student body other than English. This pretty much precludes any instruction in languages other than English. Even so there are ways in which educators and educational institutions can show respect to languages and language varieties. With respect to the latter, various ways of attending to *Patois* may generate positive results. Corson and Lemay (1986) for example cite a number of studies that explore methods for promoting Caribbean varieties of English. Ladson-Billings and Henry (1990) describe a number of ways in which successful teachers of Black students use Caribbean varieties of English to help reinforce the children's identity and provide a bridge between the language of the home and the language of the dominant culture. Morrison *et al.* (1991) introduced a special program to Caribbean speakers. In doing so they sought ways to encourage free expression in a setting where students were learning standard English, while at the same time respecting and reinforcing children's pride in their own variety. This program featured an emphasis on reading activities, narratives, story-telling, and the development of language skills. Corson and Lemay (1996) observe that the results of this study suggest that assisting teachers to help students who regularly employ non-standard English varieties to focus on rich language acquisition activities can produce meaningful changes in the children's speaking, thinking, and writing in both varieties.

While many scholars and practitioners recognize the academic value of instruction in home languages or varieties, not everyone supports efforts of this nature. With respect to instruction in varieties, for example, some who look to enhance the opportunities of minority variety or language speakers may not favour the use of *Patois* in the classroom. In Britain, for example, parents and sociologists believe that such efforts are tokenistic and doomed to failure. Citing Stone and Carby, Edwards (1986) asserts that the introduction of *Patois* is simply an attempt to defend the legitimate culture of the school against the 'heretical' culture of Black people, and that it will do little to remove the racist attitudes in school and society which are the most serious obstacles to social equality for Black people.

This does not mean, however, that there is nothing that the school as a whole or teachers individually can do to acknowledge, and thereby value, student languages and dialects. One place to start is with both student and teacher knowledge. Educational programs need to begin to encourage minority dialect and language students to believe in themselves. Educators need, as Walsh (1991) contends, to invite them to believe that they have knowledge. Students need to understand, furthermore, that their knowledge, just like any other form of knowledge, is valuable. It means, Toohey (1987) maintains, not necessarily understanding or knowing the right words, but knowing that they have a right to words. She argues that reading and writing programs for speakers of non-English or non-standard varieties of English must aim at increasing the confidence of learners over finding their own forms of comprehension and also their belief in the importance of expressing their own particular experiences and perceptions. Finally Corson (1993) maintains that for this type of valuing to count it must be carried on in a genuinely critical context. This requires that children need to become aware of the social and historical factors that have combined to make one variety of language or dialect more appropriate in contexts of prestige, while relegating other varieties to marginalized settings.

In order to be in position to help students in this regard, teachers need to be able to understand linguistic matters themselves. They must become aware of the conditions of language development and use preferred in their classrooms. Educators need to become aware of both the technical and symbolic aspects of students' linguistic practices. With regard to the former, Rickford (1997) and Corson (1993) recommend that teachers acquire an understanding of the variation of language practices, even in what may be superficially monolinguistic settings, and of the relationships between these variants and standard English. It is important for them to know, in the case of non-standard English variations, that there are enduring patterns that underlie these forms of speech. At Suburbia, for example, it would be important for teachers to understand that *Patois* has a legitimate structure to it, one which has evolved over a period of many years.

It is also important for teachers to understand the symbolic functions that language plays in the lives of students. They need to be aware of the rewards and penalties that await students when they speak, or attempt to speak, in standard English or in their mother tongues. It would be helpful at Suburbia, for example, if teachers could understand what Chinese and other non-English speaking students can gain from speaking their mother tongue in the classroom and hallways, and the penalties they are likely to pay for trying to speak English to teachers or to their friends (Goldstein, 1997). These teachers might also benefit from a knowledge that *Patois* and other non-standard variety speakers may regard their speech as an act of defiance, and its features as signs of friendship and solidarity among fellow speakers (Edwards, 1986). Such speakers may also have an ambivalent attitude toward language. As a consequence, they may be reluctant in some circumstances to admit using a stigmatized variety of language.

Toohey (1987) maintains that in order to impart to students the importance of their language and the culture and knowledge associated with it, teachers need to do much more than to document how students' dialects and/or language differs in a structural sense from standard or dominant varieties. She contends that it is essential for teachers to know something of what their students know, and of how students form this knowledge. Toohey recommends Heath's (1983) example of teachers helping students take community knowledge and reformulate it into the language of schooling as one method of acquiring this kind of knowledge (see also Ryan, 1994a). In this setting teachers were convinced that learners brought valuable knowledge to the educational process, and as a consequence, were actively engaged with students in validating and building on this knowledge. Their conviction that these students knew something was not based on abstract liberal sentiments or a detailed knowledge of the grammatical features of the students' variety, but can rather be traced to the fact that they had learned something of what the students knew and had become more familiar with the ways in which their students communicated.

Corson (1998) recommends a wide range of policies and practices designed to promote the value of non-English languages and language varieties and the speakers of these varieties. These policies and practices target staff and visitors, curriculum and teaching, parents and communities, professional development, and school organization. Among other ideas, Corson (1998) recommends that schools:

- recruit people who can tutor fluently those students whose first language is not standard English;

- appoint as many staff as possible who share students' language and culture;

- invite guests who represent various student cultures and language groups;

- employ professionals who understand the influence of home language and culture on students' development;

- provide leaders, mentors, and models of culturally sensitive practices;

- make wide use of the language and skills of community members in the school;

- involve children and parents together in family literacy programs;

- arrange for professional development that explores the languages and language varieties used by students;

- base management on clear principles that promote culturally sensitive practices;

- provide bilingual or multilingual signs that welcome people to the school;

- use a variety of languages in school newsletters;

- involve various language communities in the school's management; and

- ask teachers to allow the minority languages to be used freely whenever possible.

Knowledge and Discourse

So far the suggestions for schools have centered on the kinds of things educators can do. Ideally these practices will make it possible for alternative discourses and voices to surface, both in schools and out, in ways that work for traditionally marginalized groups. There are, however, other forms of discourse that have the potential to work in the interests of these groups. These are the discourses of social science. Social scientists have the opportunity to assist in the work of both revealing and circulating alternative discourses and voices. The very nature of their work puts them in a position to uncover and explore those often hidden forms of meaning, and to disseminate them well beyond the local contexts of their use. It is in this regard that Corson (1998) calls for the development of a knowledge base to assist in the promotion of diversity in education. Social scientists, however, would not be expected to follow the illusory tradition of so-called neutrality in these sort of inquiries. Indeed such neutrality has more often than not masked approaches that have obscured and silenced the voices of marginalized groups (Kirby & McKenna, 1989). Instead social scientists need to abandon such neutrality pretensions and explicitly declare their intentions to work to improve opportunities for marginalized groups.

There are a number of ways in social scientists can help to uncover and circulate alternative discourses. Corson (1998) identifies two. The first is to work from a critical perspective. This means employing techniques that accompany approaches such as critical ethnography and critical discourse analysis. Those who work in these traditions explore hidden or taken-for granted relationships of power, examine social injustices, link the wider social patterns and structures to local practices, look into history, take seri-ously the perceptions of the powerless, negotiate research outcomes with participants, cooperate with participants in research, and of course, work to see that the voices of the marginalized are heard beyond their local settings. A second alternative is for social scientists to help practitioners conduct their own research (see also Ryan, 1995). Teachers are in a good position to generate knowledge of their particular situations, knowledge that will help them recognize and challenge oppressive discourses and supplant these with alternative discourses once they have research skills at their disposal. It is here that academics can provide some guidance. They can share their expertise, provide guidance or offer to cooperate with teachers.

Conclusion

Practices of representation play a crucial role in the lives of all men, women and children. This is because the ways in which individuals and groups of individuals are depicted will dictate the manner in which they are treated. If, for example, certain groups are portrayed in a negative manner, if the ways in which they choose to represent themselves are not valued or the languages they employ to shape representations are looked down upon, then they will not experience the same kinds of opportunities and fortunes that other groups do. This is particularly true in educational institutions like Suburbia where representational practices extend advan-tages to some and disadvantages to others. Schools like Suburbia that genuinely wish to optimize the life chances of all of their students need to find ways to allow the discourses and voices of traditionally marginalized groups to compete on an equal footing with other discourses. To achieve this, educators need to provide the conditions necessary to enable both teachers and students to recognize, understand, and challenge oppressive discourses and replace them with alternatives that will allow the voices of groups normally silent to be heard. The strategies outlined above represent merely a starting-point for this very challenging task. There is a long way to go.

Notes

1. The power of media discourse lies, in part, in its ability to remain hidden. This capacity rests with its power to transform sense made from a particular position, and with particular interests in mind, into common sense (Fiske, 1996).
2. Peshkin (1991) notes that improvements in the relationships between different groups over the years in the school he studied came about as community representatives of non-European heritage came to power.

References

Adorno, T.W., Frenkel-Brunswick, F., Levinson, D. and Sanford, R.N. (1950) *The Authoritarian Personality*. New York: Basic Books.

Alladin, I. (1996) *Racism in Candian Schools*. Toronto: Harcourt Brace.

Allen, A. (1995) Constructing meaning: The responses of emergent readers to black images in children's picture-books. MA thesis, University of Toronto.

Alleyne, M. (1976) Dimensions and varieties of West Indian English and the implications for teaching. *TESL Talk* 7 (1), 35–62.

Allport, G. (1954) *The Nature of Prejudice*. Cambridge: Addison-Wesley.

Andersen, R. (1995) *Consumer Culture and TV Programming*. Boulder, Colo.: Westview Press.

Anderson, W.A. (1990) *Reality Isn't What It Used to Be*. San Francisco: Harper.

Ang, I. (1995) *Living Room Wars: Rethinking Media Audiences for a Postmodern World*. London: Routledge.

Angus, L (1986) Research traditions, ideology and critical ethnography. *Discourse* 7, 61–77.

Angus, L. (1987). A critical ethnography of continuity and change in a Catholic school. In R. MacPherson (ed.) *Ways and Meanings of Research in Educational Administration* (pp. 25–52). Armidale: University of New England Press.

Anthony, S. (1998) Black-eyed Susan: 'Blue-eyed' schools: Academically-oriented Black girls in school. PhD thesis, University of Toronto.

Anyon, J. (1979) Ideology and United States history textbooks. *Harvard Educational Review* 49 (5), 361–386.

Appadurai, A. (1990) Disjuncture and difference in the global cultural economy. *Theory, Culture and Society*, 7 (2/3), 295–310.

Apple, M. and Christian-Smith, L. (1991) The politics of the textbook. In M. Apple and L. Christian-Smith (eds) *The Politics of the Textbook* (pp. 1–21). New York: Routledge

Apple, M. (1985) The culture and commerce of the textbook. *Journal of Curriculum Studies* 17 (2), 147–162.

Australian Bureau of Statistics (1995) *1995 Year Book Australia*. No. 77. Canberra: Australian Bureau of Statistics.

Bakhtin, M. (1981) *The Dialogic Imagination: Four Essays*. Austin: University of Texas Press.

Barman, J., Hebert, Y. and McCaskill, D. (eds) (1986) *Indian Education in Canada (Vol. 1): The Legacy*. Vancouver: University of British Columbia Press.

Barthes, R. (1972) *Mythologies*. London: Cape.

Baudrillard, J. (1981/1994) *Simulacra and Simulation*. Ann Arbor: University of Michigan Press.

Baudrillard, J. (1983) *Simulations*. New York: Semiotext.

Baudrillard, J. (1988) *America*. London: Verso.

Bernstein, R. (1990) The arts catch up with a society in disarray. *The New York Times* (pp. 1, 12–13), 2 September.

Bissoondath, N. (1994) *Selling Illusions: The Cult of Multiculturalism in Canada.* Toronto: Penguin.

Bloom,A. (1987) *The Closing of the American Mind.* New York: Simon & Schuster.

Bogdan, R. and Biklen, S. (1998) *Qualitative Research for Education: An Introduction to Theory and Methods.* Toronto: Allyn & Bacon.

Bourdieu, P. (1991) *Language and Symbolic Power* (G. Raymond and M. Adamson, trans.) Introduced by J.B. Thompson (ed.) Cambridge: Harvard University Press.

Boutte, G. and McCormick, C. (1992) Authentic multicultural activities. *Childhood Education* 68 (3), 140–144.

Boutte, G. (1992) Frustrations of an African-American parent: A personal and professional account. *Phi Delta Kappan* 73 (10), 786–788.

Brighton, L. (1994) Perceptions of 'White minority' students in a racially diverse secondary school. Masters research paper, Ontario Institute for Studies in Education.

Britzman, D., Santiago-Valles, K., Jimenez-Munoz, G., and Lamash, L. (1993) Slips that show and tell: Fashioning multiculture as a problem of representation. In C. McCarthy and W. Crichlow (eds) *Race, Identity and Representation in Education* (pp. 188–200). London: Routledge.

Burbules, N. (1995) Postmodern doubt and philosophy of education. Unpublished paper.

Carey, E. (1998) Minorities set to be majority. *The Toronto Star* (p.1), 7 June.

Carrington, B. and Short, G. (1989) *'Race' and the Primary School: Theory into Practice.* Windsor: NFER—Nelson.

Cassidy, F. (1961) *Jamaica Talk.* London: Macmillan.

Castle, K. (1993) The imperial Indian: India in British history textbooks for schools, 1880–1914. In J.A. Mangan (ed.) *The Imperial Curriculum: Racial Images and Education in the British Colonial Experience* (pp. 23–39). New York: Routledge.

Cherryholmes, C. (1994) Pragmatism, poststructuralism and socially useful theorizing. *Curriculum Inquiry,* 24 (2), 193–213.

Clegg, S. (1990) *Modern Organizations: Organizational Studies in the Postmodern World.* London: Sage.

Corson, D. (1993) *Language, Minority Education and Gender: Linking Social Justice and Power.* Clevedon: Multilingual Matters.

Corson, D. (1995) Discursive power in educational organizations: An introduction. In D. Corson (ed.) *Discourse and Power in Educational Organizations* (pp. 3–15). Toronto: OISE Press.

Corson, D. (1998) *Changing Education for Diversity.* Philadelphia: Open University Press.

Corson, D. and Lemay, S. (1996) *Social Justice and Language Policy in Education: The Canadian Research.* Toronto: OISE Press.

Cousins, M. and Houssain, A. (1985) *Michel Foucault.* London: Macmillan.

Craig, D. (1976) Bidialectal education: Creole and Standard in the West Indies. *International Journal of the Sociology of Language* 8, 94–134.

Cummins, J. and Swain, M. (1986) *Bilingualism in Education: Aspects of Theory, Research and Practice.* London: Longman.

Cummins, J. (1986) Empowering minority students: A framework for intervention. *Harvard Educational Review*, 56, 18–36.

Cummins, J. (1995) Discursive power in educational policy and practice for culturally diverse students. In D. Corson (ed.) *Discourse and Power in Educational Organizations* (pp. 191–210). Toronto: OISE Press.

Dei, G. (1995) *Drop Out or Push Out? The Dynamics of Black Students' Disengagement from School.* Toronto: Ontario Institute for Studies in Education.

Dei, G. (1996a) *Anti-Racism Education: Theory and Practice.* Halifax: Fernwood.

Dei, G. (1996b) Black/African-Canadian students' perspectives on school racism. In I. Alladin (ed.) *Racism in Canadian Schools* (pp. 42–61). Toronto: Harcourt Brace.

Denzin, N. (1991) *Images of Postmodern Society: Social Theory and Contemporary Cinema.* London: Sage.

Department of Education and Science (1985) *Education for All.* London: HMSO.

Drake, S. and Ryan, J. (1994) Narrative and knowledge: Inclusive pedagogy for contemporary times. *Curriculum and Teaching* 9 (1), 45–56.

Dreyfus, H. and Rabinow, P. (1982) *Michel Foucault: Beyond Structuralism and Hermeneutics.* Brighton: Harvester Press.

Drucker, P. (1993) *Post-Capitalist Society.* New York: Harper.

Eco, U. (1989) *The Open Work.* Cambridge, MA: Harvard University Press.

Edwards, J. (1989) *Language and Disadvantage.* London: Cole & Whurr.

Edwards, V. (1986) *Language in a Black Community.* Clevedon: Multilingual Matters.

Eitzen, D.S. (1992) Problem students: The sociocultural roots. *Phi Delta Kappan* April, 384–590.

Ellsworth, E.I. (1993) 'I pledge allegiance': The politics of reading and using educational films. In C. McCarthy and W. Crichlow (eds) *Race, Identity and Representation in Education* (pp. 201–219). London: Routledge.

Elrich, M. (1994) The stereotype within. *Educational Leadership* 51 (8), 12–15.

Erickson, F. (1987a) Conceptions of school culture: An overview. *Educational Administration Quarterly* 23 (4), 11–24.

Erickson, F. (1987b) Transformation and school success: The politics of culture and educational achievement. *Anthropology and Education Quarterly* 18 (1), 335–356.

Featherstone, M. (1991) *Theories of Consumer Culture and Postmodernism.* London: Sage.

Firth, S. and Darlington, R. (1993) Racial stereotypes in the Australian curriculum: The case study of New South Wales. In J.A. Mangan (ed.) *The Imperial Curriculum: Racial Images and Education in the British Colonial Experience* (pp. 79–92). New York: Routledge.

Fishman, J. (1956) An examination of the process and functioning of social stereotyping. *Journal of Social Psychology* 43, 27–46.

Fiske, J. (1996) *Media Matters: Race and Gender in US Politics.* Minneapolis: University of Minnesota Press.

Fitzgerald, T. (1991) Media and changing metaphors of ethnicity and identity. *Media, Culture and Society* 13, 193–214.

Foucault, M. (1970) *The Order of Things: An Archeology of the Human Sciences.* New York: Vintage Books.

Foucault, M. (1972) *The Archeology of Knowledge.* London: Tavistock.

Foucault, M. (1979) *Discipline and Punish: The Birth of the Prison.* New York: Pantheon Books.

Foucault, M. (1980) *Power/Knowledge: Selected Interviews and Other Writings 1972–1977*. New York: Pantheon Books.

Foucault, M. (1988) *Madness and Civilization: A History of Insanity in the Age of Reason*. New York: Random.

Friedman, J. (1990) Being in the world: Globalization and localization. *Theory, Culture and Society* 7 (2/3), 311–328.

Geertz, C. (1973) *The Interpretation of Cultures*. New York: Basic Books.

Ghosh, S. (1993) 'English in taste, in opinions, in words and intellect': Indoctrinating the Indian through textbook, curriculum and education. In J.A. Mangan (ed.) *The Imperial Curriculum: Racial Images and Education in the British Colonial Experience* (pp. 175–193). New York: Routledge.

Gibson, M. (1976) Approaches to multicultural education in the United States: Some concepts and assumptions. *Anthropology and Education Quarterly* 7 (4), 7–18.

Giddens, A. (1979) *Central Problems in Social Theory*. Berkeley: University of California Press.

Gillborn, D. (1995) Racism, modernity and schooling: New directions in antiracist theory and practice. Paper prepared for the Annual Meeting of the American Educational Research Association, San Francisco.

Gilman, S. (1985) *Difference and Pathology: Stereotypes of Sexuality, Race and Madness*. Ithaca: Cornell University Press.

Giroux, H. (1991) Postmodernism as border pedagogy: Redefining the boundaries of race and ethnicity. In H. Giroux (ed.) *Postmodernism, Feminism and Cultural Politics: Redrawing Educational Boundaries* (pp. 217–256). Albany: SUNY Press.

Giroux, H. (1993) *Living Dangerously: Multiculturalism and the Politics of Difference*. New York: Peter Lang.

Goldstein, T. (1997) Bilingual life in a multilingual high-school classroom: Teaching and learning in Cantonese and English. *The Canadian Modern Language Review* 53 (2), 356–372.

Goody, J. and Watt, I. (1968) The consequences of literacy. In J. Goody (ed.) *Literacy in Traditional Societies*. Cambridge: Cambridge University Press.

Goody, J.R. (1977) *The Domestication of the Savage Mind*. Cambridge: Cambridge University Press.

Gould, S.J. (1981) *The Mismeasure of Man*. New York: W.W. Norton.

Gould, S.J. (1994) The eometer of ace. *Discovery* November, 65–69.

Government of Ontario (1980) *Race, Religion, and Culture in Ontario School Materials: Suggestions for Authors and Publishers*. Toronto: Ministry of Education.

Grossberg, L. (1993) Cultural studies and/in new worlds. In C. McCarthy and W. Crichlow (eds) *Race, Identity and Representation in Education* (pp. 89–105). London: Routledge.

Gue, L. (1975) Patterns in Native education. *CSSE Yearbook* 1, 7–20.

Hall, S. (1980) Teaching racism. *Multiracial Education*, 9 (1), 3–13.

Hall, S. (1991a) The local and the global: Globalization and ethnicity. In A.D. King (ed.) *Culture, Globalization and the World-System: Contemporary Conditions for the Representation of Identity* (pp. 19–39). Birmingham: State University of New York.

Hall, S. (1991b) Old and new identities, old and new ethnicities. In A.D. King (ed.) *Culture, Globalization and the World-System: Contemporary Conditions for the Representation of Identity* (pp. 41–68). Birmingham: State University of New York.

Hall, S. (1997a) The work of representation. In S. Hall (ed.) *Representation: Cultural Representations and Signifying Practices* (pp. 13–74). London: Sage.

Hall, S. (1997b) The spectacle of the 'other'. In S. Hall (ed.) *Representation: Cultural Representations and Signifying Practices* (pp. 223–290). London: Sage.

Handscombe, J. (1989) Mainstreaming: Who needs it? In J. Esling (ed.) *Multicultural Education and Policy: ESL in the 1990s*. Toronto: OISE Press.

Hargreaves. A. (1994) *Changing Teachers, Changing Times: Teachers' Work and Culture in the Postmodern Age*. Toronto: OISE Press.

Harvey, D. (1989) *The Condition of Postmodernity*. Cambridge: Blackwell.

Havelock, E.A. (1978) *The Greek Conception of Justice: From Its Shadow in Homer to Its Substance in Plato*. Cambridge, MA: Harvard University Press.

Heath, S. (1983) *Ways with Words: Ethnography of Communication in Communities and Schools*. Cambridge: Cambridge University Press.

Heath, S.B. and McLaughlin, M.W. (eds) (1993) *Identity and Inner-City Youth: Beyond Ethnicity and Gender*. New York: Teachers College Press.

Henriques, J. (1984) Social psychology and the politics of racism. In J. Henriques, W. Holloway, C. Urwin, C. Venn and V. Walkerdine (eds) *Changing the Subject: Psychology, Social Regulation and Subjectivity* (pp. 60–89). London: Methuen.

Henwood, K., Giles, H., Coupland, J. and Coupland, N. (1993) Stereotyping and affect in discourse: Interpreting the meaning of elderly, painful self-disclosure. In D. Mackie and D. Hamilton (eds) *Affect, Cognition, and Stereotyping: Interactive Processes in Group Perception* (pp. 269–296). Toronto: Academic Press.

Herrnstein, R. and Murray, C. (1994) *The Bell Curve: Intelligence and Class Structure in American Life*. New York: The Free Press.

Hirsch, E.D. (1987) *Cultural Literacy*. Boston: Houghton Mifflin.

Hoffman, D. (1997) Diversity in practice: Perspectives on concept, context and policy. *Educational Policy* 11 (3), 375–392.

Hudak, G.M. (1993) Technologies of marginality: Strategies of stardom and displacement in adolescent life. In C. McCarthy and W. Crichlow (eds) *Race, Identity and Representation in Education* (pp. 172–187). London: Routledge.

Ibrahim, A. (1997) Becoming Black: Race, language, culture, and the politics of identity: African students in a Franco-Ontarian high school. Unpublished PhD thesis, University of Toronto.

Jameson, F. (1984) Foreword to J. Lyotard *The Postmodern Condition: A Report on Knowledge*. Minneapolis: University of Minnesota Press.

Jeffcoate, R. (1979) *Positive Image*. London: Writers and Readers.

Kehoe, J. (1985) *Ethnic Prejudice and the Role of the School*. Toronto: North York.

Kirby, S. and McKenna, K. (1989) *Experience, Research, Social Change: Methods from the Margins*. Toronto: Garamond.

King, J. (1992) Diaspora literacy and consciousness in the struggle against miseducation in the Black community. *Journal of Negro Education* 61 (3), 317–340.

Klein, G. (1985) *Reading into Racism: Bias in Children's Literature and Learning Materials*. Boston: Routledge.

Kroeber, A. and Klockholm, C. (1952) Culture: A critical review of concepts and definitions. *Peabody Museum Papers* XLVII, Harvard University Press.

Labov, W. (1982) Objectivity and commitment in linguistic science: The case of the Black English trial in Ann Arbor. *Language in Society* 11, 165–201.

Laclau, E. and Mouffe, C. (1990) Post-Marxism without apologies. In E. Laclau (ed.) *New Reflections on the Revolution of Our Time*. London: Verso.

Ladson-Billings, G. and Henry, A. (1990) Blurring the borders: Voices of African liberatory pedagogy in the United States and Canada. *Journal of Education* 172 (2), 72–88.

Lash, S. (1988) Discourse or figure? Postmodernism as a 'regime of signification'. *Theory, Culture & Society* 5, 311–336.

Lee, H. (1960) *To Kill a Mockingbird.* New York: Warner.

Lee, S. (1996) *Unraveling the 'Model Minority' Stereotype.* New York: Teachers' College Press.

Levine, R. and Campbell, D. (1972) *Ethnocentrism: Theories of Conflict, Ethnic Attitudes, and Group Behavior.* New York: Wiley.

Lewis, M. (1987) Native images in children's books. In J. Young (ed.) *Breaking the Mosaic: Ethnic Identities in Canada.* Toronto: Garamond.

Lidchi, H. (1997) The poetics and politics of exhibiting other cultures. In S. Hall (ed.) *Representation: Cultural Representations and Signifying Practices* (pp. 151–222). London: Sage.

Lippmann, W. (1922) *Public Opinion.* New York: Harcourt Brace.

Lorrimore, R. (1994) *Mass Communications: A Comparative Introduction.* Manchester: Manchester University Press.

Lowe, D. (1995) *The Body in Late Capitalist USA.* Durham: Duke University Press.

Lucy, J. (1992) *Language, Diversity and Thought: A Reformulation of the Linguistic Relativity Hypothesis.* Cambridge: Cambridge University Press.

Lyotard, J. (1984) *The Postmodern Condition: A Report on Knowledge.* Minneapolis: University of Minnesota Press.

Mackie, M. (1973) Arriving at 'truth' by definition: The case of stereotype inaccuracy. *Social Problems* 20, 431–447.

Mangan, J.A. (1993) Images for confident control: Stereotypes in imperial discourse. In J.A. Mangan (ed.) *The Imperial Curriculum: Racial Images and Education in the British Colonial Experience* (pp. 6–22). New York: Routledge.

May, S. (1994) *Making Multicultural Education Work.* Clevedon: Multilingual Matters.

McCarthy, C. and Crichlow, W. (1993a) Introduction: Theories of identity, theories of representation, theories of race. In C. McCarthy and W. Crichlow (eds) *Race, Identity and Representation in Education* (pp. xiii–xxix). London: Routledge.

McCarthy, C. and Crichlow, W. (eds) (1993b) *Race, Identity and Representation in Education.* London: Routledge.

McCarthy, C. (1993) After the canon: Knowledge and ideological representation in the multicultural discourse on curriculum reform. In C. McCarthy and W. Crichlow (eds) *Race, Identity and Representation in Education* (pp. 289–305). London: Routledge.

McDiarmid, G. and Pratt, D. (1971) *Teaching Prejudice: A Content Analysis of Social Studies Textbooks Authorized for Use in Ontario.* Toronto: Ontario Institute for Studies in Education Curriculum Series 12.

McGeorge, C. (1993). Race, empire and the Maori in the New Zealand primary-school curriculum, 1880–1940. In J.A. Mangan (ed.) *The Imperial Curriculum: Racial Images and Education in the British Colonial Experience* (pp. 64–78). New York: Routledge.

McLaren, P. (1995) White terror and oppositional agency: Towards a critical multiculturalism. In P. McLaren, R. Hammer, D. Sholle and S. Reilly (eds) *Rethinking Media Literacy: A Critical Pedagogy of Representation.* New York: Peter Lang.

McLaughlin, B. (1986) Multilingual education: Theory East and West. In B. Spolsky (ed.) *Language and Education in Multilingual Settings* (pp. 32–52). Clevedon: Multilingual Matters.

McLuhan, M. (1973) *Understanding Media*. London: Abacus.

McRobbie, A. (1978) Working-class girls and the culture of femininity. In Centre for Contemporary Cultural Studies (ed.) *Women Take Issue*. London: Hutchinson.

Merelman, R. (1995). *Representing Black Culture: Racial Conflict and Cultural Politics in the United States*. New York: Routledge.

Merriam, S. (1988) *Case Study Research in Education: A Qualitative Approach*. San Francisco: Jossey-Bass.

Miles, R. (1993) *Racism after 'Race Relations'*. New York: Routledge.

Miller, A.G. (1982) Historical and contemporary perspectives on stereotyping. In A.G. Miller (ed.) *In the Eye of the Beholder: Contemporary Issues in Stereotyping* (pp. 1–40). New York: Praeger.

Moore, K. (1992) Racial bias in children's textbooks. MA thesis, University of Toronto.

Morely, D. and Robins, K. (1995) *Spaces of Identity: Global Media, Electronic Landscapes and Cultural Boundaries*. London: Routledge.

Morgan, R. (1995) Television, space, education: Rethinking relations between schools and media. *Discourse* 16 (1), 39–57.

Morrison, D., Luther, M. and McCullough, J. (1991) Language programming with dialect students. *Orbit* 22 (3), 8–9.

Natsoulas, A. and Natsoulas, T. (1993) Racism, the school and African education in colonial Kenya. In J.A Mangan (ed.) *The Imperial Curriculum: Racial Images and Education in the British Colonial Experience* (pp. 108–134). New York: Routledge.

Nieto, S. (1992) *Affirming Diversity: The Sociopolitical Context of Multicultural Education*. New York: Longman.

North York Board of Education (1985) *Guidelines for Assessing Learning Materials*. Toronto: North York Board of Education Curriculum and Staff Development Series.

O'Connor, T. (1989) Cultural voice and strategies for multicultural education. *Journal of Education* 171 (2), 57–74.

O'Neil, P. (1984) Prejudice towards Indians in history textbooks: A 1984 profile. *The History and Social Science Teacher* 20 (1), 33–39.

Ogbu, J. (1992). Understanding cultural diversity and learning. *Educational Researcher* 21 (8), 5–14.

Okath, P. (1993) The creation of a dependent culture: The imperial school in Uganda. In J.A. Mangan (ed.) *The Imperial Curriculum: Racial Images and Education in the British Colonial Experience* (pp. 135–146). New York: Routledge.

Olneck, M. (1990) The recurring dream: Symbolism and ideology in intercultural and multicultural education. *American Journal of Education*, 98 (2), 147–174.

Omni, M. and Winant, H. (1986) *Racial Formation in the United States*. London: Routledge.

Ontario Ministry of Education and Training (1993) *Antiracism and Ethnocultural Equity in School Boards: Guidelines for Policy Development*. Toronto: Ontario Ministry of Education and Training.

Ornstein, A. (1992) The censored curriculum: The problem with textbooks today. *NASSP Bulletin* November 76 (547), 1–9.

Owen, D. (1994) *Population Trends*. Winter 78, 23–33. Office of Population Censuses and Surveys (OPCS) London: HMSO.

Pahl, R. (1995) The image of Africa in our classrooms. *The Social Studies* 86 (6), 245–247.

Peshkin, A. (1991) *The Color of Strangers, the Color of Friends*. Chicago: University of Chicago Press.

Philip, M. (1988) All my children. In *The Role of the Reader in the Curriculum: The Third Report* (pp. 106–112). Toronto: North York Board of Education Curriculum and Staff Development Series.

Philips, S. (1983) *The Invisible Culture: Communication in Classroom and Community on the Warm Springs Indian Reservation*. New York: Longman.

Pinar, W. (1993) Notes on understanding curriculum as a racial text. In C. McCarthy and W. Crichlow (eds) *Race, Identity and Representation in Education* (pp. 60–70). London: Routledge.

Poster, M. (1995) *The Second Media Age*. Cambridge: Polity Press.

Prentice, A. (1977) *The School Promoters: Education and Social Class in Mid-Nineteenth-Century Upper Canada*. Toronto: McClelland and Stewart.

Rattansi, A. (1992) Changing the subject? Racism, culture and education. In J. Donald and A. Rattansi (eds) *Race, Culture and Difference* (pp. 11–48). London: Sage.

Rickford, J. (1997) Unequal partnership: Sociolinguistics and the African American speech community. *Language in Society* 26, 161–197.

Rizvi, F. (1993) Critical introduction to B. Troyna *Racism and Education* (pp. 1–17). Bristol: Open University Press.

Roberts, P. (1988) *West Indians and Their Language*. New York: Cambridge University Press.

Robertson, L. (1998) Responses to equity in-service. EdD thesis, University of Toronto.

Ruchames, L. (1969) *Racial Thought in America: A Documentary History*. Amherst: University of Massachusetts Press.

Rushdie, S. (1990) In good faith. *Independent on Sunday*, 4 February.

Ryan, J. (1989) Disciplining the Innut: Normalization, characterization and schooling. *Curriculum Inquiry*, 19 (4), 379–403.

Ryan, J. (1992a) Eroding Innu cultural tradition: Individualization and communality. *Journal of Canadian Studies* 26 (4), 94–111.

Ryan, J. (1992b) Formal schooling and deculturation: Nursing practice and the erosion of Native communication styles. *Alberta Journal of Educational Research* 38 (2), 91–103.

Ryan, J. (1994a) Organizing the facts: Aboriginal education and cultural differences in school discourse and knowledge. *Language and Education* 8 (4), 251–271.

Ryan, J. (1994b) Transcending the limitations of social science: Insight, understanding and the humanities in educational administration. *Journal of Educational Thought* 28 (3), 225–244.

Ryan, J. (1995) Order, anarchy and inquiry in educational administration. *McGill Journal of Education* 30 (1), 37–59.

Ryan, J. (1996a) Organizing for teaching and learning in a culturally diverse school setting. *Multicultural Education Journal* 14 (1), 15–32.

Ryan, J. (1996b) Restructuring First Nations' education: Trust, respect and governance. *Journal of Canadian Studies* 31 (2), 115–132.

Ryan, J. (1996c) The new institutionalism in a postmodern world: De-differentiation and the study of institutions. In R. Crowson, W.L. Boyd and H. Mawhinney (eds) *The Politics of Education and the New Institutionalism: Reinventing the American School* (pp.189–202). London: Falmer.

Ryan, J. (1997) *Principals' Problem-Solving Practices in Schools with Diverse Ethnocultural Student Populations.* Toronto: Final Report for Social Sciences and Humanities Council of Canada.

Ryan, J. and Drake, S. (1992) Narrative and knowledge: Teaching educational administration in a postmodern world. *Journal of Educational Administration and Foundations* 7 (2), 13–26.

Ryan, J., Wignall, R. and Moore, S. (1995) *Teaching and Learning in a Multi-ethnic School.* Toronto: Ontario Ministry of Education and Training.

Sadker, D. and Sadker, M. (1994) *Failing at Fairness: How America's Schools Cheat Girls.* Toronto: Maxwell MacMillan.

Said, E. (1978) *Orientalism.* Harmondsworth: Penguin.

Saussure, F. de (1974) *Course in General Linguistics.* London: Fontana.

Scarman, L. (1981) *The Brixton Disorders: 10–12 April 1981.* London: HMSO.

Schlesinger, Arthur M., Jr (1991) *The Disuniting of America.* Knoxville, TN: Whittle Direct Books.

Schutz, A. (1967) *The Phenomenology of the Social World* (G. Walsh and F. Lehnert, trans.) Evanston, IL: Northwestern University Press.

Scollon, R. and Scollon, S. (1981) *Narrative, Literacy, and Face in Interethnic Communication.* Norwood, NJ: Ablex.

Shohat, E. and Stam, R. (1994) *Unthinking Eurocentrism: Multiculturalism and the Media.* New York: Routledge.

Sholle, D. and Denske, S. (1995) Critical media literacy: Reading, remapping, rewriting. In P. McLaren, R. Hammer, D. Sholle and S. Reilly (eds) *Rethinking Media Literacy: A Critical Pedagogy of Representation* (pp. 7–31). New York: Peter Lang.

Sholle, D. (1995) 'Buy our news': The melding of news, entertainment and advertising in the totalized selling environment of the postmodern market. In P. McLaren, R. Hammer, D. Sholle and S. Reilly (eds) *Rethinking Media Literacy: A Critical Pedagogy of Representation* (pp. 145–170). New York: Peter Lang.

Shreeve, J. (1994) Terms of estrangement. *Discover* November, 57–63.

Simon, R. (1992) *Teaching Against the Grain: Texts for a Pedagogy of Possibility.* Toronto: OISE Press.

Sleeter, C. and Grant, C. (1987) An analysis of multicultural education in the United States. *Harvard Educational Review* 57 (4), 421–444.

Sleeter, C. and Grant, C. (1991) Race, class, gender and disability in current texts. In M. Apple and L. Christian-Smith (eds) *The Politics of the Textbook* (pp. 78–110). New York: Routledge.

Sleeter, C. (1989) Multicultural education as a form of resistance. *Journal of Education* 171 (3), 51–71.

Smart, B. (1993) *Postmodernity.* New York: Routledge.

Smith, A. (1990) Towards a global culture? *Theory, Culture and Society* 7 (2/3), 171–191.

Solomon, P. (1992) *Black Resistance in High School: Forging a Separatist Culture.* Albany, NY: State University of New York Press.

Speicher, B. and McMahon, S. (1992) Some African-American perspectives on Black English vernacular. *Language in Society* 21, 383–407.

Stake, R. (1994) Case studies. In N. Denzin and Y. Lincoln (eds) *Handbook of Qualitative Research* (pp. 236–246). Thousand Oaks, CA: Sage.

Statistics Canada (1990) *Canada Year Book*. Ottawa: Ministry of Supply and Services.

Statistics Canada (1993) *Ethnic Origin*. Ottawa: Ministry of Industry, Science and Technology.

Statistics Canada (1994) *Television Viewing Habits*. Ottawa: Ministry of Industry, Science and Technology.

Statistics Canada (1997) *1996 Census: Immigration and Citizenship*. Ottawa: Ministry of Industry, Science and Technology.

Taylor, C. (1991) *The Malaise of Modernity*. Concorde, Ontario: Anasi.

Thorne, S. (1998) Bridging the gap: Newspaper tackles tough racial issues. *Peterborough Examiner* (p. 1b), 6 February.

Tierney, W. (1993) *Building Communities of Difference: Higher Education in the Twenty-First Century*. Toronto: OISE Press.

Toohey, K. (1987) Minority educational failure: Is dialect a factor? *Curriculum Inquiry* 16 (2), 127–145.

Troyna, B. (1993) *Racism and Education*. Philadelphia: Open University Press.

Turner, T. (1993) Anthropology and multiculturalism: What is anthropology that multiculturalists should be mindful of it? *Cultural Anthropology* 8 (4), 411–429.

United Nations Yearbook (1994) Vol. 48. The Hague: Martinus Nijhoff.

United States Bureau of the Census (1995) *Statistical Abstract of the United States:1995* (115th edn). Washington, DC: US Bureau of the Census.

Usher, R. and Edwards, R. (1994) *Postmodernism and Education*. London: Routledge.

Verma, G., Zec, P. and Skinner, G. (1994) *The Ethnic Crucible: Harmony and Hostility in Multi-ethnic Schools*. London: Falmer.

Vogel, V. (1968) The Indian in American history textbooks. *Integrated Education* 6 (3), 16–32.

Walker, S. (1993) Tarzan in the classroom: How 'educational' films mythologize Africa and miseducate Americans. *Journal of Negro Education* 62 (1), 3–23.

Wallace, M. (1993) Multiculturalism and oppositionality. In C. McCarthy and W. Crichlow (eds) *Race, Identity and Representation in Education* (pp. 251–261). London: Routledge.

Walsh, C. (1991) *Pedagogy and the Struggle for Voice: Issues of Language, Power, and Schooling for Puerto Ricans*. Toronto: OISE Press.

Wax, M. (1993) How culture misdirects multiculturalism. *Anthropology and Education Quarterly* 24 (2), 99–115.

West, C. (1991) Decentering Europe. *Critical Quarterly* 33 (1), 1–26.

West, C. (1994) *Race Matters*. New York: Vintage.

Wexler P. (1982) Structure, text, and subject: A critical sociology of school knowledge. In M. Apple (ed.) *Cultural and Economic Reproduction in Education* (pp. 275–303). London: Routledge.

Wexler, P. (1992) *Becoming Somebody: Toward a Social Psychology of School*. London: Falmer.

Whately, M. (1988) Photographic images of Blacks in sexuality texts. *Curriculum Inquiry* 18 (2), 137–155.

William, R. (1981) *Culture*. Glasgow: Fontana.

Williams, R. (1958) *Culture and Society*. London: Chatto & Windus.

Willinsky, J. (1994) After 1492–1992: A post-colonial supplement for the Canadian curriculum. *Journal of Curriculum Studies* 26 (6), 613–629.

Willis, P. (1977) *Learning to Labour: How Working-Class Kids Get Working-Class Jobs.* Westmead, England: Saxon House.

Wilson, A. (1995) Teaching about Africa: A review of middle/secondary texbooks and supplemental materials. *The Social Studies* 86 (6), 253–259.

Wilson, C. and Gutierez, F. (1995) *Race, Multiculturalism and the Media: From Mass to Class Communication.* London: Sage.

Wittgenstein, L. (1972) *Philsophical Investigations.* Oxford: Blackwell.

Wong, P. and Cowan, G. (1998) Attitudes, values and student outcomes: A framework for analyzing the impact of multicultural education programs. Paper presented at the Annual Meeting of the American Educational Research Association, San Diego.

Yin, R. (1994) *Case Study Research and Design.* Thousand Oaks, CA: Sage.

Young, A. (1989) Television viewing. *Canadian Social Trends* Autumn, 14–15.

Young, R.J.C. (1995) *Colonial Desire: Hybridity in Theory, Culture and Race.* New York: Routledge.